Lyn Hall's
COOKERY COURSE

Lyn Hall's
COOKERY COURSE

Foreword by Nigel Slater

conran OCTOPUS

Dedication

To Jenni Muir, without her support
and guidance, this book would not
have been published

Publishing Director: Lorraine Dickey

Senior Editor: Katey Day

Managing Editor: Jenni Muir

Art Director: Chi Lam

Art Editor: Alison Fenton

Photography: Jean Cazals

Stylist: Sue Rowlands

Senior Production Controller:

   Angela Couchman

Published in 2004 by
Conran Octopus Limited
A part of Octopus Publishing Group
2–4 Heron Quays
London E14 4JP

www.conran-octopus.co.uk

ISBN 1 84091 348 7

British Library Cataloguing-in-Publication Data
A catalogue record for this book is available from the
British Library

Printed and bound in China

CONTENTS

Foreword by Nigel Slater

I cannot begin to tell anyone how much pleasure I get from cooking. Not simply from putting the finished dish on the table for friends and family but from the actual process of cooking. The feel of warm dough in my hands, grating an orange or taking a sizzling roast from the oven. Cooking is something that goes beyond the practical need of making something to eat; it is also a source of great pleasure and joy.

There is always talk about whether cooking is an art or a science or, as some suggest, simply a gift. It is a discussion I tend to stay out of. What I am certain of is that the ability to cook is more a matter of confidence than anything else. I remember to this day the first cake I ever baked. I had been told that baking is very different from any other type of cooking and that my efforts would probably lead to disaster first time. I had also picked up the idea that recipes in books rarely worked. As it happened I did find it intimidating and was worried that everyone would see my failure and make fun of it. The reality couldn't have been more different. My cake turned out like a dream, golden-topped and with big, soft crumbs. I couldn't have been prouder when I took my handiwork from the oven and could barely conceal my joy when everyone tucked into it. That one small success gave me the confidence to move on to other cakes and then to bread and then to everything else. All I needed was that one success.

I passionately believe that confidence plays a bigger part in learning to cook than any other single thing. But where does that confidence come from? Ideally, you will have a teacher by your side, a teacher who you like and trust, watching your every move and pushing you gently in the right direction. All very well for those with the time to attend cooking school. And what about those who can't, or would rather learn to cook in their own home with their own equipment?

Most, though certainly not all cookery books, are written in such a way than anyone with a grasp of the basics can expect to be able to follow the recipes. The tricky thing is getting the opportunity to learn those basics. There are thousands of cookery books published each year, yet very few are actually capable of teaching you how to cook. It takes a very special cook and writer indeed to do that. I believe that Lyn is one of the few people who have the ability not just to teach but to warmly instil confidence in any new cook. She has the knack of holding your hand but not so tightly that you feel you cannot do things for yourself.

When I saw the plans for this book I saw immediately that it was something special. Not simply that the clear, step-by-step pictures had a certain reality to them, but also that the voice with which you are taken through the basics is reassuring enough to take you further than you thought you could ever go. The simple truth is that Lyn teaches you to cook rather than to simply follow a recipe.

This book succeeds where others have failed. I have struggled for years to describe the difference between a gentle and a brisk simmer. Lyn does it simply by describing the movement of the bubbles as 'slow-rising' or 'energetic'. Suddenly everything is as clear as crystal. Yet while the book addresses the basics and teaches us why as well as how, the dishes are far from mundane. This is thoroughly modern, exciting cooking, with original recipes to compliment the classics that we all should have in our repertoire. Dishes such as Persian chicken pilau with pistachios and barberries and a khoresh of duck with orange, rose petals and cardamom are a world away from the run-of-the-mill cookery school classics.

I wish so much that there had been a book like this when I was learning to cook. Much of my learning was done by stern-faced cooks with intimidating text books. I got there, but how much more pleasure I would have had with a book like this. I have said enough, it's time to roll up your sleeves and get started on what may well be the most rewarding thing you will ever do.

PART ONE

Principles

"Lyn Hall's explanations and techniques are second to none."
Mary Berry

Equipment

I have cooked in private mansions where the oil paintings on the drawing room wall were worth millions, and all I could find to warm up the christening scones were some vile, rusty, buckled baking sheets. It amazes and saddens me that a family will spend £19–£25 on a joint of meat to roast every weekend, yet never skip the joint for just one week, have a cheaper meal, and spend the same amount on a decent roasting tray that will last them for 25 years.

With good equipment, cooking is lifted from a chore to a joy. Well-designed equipment looks after you, and often doubles-up its duties, taking on several tasks. Equipment has to work for me – and you – in a strong, sturdy, helpful and completely reliable way. In my kitchen, a non-stick pan does not have separate utensils, it gets the same whisk and fish slice used in it as the other saucepans in my kitchen.

The materials from which equipment is made can have a huge effect on how it helps you, and what that equipment does best in the kitchen. And at the end of the day, 95 per cent of it has to go in the dishwasher, which does an unparalleled job of washing, drying, sterilising and polishing. So I tend to go for materials such as stainless steel, heat-proof glass, enamelled cast iron and steel, and porcelain.

For really enjoyable cooking, equipment has to be kept out and around you, ready to grab, so last but not least, it has to look sleek, beautiful and tempting to use.

You never can have enough

Bowls Stainless steel with a pouring lip, light but strong, which stack in a nest are my first choice. Ingredients look stunning in glass. It makes you want to get your hands on them and into them. Pyrex bowls are also good for using as the top part of a double boiler. A number of small plastic bowls are also useful for the measuring out of ingredients. Those left over from purchased Christmas puddings are ideal. Make sure you have mixing bowls ranging from 30cm/12in to 15cm/6in diameter.

Sieves Two types are essential. Stainless steel mesh, which are woven as fine as muslin, from 13cm/5in to 9cm/3½in diameter for straining custards, broths, sauces and gravies. You also need one or two flour and sugar sieves, with larger mesh, like the one on the cover, for baking.

Oven trays These are an expensive but important investment nevertheless. If you buy one or two per year, you will soon have six, which is all you need. The best are black, heavy and non-stick, and no smaller than 23 x 33cm/9 x 13in. Not only are they essential for baking, you can use them to group and move ingredients around the kitchen. I use Tefal non-stick, which are light, when working with trays of canapés, and before and after frying ingredients in batches. In ovens hotter than 180°C/350°F/ Gas 4, the heavier anodized aluminium baking trays serve

In the drawer

Kitchen foil
Greaseproof paper or waxed paper
Plastic wrap or cling film
Silicone or parchment paper
Bake-o-Glide or black Teflon liners
Roasting bags
String
Ziploc bags

Picture captions
Top to bottom: timer,
kitchen scissors (left)
corkscrew (right),
horseshoe peeler, nutmeg
grater, Microplane fine
grater, paring knife,
carving knife, chef's fork.

well for toasting, baking and cooking under the grill {broiler}. Use a Teflon liner with them for complete ease of cleaning.

Measuring jugs You need several of different sizes and capacities for measuring out liquids and holding them until use. Make a collection of clear Pyrex glass, in which liquids shimmer and the amounts are easy to read at a glance, plus a few plastic jugs that will bounce on a hard kitchen floor, and some stainless steel jugs, which will last forever.

Tea towels Pure Irish linen tea towels are a luxury. Flax, from which linen is made, grows in water, loves to be soaked, and is wonderfully strong. You can get by with a snowy pile of tea towels made from a respectable mix of cotton and linen. The less expensive blend works well, especially for polishing glasses. Ironed tea towels dry more efficiently as all the fibres are pressed in the same direction.

Electrical goods

When friends come round for a midweek supper and everyone has been up to their eyes in work, they cannot believe how anyone can possibly get a three-course meal on the table in such short time. One of the secrets is using good electrical equipment.

For these items to really work for you, they should be out on your counter, ready to whizz at the flick of a switch. I would not be without my:

Food processor Purée, grind Thai curry pastes, make eggy sauces. I also cannot do without its citrus squeezer attachment, which is

indispensable at Christmas with those never-ending oranges and lemons in festive recipes, and juice required to ward off 'flu.

Blender Essential to blend soups, sauces and smoothies to a perfectly velvety texture.

Stick blender Make soups and sauces in the saucepans (resulting in less washing up), to smooth out lumpy sauces, and those which have been frozen. When zapped with bubbles using this machine to create a cappuccino effect, some creamy sauces appear much lighter. Use the stick blender in a tall narrow beaker or jug for the best results.

Electric steamer A stand-alone steamer allows you to make a complete healthy dinner without using the hob. It is also useful for those times when the hob is full, as it allows extra ingredients to be cooked independently. With two stainless steel tiers, an alarm to prevent the water boiling dry, and a keep-warm facility, my

Magimix steamer certainly earns its place on the worktop.

Electric mixer This will include a whisk, mixing blade, and a metal mixing bowl. Nothing creams butter and sugar for cakes as effortlessly as a proper mixer, and you are less inclined to skimp on the time required when there is a quiet steady purring in the background. Nothing beats egg whites and sugar to a firm snow as efficiently as my Kitchen Aid, and it comes with a useful set of attachments too.

Knives

Dearest to every cook is his or her set of knives. However small your collection, look after it carefully, and buy each new knife thoughtfully. Bad knives crush and pulp ingredients, making them look hashed, rather than sliced. Good knives on the other hand cut cleanly and thinly, so the food looks beautiful, people gasp at your skill, and you will find them a joy to use.

I love JA Henckels' knives, made from a mix of soft carbon steel, for easier sharpening, and chrome, which keeps them bright. For dash and dazzlement, I like to use my Japanese Kyocera fine ceramic kitchen knife which, being ceramic, cannot be dropped on the floor or it will shatter.

Each knife is designed for a different task. The weight of the handle plays an important part in chopping and cutting, and is just as important as the blade. If you don't enjoy holding your knife, you cannot begin to enjoy cooking. Go back to the shop and try another brand.

Pots and pans

You need a range of saucepans made from a selection of metals. My first choice for every day cooking is stainless steel. Nothing beats it for cleanliness and hardiness. It can be scoured to within an inch of its life and boiled dry, usually without causing any change whatsoever in its appearance.

The disadvantage of stainless steel is that it is not a good conductor of heat, which is why you must ask about the 'sandwich' when you purchase a stainless steel saucepan. This is the conducting layer of aluminium or copper inside the saucepan, invisible, but powerful. Good saucepans are fully lined across base and sides, others have linings in the base only, and many are not lined at all. Look for flush riveting and welding, and no 'joins' in which bacteria can gather.

A saucepan in which you make a sauce is different from that in which you poach eggs, boil water or vegetables, or make a stock, soup or stew. A true saucepan is not very deep, has curved sides to allow the hand-whisk and spatula to work smoothly against its sides, and allows plenty of room for thickening of the sauce by evaporation.

All well-designed saucepans have hollow handles, which don't get hot or burn your hands while you cook. Remember when buying to get a steamer insert and lid that fit the pan snugly. Saucepan lids are not easy to store, but thankfully you only need three or four in varying sizes. Toughened glass is best, as

you can see what is going on in the pan at every stage of cooking.

A large yet fairly light pot is essential for boiling pasta and blanching vegetables, and this will be made easier if you also purchase a blanching basket.

If you plan on giving regular parties, make sure you have enough pans of generous size. It is difficult, and a drudge, to cook for large parties using small saucepans, and few things irritate me more than food boiling over and falling out of pans that are too small for the job.

Buy top quality saucepans and they will return the investment by becoming family heirlooms. Non-stick pans on the other hand are likely to need replacing from time to time.

For successful stews and pot-roasts, good enamelled cast-iron cocottes [Dutch ovens] and matching heavy lids are vital. Try to buy at least one very large pot for parties, and a smaller version for making dinner for six. If you particularly like poultry and game, one or two oval cocottes will be very useful.

Electronic

Scales Although a set of large spring scales is essential for weighing large items, it is also important to have a set of digital scales for accurate measurement of tiny quantities, light foods, and those ingredients requiring precision. Be careful what you buy: some inexpensive digital scales work only in increments of 5g or ¼oz.

Timers These are indispensable if you are still cooking when your guests arrive, or when the phone

Using this book

Unless otherwise stated:
All ingredients are fresh, not frozen.
All ingredients are raw, not cooked.
Eggs are British medium size.
Herbs are fresh herbs.
Ovens and grills [broilers] are always preheated.

Use one set of measurements (metric, imperial or US cups) when using recipes.
Pints are British pints and equivalent to 20floz.
Cups are US cups and equivalent to 8floz.
Tablespoon measures are 15ml.
Teaspoon measures are 5ml.

never stops rining while you are trying to cook. Make sure you have a selection of battery operated and non-battery timers.
Probe thermometer This is the very best thing for ascertaining when meat or poultry is cooked to rare, medium or well-done. It is also the only reliable way of telling when meat or fish that has been baked in pastry is ready.

Equipment for baking

Bakeware seems to get more glamorous every year. Anodized aluminium products look the sleekest on the shelves, but you can still cook pastries, cakes and quick breads just as well in silvered tinware. The most important thing is that the tin needs to conduct heat very quickly through to the pastry, and when it comes out of the oven, it must cool just as quickly. Remember that pies and tarts tend to get sliced while still on the tin's metal base, which will destroy cheaper kinds of non-stick cookware.

A word on shopping

Test pieces when shopping for supreme comfort and a good grip in the hand. People have personal preferences. If you're considering a peeler, hold it and imagine peeling large, heavy celeriac, or the knobbly bits of Jerusalem artichokes with it. Don't hesitate to take equipment back if it doesn't work or suit your hands, a good supplier will understand.

Kitchen storage

In my tiny kitchen the equipment is stored in such a way that all is to hand. Please don't tell my neighbours, but I have cooked for hundreds of people, safely and happily in this space.

Two hugely important yet often unnoticeable features of a happy working kitchen are the position of the waste bin, and the provision of a 'tray space'. This is an area to store trays, baking sheets, oven shelves, cake racks, boards and so on, neatly on their sides when not in use.

Shallow vertical storage helps house everything up to the ceiling, behind cupboard doors, or out on display. Place the less-used items, but not heavy ones, at the very top.

Consider grouping equipment together and keeping it elsewhere. Heavy stewpots, large cake pans and items used for annual feasts and festivals could be stored in a utility room or under the stairs. Much is of such disparate size and shape it is impossible to store neatly without damage, so gather items together in labelled stacking plastic boxes. A box for pastry, for example, could contain the rolling pin, baking rice, and your full range of tartlet and quiche tins. Bring the whole box in when you need it, and store it out of sight when you don't.

Finally, no matter how exquisite your equipment, and how much it has cost, remember your hands are indispensable. Only your fingers can sense when to scrape the batter from the sides of the bowl and place it in a food processor to achieve a perfectly smooth mix. It's your hands, when combined with good equipment, that make cooking such an utterly absorbing and delightful activity.

Cooking techniques

Learning to cook is not dissimilar to learning to drive a car. The more you do it, the better you get, but you cannot get better unless you do it. Each time I buy a new car, it seems to spend quite a bit of time in the bodyshop, repainting scrapes and replacing the wing-mirrors (ahem). Obviously I have not got the feel of it, and my judgment is flawed. Cooking is the same, but thankfully the early mistakes aren't so expensive to put right, and most of the time they're perfectly edible.

Knowing when something is cooked perfectly is as important as knowing how to cook it. If you understand both, you are well on your way to success.

Cooking to the right degree of doneness is a combination of feel, knowledge, experience and judgment. If you have lived with someone who cooks, you will automatically pick up much of it. But if you are a self-taught cook, or about to become one, take heart: success is achieveable.

No two ovens are alike, pots and pans have different shapes and are made of different metals. Food is a product of nature and like nature, can be unpredictable. All these have an effect on cooking times and temperatures. After you have been cooking for a while, you will accumulate your own knowledge and judgment. How will you know? The day you turn around in mid-sentence and reach into the oven for a perfectly cooked cake, soufflé or roast, just before the pinger goes off.

Most ingredients are done when they are fully cooked and piping-hot all the way through. It is usually fashion that decrees which foods are served rare, barely warm or bleeding. At present, fashion favours crunchy, undercooked vegetables, especially greens, but occasionally it is equally good to have soft root vegetables that can be crushed with a fork.

Try to use at least two methods of testing for doneness when learning to cook. More details for specific ingredients and recipes are given later, but the most common techniques are:

Skewer: plunge a fine metal skewer into the deepest part of the food, avoiding any bone and fat, and hold it there for 2 seconds. Remove and press the skewer against your wrist. The point should feel piping hot for well-done. For fish and meat cooked rare, it should simply feel hot. To re-test, hold the skewer under cold running water then repeat.

Weighing and calculating: this is necessary for joints of meat in order to estimate the cooking time. Refer to a roasting chart (page 218), or follow the calculation given in your recipe.

Thermometers: for meat and poultry, a probe thermometer with large digital display is easy to use, accurate and foolproof.

Feeling: cuts of meat and fillets of poultry and fish can be tested by gentle finger pressure. It is easy to do, but requires experience.

Biting: lift vegetables, pasta, grains and pulses from the pan, cool briefly, then bite into them to gauge firmness.

Remember to

Read the recipe all the way through before you begin, to get a clear overview of what is involved.

Adjust the seasoning to suit your taste. It is probably the most important thing you do when cooking. Salt and pepper, when used carefully, enhance the flavours of the ingredients. Taste at each stage of cooking, adding just a little salt and pepper each time, until you are pleased with the result.

Boiling and simmering

Best foods for boiling and simmering

Starting with boiling liquid:
Vegetables such as leeks, courgettes [zucchini], kohlrabi, green beans, new potatoes, cabbage
Pasta and **rice**

Starting with a cold liquid:
Pulses
Large potatoes peeled and cut up evenly
Large root vegetables peeled and cut up evenly
Stocks

Picture captions
1 *You only need to use a cover when cooking rice by the absorption method, or when boiling pulses or root vegetables.*
2 *A rolling boil, also known as a fast or hard boil, is required for dried pasta, grains and for reducing and thickening sauces and stocks.*
3 *Stocks should be gently simmered during making, but once completed and strained of solids, they can be boiled vigorously.*

You can boil just about anything. At one time, an entire dinner was often boiled in a three-legged pot. A thick slab of bacon on the base, root vegetables on top, and savoury and sweet puddings, tied separately in cloths, hung from the sides. For our purposes boiling makes carbohydrate-rich foods such as rice, pasta and pulses, thick and fluffy. It softens the texture and mellows the flavour of fibrous vegetables such as fennel and cabbage. Boiling reduces stock and sauces, strengthening their flavour, and it thickens sauces containing a little starch such as cornflour [cornstarch]. Boiled, dried pasta takes about 10–11 minutes, crunchy green vegetables take as little as 30 seconds depending on their type, and stock up to three hours.

You need A large, deep pan, not too heavy, with handles either side so you can lift it easily when it is full of water and ingredients. The one you would normally use for cooking pasta is perfect.
• For pasta and some vegetable varieties, a blanching basket. Use a pasta pan insert or wire-mesh chip basket.
• A lid or plate to cover the pan.
• A large sieve or colander for draining, although it is also possible to drain some small items using a tilted saucepan lid.
• A timer.

To boil Fill the pan with water no more than three-quarters full, so that the liquid, when it reaches a tumultuous, rolling boil, will not overflow and drown the gas or electrics. Turn on the extractor or open nearby windows. Bring the water to a boil, covered with a lid or plate to save energy and speed up the process, or boil it in a kettle first and add it to the pan. Stock can be used instead of water.

If you are cooking vegetables and pasta, add enough salt for the water to taste as salty as the sea, before it has reached the boil, or it will froth and foam.

Once the water is at a rolling, vigorous boil (100°C/212°F) place your pasta or vegetables in the basket, lower them into the boiling water, and adjust the heat so it maintains a steady boil. Time the cooking. I tend to boil food with the lid off so I can see what is happening; it helps to make instant judgements.

Test for doneness by tasting and biting the food to test the texture. Also watch the colours. Then immediately lift out the basket, draining off the water.

To simmer Simmering occurs at 97°C/207°F, when the temperature drops beneath a rolling boil but there are still bubbles on the surface of the liquid. Energetic bubbles are termed a brisk simmer and slowly rising bubbles are called a gentle simmer. Unlike a rolling boil, simmering may go on for hours and is useful for cooking many vegetables and fruits, as well as for making stock.

Advantages Boiling causes starch cells to swell and therefore soften the texture of rice, potatoes and pasta. It softens the cellulose in vegetables, making them more digestible. Boiling also destroys harmful bacteria in food, and rapid boiling for 10-15 minutes kills the toxins in certain pulses. Rapid boiling is one of the most useful ways of thickening sauces, whether by reducing and intensifying the liquid, or by the addition of cornflour. It is also essential for burning the alcohol out of wines and spirits. Simmering is essential for

making stocks and brings an appetising softening of texture and flavour to most vegetables.

With or without a cover? In most cases, boiling without a cover is preferable because it makes it easier to control the cooking. In the case of green vegetables, acids can accumulate beneath the lid, causing the vegetables to change from bright green to khaki. Sauces and stocks are best left uncovered to prevent cloudiness. Using a cover allows ingredients such as rice to absorb

the liquid and cook evenly, preventing toughness and hardness. It also speeds up the cooking process, saves energy, and in some cases the food may retain more nutrients and colour.

Points to remember Prolonged boiling of vegetables and pasta will make them soft and mushy, grains of rice will turn into a sticky mass, and protein-rich foods such as eggs will become

hard and rubbery, so it is crucial to observe cooking times.

• It is important that ingredients are boiled or simmered at the appropriate rate. A rapid boil is suitable only for dry pasta and grains, while a steady boil is required for potatoes, root vegetables, pulses, some stews, and soups containing potato. A few vegetables require brief, rapid boiling then refreshing, a slightly different process known as blanching (see overleaf).

• As a general rule, small items of food are added to boiling water and large items of food are put in cold water then brought to a boil.

• Vegetable boiling water contains valuable nutrients, so don't throw it down the sink. Re-use it for a gravy or sauce.

• When using the same pot of water to cook various vegetables, start with those with the mildest, sweetest flavour, removing them with a perforated spoon as they become cooked, and finish with pungent brassicas and asparagus.

• Food will continue to cook in residual heat while you are draining it, so be quick, and allow for this continued cooking when you test for doneness.

• The greater the proportion of water to food, the more likely you are to retain the heat of the water when cold food is added to the boiling liquid.

• Adding a wedge of lemon, or a knife-tip of cream of tartar when boiling turnips and cauliflower keeps them white and glossy.

• It is essential to boil leftover soups or stews before eating them to destroy any potentially harmful bacteria.

Blanching in water

Blanching has several meanings. One method involves cooking slightly by the quickest possible immersion of the food, usually vegetables, in rapidly boiling water. With vegetables that are preferred crisp and al dente, this is all the cooking required. Other vegetables may be blanched then refereshed in cold water, drained and cooked normally. Another type of blanching, sometimes called par-boiling, aims to draw out unwanted flavours from ingredients such as hams, gammons, and cuts of bacon, and strongly flavoured vegetables such as turnips or mature cabbage. Meat is usually placed in cold water and brought to the boil. Potatoes are also placed in cold water and brought to the boil in order that they may be partially cooked before roasting.

Picture captions
1 The best way to blanch spinach is to place it in a colander and pour boiling water from a kettle over it.
2 Plunging blanched vegetables into a bath of iced water helps stop the cooking process quickly.

You need Depending on your ingredients, a large, deep pan, not too heavy, with handles either side so you can lift it easily when it is full.
• For some vegetables, a blanching basket. Use a pasta pan insert or wire-mesh chip basket.
• A kettle, for blanching spinach and tomatoes, or for topping up the water level when blanching vegetables in batches.
• A lid or plate to cover the saucepan and speed up boiling.
• A large sieve or colander for draining, although it is also possible to use a saucepan lid for small items.
For refreshing vegetables:
• A large and deep basin of water and, in summer, a stock of ice.
• A skimmer for lifting small items from still-boiling water.
• A colander or sieve.

To blanch When blanching vegetables in boiling water, use the ratio of 10:1 water to vegetables. Fill the pan with water no more than three-quarters full, so that the liquid, when it reaches a tumultuous, rolling boil, will not boil over and drown the gas or electrics. Turn on the extractor or open windows to prevent streaming of window panes. Bring the water to a boil, or boil it up in a kettle first and add it to the pan, then cover with the lid or a plate to save energy and to speed up the boiling process. Add enough salt for the water to taste as salty as the sea, before it has reached the boil, or it will froth and foam and risk once again drowning the power.

Once the water is at a rolling, vigorous boil (100°C/212°F) place your vegetables in the

basket and lower them into the boiling water. Lift the vegetables out when they brighten vividly and evenly in colour.

Refreshing is a step after boiling and blanching. It is done when the recipe requires it, or if you are preparing food in advance. Refreshing stops the cooking process, and needs to be done with split-second timing. It is useful for little vegetables as above, and green vegetables – not potatoes as they go gummy.

Plunge the basket of hot food into a deep basin of icy water, or place it in a sieve or colander held under running cold water. When the food is cool, drain immediately, then dry by blotting with paper towel or it will become waterlogged. Refrigerate the food in a plastic or Ziploc bag for reheating later. If you are using a microwave oven for reheating, you might store the vegetables in the serving dish. Blanching and refreshing can be done up to 5 hours in advance.

To blanch tomatoes, peaches and pistachio nuts, so that their skins slip off easily, put them in a bowl and pour over boiling water from a kettle. Leave for a few seconds, then drain and remove the skins.

A similar technique is used to blanch young spinach leaves. Place them in a colander, over a basin or sink, and slowly pour the boiling water from a kettle over the leaves, until wilted.

Another type of blanching, or part-cooking, draws out strong, bitter and salty flavours. Place the food in cold, unsalted water. Raise the heat until it boils. As

2

soon as the water boils, discard it, rinse the food, and continue with the recipe.

A more prolonged version of the above is also called par-boiling. It involves submerging potatoes and root vegetables in cold water or stock and bringing them to the boil for up to 10 minutes, before continuing to cook by another method, usually roasting. This results in even cooking all the way through. Treated this way, Puy lentils lose a lot of sludgy colour, and pulses start the process of rehydrating, to make them appetising and edible. Hams, gammons and bacon may be simmered for an hour or more to rid them of excess saltiness.

Reheating blanched vegetables It is useful to blanch vegetables then reheat them in a microwave just before serving. To do this, place the vegetables in a buttered bowl and season. If desired, add little knobs of butter or a drizzle of olive oil. Cover with plastic wrap

and reheat at full power. In a 750 watt oven, 700g/1½lb vegetables, enough to serve ten people, will take about 8 minutes to reheat; 450g/1lb vegetables, for four to six people, will take about 4 minutes. The heat distributes most efficiently in a Pyrex glass bowl covered with plastic wrap, though it is tempting to use a porcelain serving dish (providing it has no metallic decorations). Test with your finger, pressing to the bottom of all parts of the dish before serving. If after the allotted time the vegetables are not hot enough, heat for another minute.

Advantages Blanching is a very accurate way of cooking.
• It arguably preserves more of the flavour and nutrients in food.
• Blanching brightens the colour of asparagus, broccoli, all fresh beans, carrots and cabbage.
• It is an extremely useful way of preparing vegetables in advance.
• Par-boiling potatoes and parsnips before roasting lessens the fat absorbed during roasting and gives a delicious crunchy exterior and soft mealy interior.

Points to remember When using the same water to blanch a batch of different vegetables, start with those with the mildest flavour and finish with the most pungent.
• Food will continue to cook in the residual heat while you are draining, so be quick, and allow for this when testing for doneness.
• Use plenty of water. The greater the proportion of boiling water to food, the more likely you are to retain the heat of the water when cold food is added.

Poaching

Best foods for poaching

In water:
Smoked haddock
Sausages such as frankfurters
Eggs

In stock, or water flavoured with a few aromatics:
Fish including oily fish such as salmon or sea-trout, whole or cut into fillets or cutlets
Meat including fillet of beef, pork cured as for bacon, unsmoked and unsmoked hock, rolled shoulder, rolled loin, whole gammon
Chicken including breasts and whole birds
Dumplings
Fish or meat balls

In sugar syrup:
Dense-fleshed fruit such as pears, apples, peaches and apricots
Rhubarb and **quinces** and other fruit that is unpalatable when raw

I love poaching because it is one of the most simple, clean ways of cooking. The poaching water or light broth does not interfere with the flavour in any way. I find the best results come when poaching ingredients with a bold taste and rich or lubricating content, such as eggs, gammon and salmon. The calming effect as the water lazily trembles is not to be under-valued in the hectic way we live today.

You need A saucepan of appropriate size. For poaching eggs you will need a small saucepan, for bacon cuts and joints a large, deep saucepan, and for long, whole fish, a fish kettle.
• A skimmer, fish slice [spatula] or perforated spoon, with which to lift out the food.
• If poaching whole fish, you will need extra help to remove the fish or it will be in danger of breaking. Fold a piece of foil into a strap and lay it on the bottom of the pan under the length of the fish, or use a large piece of Teflon, leaving enough at the sides for you to grasp. Or wrap the fish in muslin [cheesecloth].
• A tray or plate lined with paper towel, a clean tea towel or napkin, to blot up the moisture.

To poach Heat the water, stock or syrup in the pan, then adjust the heat so it simmers briskly, with bubbles breaking the surface. Slide the food into the liquid. Adjust the heat so that the surface of the water barely moves. The surface of the water should tremble or shudder, with small bubbles occasionally breaking the surface – the ideal water temperature is between 65°-90°C/150°-190°F.

Eggs with a soft, runny yolk are poached at the lowest temperature. For cooking one or two eggs, I turn off the heat under the pan, and let the eggs cook in the residual heat.

When the food is cooked, remove it from the liquid with the skimmer, waving it gently so that the excess liquid drips back into the pan. Then lay the cooked food on a rack or tray, lined with paper towel, to drain off the remaining poaching liquid. For speed, keep small items of food on the skimmer and dab the bottom of the skimmer on a wad of paper towel.

Advantages Poaching is a pure, light method of cooking, ideal for low-fat diets and for invalids not ready to face more robust food.
• It is a sensitive way of cooking foods with delicate flavours that could otherwise be masked, and

for cooking fragile foods that would curdle if overheated.
• It is good for gentle cooking of large cuts of meat, especially salted meats and hams. Poaching helps to tenderise the flesh.

The magical exchange of flavours

Wherever possible, poach meats and fish in stock instead of water. The flavour of food lost into the stock will be replaced by the flavour of the stock. The stock will also benefit from increased flavour and, in the case of fish, becomes a fumet. Fruit salads are enhanced by cooking in a flavoured sugar syrup, such as one with star anise, ginger and/or chilli. Slipping prepared fruit into a boiling syrup gives it a chance to penetrate the delicate flesh evenly and prevent discoloration.

Points to remember Your ingredients

should be at room temperature before you begin poaching.
• When the food is small, such as fillets of fish, bring the water or stock to a brisk simmer, then slip

in the food. Immediately adjust the temperature, so the surface of the water only trembles.
• When the food is large, for example a whole salmon, place it in cold water and bring it gently to a simmer.
• Be sure to fully submerge the food. If you are poaching fruit, cover it with a disc of paper to stop it rising to the surface.
• Although it is a moist, gentle cooking method, you still need to ensure you do not overcook the food, or it will become tough.

• Food left to stand in its warm poaching liquid will continue to cook slightly after the heat source has been turned off.
• After poaching, you must drain the food well or it will be watery. Excess water will spoil the sauce on the serving plate too.
• If your stovetop is congested, you can also poach in the oven at 160°C/310°F/Gas 2 in a large roasting tray. Adjust the oven temperature so that the liquid bubbles or steams.

A temperature guide

Rolling fast boil
For pasta or blanching, 100°C/212°F

Simmer
Brisk surface movement, usually on one side of pan, 81°-90°C/177-194°F

Poach
Occasional bubble rises to surface, which trembles, 77°-80°C/170°-176°F

Slow poach
For eggs, 55°C/131°F

Picture captions
1 *When you remove the poached food, blot it on paper towel to remove the excess moisture, leaving it on the skimmer if you need to be quick.*
2 *Fish, poultry and meat benefit from poaching in a tasty aromatic liquid.*
3 *The consistency of the yolk is the key to assessing whether a poached egg is cooked. When the yolk is firm enough to be moved, your egg is ready.*

Steaming

Steaming gives a squeaky-clean texture and flavour to food. The natural salts and distinctive flavours of ingredients can be masked by other methods of cooking and, the more you steam foods, the more you will be able to taste and recognise them. Steaming can take from 7 minutes for a small fillet of fish, to an hour or so for a whole duck. It is also a successful method of blanching or part-cooking foods.

You need A large pan of boiling water, deep enough that it doesn't boil dry during cooking.
• A steamer basket, ideally stainless steel, which has a perforated base and suspends the food about 2.5cm/1in above the boiling water. There should be plenty of room within the steamer to allow the steam to circulate and to cook the food efficiently.
• A lid, preferably glass or clear plastic, which prevents the steam escaping, and allows you to see when your food is cooked.

Choice of steamer Electrical tiered steamers are excellent. They don't clutter up your stovetop, and many today include two or three tiers for cooking different ingredients, plus a rice bowl that allows you to prepare a whole meal in the one machine. Built-in oven steamers with a range of pressure settings are also great to own, as whole fish and duck can be cooked in them. Bamboo steamers are economical and work well. For small quantities of chopped vegetables you can use an expanding steamer basket that sits in the saucepan and has sides that fold out like the petals of a flower. For larger quantities, use a 'universal' steamer insert. This has a stepped base that will will fit into the top of any of your saucepans. A sieve set over a

saucepan and covered tightly with a dome of foil will do, but be sure not to burn your wrists when checking the food.

The Chinese, consummate masters of steaming, often put food, especially fish, on a plate or in a shallow dish in a wok to steam. This allows them to collect the juices of the food, which contain goodness and flavour. These juices may be added to a sauce or poured over the food when done. Fish would be served in the dish it was steamed in to prevent the flesh breaking.

To steam Bring the water in the lower pan to a boil, place the food in the steamer, cover with the lid, set the steamer over the water and

time the cooking. Do not season the food: salt and pepper will merely sit on top of it. When you lift the lid to check for doneness, remember to tilt it so that the steam wafts away from you, to avoid burning.

Advantages Steaming is nutritionally excellent. Few soluble nutrients are lost and the fat is dissolved out of the food cells.
• The food remains juicy, very little moisture is lost.
• Few smells are created in the kitchen during cooking.
• The steamer can be used for reheating cooked foods such as rice and pasta.
• It is an ideal means of warming a few dinner plates.
• It can be faster than boiling.

Points to remember The water must be boiling before the food is placed in the basket over it.
• Keep the liquid in the bottom section boiling steadily. Do not allow it to boil dry or your saucepan will be ruined.

• If you need to add more water to the base, it is essential that the water is at boiling temperature, so use your kettle to boil it first.
• Ingredients must be in one layer, and not overlapping or on top of each other, otherwise they will not cook properly.
• Food can become wet if steamed for too long, as the condensed steam that accumulates under the lid will drop back down onto the food. Protect the food with a cover of greaseproof paper or foil, cut to the required shape.
• When steaming whole fish, place a silicone mat or a folded strap of foil on the base of the basket to make it easier to lift out the fish without breaking it.
• You can prevent fish sticking to the base of the basket by placing them on on lettuce leaves, which also stop the tasty and nutritious juices escaping into the water.
• If you do not have a lid, you must cover the container tightly with something heavy, or the food at the bottom will cook while the food at the top remains raw.
• Leafy greens like spinach, which wilt and fall into a heavy clump, do not cook well in a steamer, though ribbon-cut cabbage is fine.
• You can steam over aromatic liquids based on stock or wine, so that their vapours impart flavour to the steamed ingredients.
• If you like steaming, make a point of using organic or home-grown produce, as the flavours will be much more rewarding.
• Despite the term 'steamed rice', it is best not to cook rice in a steamer. Instead use a saucepan or dedicated electric rice cooker.

Picture captions
1 *Long fillets tied in knots before steaming is an attractive way to present healthy white fish.*
2 *Ingredients for steaming should be in a single layer within the basket, however it is possible to cook an entire meal over one heat source if your steamer has two or three tiers.*

Cooking in a water bath

Cooking 'au bain-marie' or in a water bath can be performed in the oven or on the stovetop. It is a form of poaching or steaming done in a container and is especially good for delicate or heat-shy mixtures such as custards and mousses, and ingredients such as cream, cheese and chocolate. The steaming water prevents the heat of the oven curdling the ingredients. When using a bain-marie on the stovetop, the cooking takes place in a bowl or a saucepan set over a second pan containing steaming water, so that the food is surrounded by a gentle jacket of heat, which prevents burning or crusting on the bottom. A béchamel sauce, covered with buttered paper and left to mature in a double boiler for 45 minutes improves in flavour beyond recognition.

Best food for water baths

For the oven
steamed puddings
baked custards
meringues
timbales
hot mousses
some hot soufflés

For the stovetop
chocolate
eggs
heat-sensitive sauces
such as hollandaise and béchamel

Picture captions
1 *Butter wrappers cut into small squares or discs make a good cover for foods cooked in a water bath in the oven.*
2 *To unmold a cooked mousse, clamp the inverted mold tightly to the serving plate and give a short downward shake.*
3 *Stirring food such as chocolate in a double-boiler helps to keep the mixture cool and give a smooth velvety texture.*

You need For the oven, a flat, deep roasting pan.
• a large shallow porcelain dish, pudding bowl, or individual round aluminium containers. Porcelain ramekins will do, but are not so efficient at absorbing the heat, and lose it quickly when taken out of the water bath.
• A pastry brush for greasing.
• Little squares of buttered paper to cover individual servings.
• A kettle of steaming water to fill the roasting pan.
• An oven cloth or potholders.
• A small pointed knife for loosening and unmolding.
• Two sheets of newspaper for the base of the roasting pan if the food is prone to curdling.
• For the stovetop, you need a custom-made double boiler. Alternatively, a saucepan or heatproof bowl that fits comfortably into another saucepan. The lower saucepan should hold about 5cm/2in of water, giving you 2.5-5cm/1-2in of space between the water and the top saucepan.
• A whisk or wooden spoon.
• A rubber spatula.
• Buttered paper for covering purées and mashed potato, or the thinnest film of milk

To cook in a water bath in the oven

If the food is prone to curdling, place newspaper in the base of the roasting pan. If your concoction is to be turned out, brush the molds with softened butter, chill in the fridge until firm, then butter them again.

If the mixture is thick enough to hold its shape on a table knife, spread it against the sides of the mold to prevent air bubbles forming and to give a polished,

1

curvaceous finish when turned out. Fill the molds within 1cm/½in of the rim. If appropriate, top the mixture with little buttered papers to protect the surface.

Heat the oven to 160°C/310°F/ Gas 2½, or lower, and bring a kettle of water to the boil. Set the mold or molds in the roasting pan in the middle or lower part of the oven. Trying not to lose too much oven heat, pour the hot, steaming water from the kettle into the roasting pan, so that it comes two-thirds of the way up the sides of the molds.

Shut the oven door and start timing the cooking. When the dish is cooked, it will feel a delicate combination of firm and spongy in the centre when pressed with a finger. Remove the water bath from the oven and allow the dish to 'set' for 5 minutes or so in the roasting pan. It will keep perfectly warm.

To turn out individual mousses, run the tip of a small knife around the top edges, and invert onto a warm plate. Hold the mold tightly clamped to the plate and give a short, downward shake. Using the mould, guide the mousse to the centre of the plate, then lift off the mold. Use paper towel to blot away any excess melted butter.

On the stovetop Heat the water in the bottom saucepan. Place the chocolate, sauce or other food in the cold upper bowl or saucepan. Remember the upper bowl or pan should not touch the boiling water below – it is the steam generated from below that is the heat source. Stir often, scraping the sides of the upper container clean with a rubber spatula. Keep the heat very low for delicate sauces prone to curdling. In fact, it is a good idea to take the pan off the heat from time to time and cook in the residual heat.

Advantages Large items, such as steamed puddings or trays of custards and mousses need almost no attention when cooked this way in the oven, and they are ideal for a large crowd.
• Custards can easily be kept warm if there is a delay before serving or when cooking for large parties. Most mousses cooked au bain-marie are time tolerant too, and make a good starter for a special dinner party.

Points to remember The poaching takes place between 54°-57°C/ 129-134°F. At the most, you should only see tiny bubbles beading the base of the water bath. Any other movement in the water means it is too hot. If so, keep your oven door slightly ajar.

• If using tea-glasses as molds, fill the water bath as far up the sides of the glasses as you can, once it is safely in the oven. Tea-glasses are taller than normal molds and more exposed to the oven heat.
• Don't let the water evaporate entirely – it ruins the pan.
• When using a double-boiler, stir the food from time to time. This gives a velvety texture, and helps cool down the food.
• Steam, water and heat are chocolate's worst enemy, so be sure to keep them separate when using a double-boiler.

• Don't mix different types of chocolate in the same dish. Keep to one brand with the same amount of cocoa solids.
• If the chocolate seizes up into a dry claggy mass, add a few tablespoons of coffee, brandy or cream to loosen it, but just enough to make it shiny again.
• A stovetop bain-marie is a good way to keep a thick purée warm before serving, such as mashed potato or swede [rutabaga] purée.

Grilling and barbecuing

Best foods for grilling

For char-grilling or barbecuing
Fish including salmon steaks and cutlets, tuna steaks, small whole fish, tiger prawns, baby squid
Lamb steaks and chops
Brochettes of lamb, pork or chicken
Vegetables such as courgette [zucchini] and aubergine [eggplant]

For an overhead grill
Fish including salmon steaks, mackerel fillets, small whole sole and plaice
Beef steaks such as rump, sirloin, rib-eye, t-bone, or whole fillet
Lamb loin fillets, best end of neck fillets
Pork loin chops and rib chops, strips of pork fillet on skewers
Sausages
Poultry including chicken breast fillets, and marinated wings and drumsticks

Picture captions
1 *Flashing a dish of fish cloaked with hollandaise sauce under a grill before serving gives an appetising flavour amd colour.*
2 *Whole fish can be grilled but they must be small, such as sardines.*
3 *Pressing the food down firmly is essential to achieving charred lines.*

Grilling and broiling give a delicious flavour to the surface of an ingredient. A marinade or rub will provide an even tastier crust. The food to be grilled must be tender and juicy before you begin, and kept that way during cooking. Once the grill has been preheated, grilling can take anything from 2 minutes for a thinly sliced steak, to 10 minutes for pork chops. It can be done under a gas or electric grill [broiler], in a ridged grill pan on the stovetop, or on a barbecue.

You need A grill-pan for use under an overhead grill [broiler], a cast-iron ridged griddle for use on the stovetop, or a barbecue.
• Tongs, a fish slice, and a palette knife.

To grill Heat whatever you are grilling under, on or in, for at least 15 minutes before you begin. If the grill is electric, check that it does not automatically turn itself off after 15 minutes as a safety measure, just when it is perfectly hot enough to begin. On a barbecue, light the fire early, wait until the flames have died down, the coals are ash-grey, and the embers have subdued to a red-hot glow.

Place the food, brushed with oil or melted or softened butter and seasoned, on (or under) the extremely hot grill. When it is attractively charred, turn it over to the other side and repeat.

If the food needs further cooking, try to move it further away from the heat source, rather than turning down the heat of the grill. If using a griddle or a char-grill plate on top of a cooker, this is unavoidable, so you must turn down the heat.

After grilling, place the food briefly on a sheet of paper towel to blot up charred juices. Serve your food as soon as you possibly can, but allow a 7-minute wait in a warm place for grilled red meat.

Crossing the line To obtain the classic trellis pattern (quadrillage), you need a ridged grill-pan or griddle, preheated for 15-20 minutes. Before you begin, brush the item of food with plenty of melted butter or olive oil. As soon as you place the food on the hot grill-pan, press it evenly right along its length with a wooden spoon or palette knife [spatula]. When it colours (lift a corner and peep to have a look), lift and turn it cleanly, same side down, at an angle of 90°. Press and stroke it again along its length so the grill makes a criss-cross pattern. Then turn over and cook the other side.

Advantages Grilling gives superb flavour and appearance to food as the intense dry heat of the grill quickly seals in tasty juices beneath a crispy exterior.

• It is fairly simple to do.

• It is a reasonably healthy way of cooking that requires very little additional fat.

Points to remember Grilling indoors may produce clouds of smoke that tend to set off alarms, and smells that are difficult to disperse. Open the windows and turn on the extractor before you begin, and shut the kitchen door.

• The food must be tender before you begin to cook. It should be the same thickness all the way through, and not more than 5cm/2in thick.

• A boneless piece of meat can be evenly flattened by a carefully aimed bash with a frying pan. Poultry can be spatchcocked by cutting out the backbone and opening the bird out flat.

• Make sure you grill only best quality meat, marbled with fat.

• Very thin steaks do not cook well under an overhead grill [broiler] as they tend to dry out before achieving a good colour.

• Grill fish with a firm texture, not less than 2cm/¾in thick, and baste it as you grill.

• Meat or fish should be at room temperature, and dry, before you begin cooking.

• Brush the food with a good oil before you start for an appetising colour and sheen.

• Many cooks do not season the meat, fish or vegetables until after grilling, as salt draws out the juices. However, for fast grills, you may like to season before cooking – it gives a delicious flavour.

• The thinner the piece of food, the nearer it can be placed to the source of heat.

• If using an overhead grill [broiler], put the food on a rack in the grill-pan or pour out the fat from time to time during cooking.

• Use printed timings merely as a guide when grilling meat. The best way to tell if it is cooked is by feel. Press it in the centre, as this will be the last place to cook. If it is rare, it will feel very spongy. When at the medium stage, the meat will return to its former shape when pressed. If you simply cannot tell whether it is done, cut into the meat at the centre with a sharp, thin knife and have a look. All you then need to do is place a garnish over the little hole when serving.

• Grilled beef or lamb is best cooked to rare – well-done meat will be dry and tough.

• Marinate pork, chicken, thick

pieces of meat or fish for several hours in pineapple, papaya, lemon or yogurt-based marinades. These acids tenderize and start the cooking process before grilling by denaturing proteins, and help prevent the notorious charred crusts and raw interiors.

• Mediterranean vegetables such as aubergine [eggplant] also benefit from marinating.

• If you cook with gas, flames may flare up around the grill-pan as the fat ignites. Don't be frightened. Keep your stovetop clear of knick-knacks, check your pan is positioned firmly over the centre of the flame, so the flames are beneath the pan, and pour away excess fat.

• Cleaning the grill-pan or barbecue afterwards often takes longer than the brief, pleasurable moments of eating.

• If you particularly like grilling, invest in a good overhead extractor with an outside vent, ideally a retractable one that can be raised and lowered over the source of the smoke.

Roasting

Many people just place a roast in the oven and cook until it is done. This is probably because they have chosen perfect meat or poultry, have an excellent oven, and have done it for years. And so can you! A perfect item for roasting is not too small, is covered entirely in a thin layer of fat, and contains bones, along which the heat is efficiently conducted. It should be tender and juicy before you begin. The larger the joint, the longer it takes to roast, the crisper and browner the skin, the less the juices evaporate, and the more succulent the centre – and the more juices there will be to make a sauce. Of course, the larger the joint, the more there is leftover, hence the origin of the traditional English roast that supplied leftovers for the rest of the week.

Best foods for roasting

Beef including 3-5 rib roasts (no smaller), boned and rolled rib [prime rib] and sirloin [short loin], fillet
Lamb including rack of lamb, saddle [loin], leg
Pork including loin, shoulder, blade, saddle [sirloin end], fillet and rolled ham
Veal such as best end of neck [shoulder], or loin
Poultry whole chickens, guinea fowl, duck, goose, turkey and poussin, as well as chicken and duck legs
Game haunches of small deer such as roe deer, young fat pheasant, grouse, partridge
Vegetables including onions, aubergines [eggplant], courgettes [zucchini], red and yellow peppers, fennel, parsnips and potatoes

Picture captions
1 *Fat will be hot when you pour it off so a heatproof bowl is essential.*
2 *Use a chef's fork or carving fork to help you turn poultry without breaking the skin.*
3 *Vegetables can be roasted at the same time as the meat, providing the joint sits on a trivet or rack, not on the base of the roasting pan.*

You need A good oven.
• Robust roasting pans of suitable size. A joint of meat or a bird should only have about 7cm/2¾in space all round it. For roasting whole fish, you need a tray in which the fish can lie flat.
• A small, stable rack, or trivet.
• A chef's fork or carving fork, for picking up and turning birds.
• A bulb baster for removing fat, or for basting if desired.
• A small wide heatproof bowl into which to pour off hot fat.
• A probe thermometer.
• A timer.

To roast Take the meat or poultry out of the fridge 1-2 hours before cooking. It should not be chilled or damp when you begin to roast. Weigh the meat, calculate the cooking time, add on the resting time and work out when to start (see chart). Set the oven rack or tray at the height it will take the meat when on its trivet.

Preheat the oven. Add a light film of fat to the pan and season the meat. Decide whether you will brown it first, which is essential for small roasts, or make a sauce under the roast, or roast vegetables in the same pan. Joints of meat too large to be browned in a pan on the stovetop can be seared in the oven by cooking at 250°C/480°F/Gas 10, or the highest setting, for 15 minutes before lowering the temperature to finish roasting.

When the oven is hot, put in the meat and set the timer. Halfway through cooking, or as the recipe dictates, turn the meat over. Roast fish does not require turning; its structure is different and it cooks more quickly.

If the fat is burning and smoking, remove the tray from

the oven and pour off the fat, being sure to shut the oven door while you do this, or it will lose heat. Alternatively, if pouring off the fat is too awkward, such as

when roasting duck or goose on a rack at a high temperature, add water to the roasting tray to a depth of 2cm/¾in.

Test the meat for doneness 10 minutes before it should be ready. Over-cooking is irreversible, under-cooking is not. Always test your roast for doneness in two ways (see page 15), and never rely just on the calculated cooking time.

Remove the meat from the oven when done and set aside to rest for at least 20-30 minutes before carving. This essential process allows the muscle fibres to relax and the juices to flow evenly through the meat. To rest meat, you need a place that is warm, but not hot – a turned-off oven can still be too hot. I have built a shelf over the hob, beneath the extractor, just for resting meat.

Once the meat is out of the oven, transfer it to an upturned plate. This will keep it above its juices. Wrap all loosely in foil if you wish. After 15 minutes, the juices start to run. In theory, they are brown, with a rosy tinge for medium meat, and scarlet for rare meat. Don't be alarmed by the bright colour, the meat will be cooked. If it is a large joint, the meat will continue cooking in the residual heat, so allow for a 5°C/41°F increase in the internal temperature of the joint.

If you suspect the meat has gone cold, it can be reheated just before serving. Use a non-stick pan, or reheat the roasting tray, with most of the fat cleaned away, on the stove. Flash-fry the meat quickly all over to give a shine to the fat and reheat the exterior. The interior will still be warm. Remove any strings surrounding the meat and only carve when you are ready to eat.

Advantages Roasting gives the most superb flavour to good quality,

well-farmed meat, and there are few who do not relish the idea of a roast for lunch or dinner.
• Gorgeous flavours can be introduced by using a rub or simple marinade. With poultry you can slip your fingers between the skin and breast and gently push in herbs or flavoured butter.
• It is possible to cook vegetables at the same time as a joint.
• A very hot oven is the best way to cook the most tender of tender cuts such as fillet of beef or rib fillet of lamb. Both can be cooked at a high heat for the duration of the cooking time, assuming they are cooked rare or medium rare.

Points to remember Meat should always be roasted fat uppermost, unless it is encased in a layer of fat all the way around, such as a saddle of lamb. If so, turn the roast over from time to time.
• Investing in two good quality heavy roasting trays that will never buckle, one small and one large, is expensive but a prudent purchase that will last a lifetime.
• Meat and poultry with the bone in cooks more quickly than that without. The heat finds it way up the channels next to the bone. A de-boned leg or shoulder of lamb weighs approximately one-third less than a bone-in piece, but the cooking time per 450g/1lb is more than double. This is because the meat is denser, and the cooking time depends on the thickness of the cut, rather than its length.
• Organic and naturally reared meat may take longer to cook than intensively farmed meat, and you may need to drop the temperature a little as it cooks.

Pan-roasting

**Best foods for
pan-roasting**

Fish including small sea
bass, whole or filleted,
turbot and halibut
fillets, salmon fillet
Beef cuts such as a
thickly cut t-bone or
wing rib, fillet of beef
centre cut (the log), or
châteaubriand
Lamb cuts including
loins or cannons, short
saddles, lamb noisettes
Pork fillet, stuffed or
plain
Poultry cuts such as
chicken breasts (stuffed
or plain), or breasts of
duck or guinea fowl.

Picture captions
*1 Buttered paper helps to
keep lean foods such as
fish moist during the
second phase that takes
place in the oven.*
*2 Test for doneness by
pressing the centre of your
poultry, meat or fish. It
will feel spongy when rare.*

When you want to cook a little roasting cut, too small for your
roasting pan, but nearly 5cm/2in thick, choose to pan-roast. The
technique may be unfamiliar in many homes, but is commonly used in
restaurants. It's one of my favourite cooking methods, perfect for
mid-week suppers, and very handy when cooking for just one or two
people. If you have the time, marinating the food before pan-roasting
gives it extra flavour and helps to form the basis of a sauce.

You need A frying pan with a metal
or other ovenproof handle. The
pan must hold the food snugly.
• Tongs and a fish slice [metal
spatula].
• A heatproof bowl for hot fat.
• Buttered paper for lean foods.

To pan-roast Preheat your oven to
220°C/425°F/Gas 7, and place a
shelf just beaneath the top of the
oven. Preheat the frying pan. If
the meat or poultry has a cover of
fat, score it lightly with the point
of a knife to enable the fat to run.
Do not add fat or oil to the pan if
the meat has a coating of fat.
  Brown meat carefully, placing
the fat-side down first and
pressing it firmly into the frying
pan. Pour off the fat as it collects.

Turn the food fat-side uppermost,
transfer the pan to the oven to
roast for about 7 minutes.
  To pan-roast fish, pour a very
thin film of oil into the pan. Press
the fillet down firmly, skin-side
first if it has one, for 2-3 minutes.
Pour off any burning fat, then
cover with buttered paper and
roast for about 6 minutes.

Advantages If the fat splutters, it
does so in the oven
• It is easy to make a sauce by
deglazing the pan.
• Washing up is simple and quick.

Points to remember Once you have
taken the pan from the oven,
keep the handle covered with a
cloth, to protect your hands.

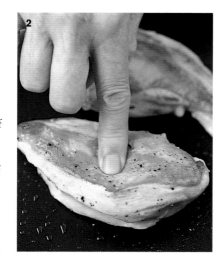

Deglazing

Deglazing is a process in which the delicious, tasty brown bits, formed in the base of a frying or roasting pan during cooking, are scooped up and dissolved in a little liquid and incorporated into a sauce or gravy. It can also be used as a means of providing extra flavour for stocks. Adding liquid to the pan and stirring vigorously helps dissolve the caramelized cooking juices and can be done while the meat is resting, with the bonus that the liquid chosen will help enhance the flavour.

You need A frying pan or roasting pan with crusty sediment, not charred or burned.
- A flat-ended wooden spoon or bamboo rice paddle.
- A very fine mesh sieve.
- A container in which to store the deglazed juices, if they are not to be used immediately.

To deglaze Pour off as much fat as possible from the pan, then place the pan on top of the stove. Dab at any remaining fat with a paper towel. Add the stock or liquid, up to a depth of 2.5cm/1in and allow it to bubble over a brisk heat. Using a flat-ended wooden spoon, scrape up the sediment from the base of the pan. Let the mixture bubble some more, until it reduces in volume.

When it tastes good and concentrated (it usually just coats a spoon at this stage), strain the mixture through a fine meshed sieve before using as part of a sauce or gravy, or adding to stock. If there are only two diners, this alone can be an ideal sauce and served immediately. If not, store for another occasion.

Advantages Deglazing enables you to use one of the tastiest parts of roast meat, in liquid form.
- It is one of the quickest ways to make a hot sauce to accompany meat, poultry or fish that you have just fried or pan-roasted.
- It gives depth to a sauce or stock.
- It forms the basis of the most delicious traditional gravy.
- The results can be frozen for use on another occasion.
- It cleans the pan better than any dishwasher, which often strips the surface off the metal.

Points to remember If the sediment has burned, and you use it, it will bring an irreversible flavour of 'cinders' to your sauce. Taste it before trying to deglaze as looks can be deceptive.
- Consider the deglazing liquid as a part of the sauce only. Sometimes you may be lucky and it will taste good enough to serve immediately; other times it may be sour, too black, or too thin. Sometimes there is simply not enough of it to go round.
- If you have used honey as a glaze or marinade, it may cook to a black and charred lining on the roasting tin, but it might not be bitter. Taste first.
- Roasting without a rack results in more crusty bits in the bottom of the roasting pan.
- If the fat left in the pan after the initial cooking is very pale, it can be strained into a clean jar and, when cold, stored in the fridge for another occasion.

Best liquids for deglazing

Stock especially one chosen to match the food cooked in the pan
Water including leftover vegetable cooking water
Wines including red or white wines
Fortified wines such as Amontillado sherry, Madeira and Marsala
Lemon juice
Cream

Braising and pot-roasting

Braising and pot-roasting are very similar cooking techniques that usually involve cooking in a heavy, lidded pot with aromatic flavourings such as vegetables and herbs. Braising is a moist process that always results in tender meat, fish or poultry, and intensely flavoured and perfumed juices. Liquid is added and the cooking is slow, to meld the ingredients and create a memorable flavour. Pot-roasting, my favourite way of cooking lean foods such as guinea fowl and feathered game, requires no liquid, or very little. I also prefer to use a much higher temperature than for braising.

Best foods for braising

Fish such as salmon, sea-bass, sea-trout, snapper, bream, conger eel, small shark, hake, haddock, monkfish
Beef, usually boned and rolled, with most of the fat removed. Use chuck, brisket, topside and silverside, thick flank
Lamb and mutton shoulder, boned and rolled
Pork boned and rolled loin and shoulder
Veal shoulder or breast
Vegetables such as celery, cardoons and fennel

Best foods for pot-roasting

Whole fish
Beef top rump
Veal cushion of veal, boned and rolled
Poultry including whole chicken, poussin, guinea fowl, young pheasants, partridge, grouse and quail

Picture captions
1 A Teflon liner placed in the bottom of the pot will help you lift out a whole braised fish after cooking.
2 Slide strips of paper towel across the surface of the sauce to remove every last trace of fat.

You need A large pot with a heavy lid, sometimes called a cocotte, for cooking meat, birds and whole fish.
• For a quick braise of fish fillets, use a sauté or frying pan with a glass lid, or a wok.
• A disc of buttered greaseproof or silicone paper, cut to fit the diameter of the pan, or leftover butter wrappers.
• If cooking a whole fish, something to help lift it out of the pan without breaking.
• For braising, a fish slice [metal spatula], sieve, bamboo rice paddle, or straight-sided wooden spoon, and a sauce whisk.
• For pot-roasting, a bulb baster and chef's fork.

To braise Place the meat, fish or poultry in a suitable pot. If using meat, brown it first, for a richer flavour and a darker gravy. Add aromatic vegetables that knit well together, saving some for the top. The fit must be snug. Tuck in herbs: oregano, tarragon, bay, fennel or parsley, splash over enough stock and wine to come one-half or one-third up the side of the main ingredient, but not more. Cover with buttered paper, place a tight-fitting lid on the pot, and begin the cooking gently on top of the stove, until the pot is hot. If you are cooking meat, transfer the pot to a preheated oven no higher than 170°C/325°F/Gas 3 and cook until very tender, turning the meat once or twice during cooking. Try not to lift the lid too often, just let the food cook peacefully in the steam generated by the liquid and vegetables.

After removing the braised item, make a sauce by rapidly boiling the remaining ingredients on the stovetop, stirring from time to time, until the cooking liquid has reduced. Scrape the tasty sediment from the bottom and sides of the pot. Cream and more alcohol can be added at this stage. Strain the sauce through a fine mesh sieve, mashing the aromatic ingredients to extract the very last traces of flavour – this will help thicken the sauce too. Discard the sieve's contents.

Remove the pot from the heat and allow the sauce to settle. Spoon off as much fat as possible from the surface of the sauce, tilting the pot to one side. If desired, you can remove the final traces of fat by running wide strips of paper towel across the surface. Then reheat the sauce until piping hot, whisking well, and serve with the braised item.

To pot roast Preheat the oven to 220°C/425°F/Gas 7. Butter meat or poultry liberally to give a rich caramel note to the juices created during roasting. Place the main ingredient on a bed of chopped or sliced vegetables and herbs such as fennel, bay and oregano. This bed may include unsmoked bacon or cooked ham, or oranges and lemons for poultry and game. Save some of this mixture to scatter over the top. Season with salt and cracked peppercorns.

When you have a cosy fit in the pot, cover with buttered paper, then the lid and place in the oven. Turn meat over once or twice during cooking. Use a bulb baster to suck up the juices collecting at the base of the pot and drizzle them over the roast 3-4 times during cooking, otherwise keep the lid firmly on the pan.

Birds should be crammed in snugly, cracking down on the breast-bones to ensure a tight fit. I generally roast birds for just over half the cooking time with one leg uppermost, then most of

the remaining time with the other leg uppermost, and finish with the birds breast up, uncovered, at the top of the oven, turned to the hottest possible temperature, to brown the breasts. Use a chef's fork to turn them during cooking.

When all is fork-tender, remove the main ingredient from the pot and start to carve. Deglaze the pot with a decent splash of brandy, Madeira, or Amontillado sherry and simmer until you have just a few spoonfuls left. Spoon the hot buttery juices (not quite a sauce, but delicious nonetheless) over each plate, and serve on a bed of the aromatics, which (unlike braising) are not past their prime.

Advantages A minimum of attention is required from the cook when braising and pot-roasting.
• Cheap flavourful meat and fish can be used.
• Braising fish fillets is very quick.
• A sauce is formed naturally.
• A braise can wait in the pot if a

meal is delayed, with minimum loss of quality, even if the main ingredient has been sliced and portioned.
• Pot-roasts do not dry out. The food is protected from the dry heat of the oven, and cooks in its own steam.
• The intensely-flavoured juices generated by a pot-roast are integral to the main ingredient, celebrating its flavour and quality.
• It is an unfussy way of cooking.

Points to remember Braising is not a quick method of cooking meat. Only tougher cuts are suitable for braising, so tenderising them takes a long time. The meat should not be served pink.
• Meat is generally braised whole, often boned and rolled, and can be browned all over before braising.
• It is best to remove most of the fat from meat before braising.
• Braising is gentle. The surface of the liquid for fish should barely shudder, in meat cooking the stock should tick over with small steady bubbles.
• When pot-roasting, be careful that the sauce does not boil away entirely while you are carving.
• If there is a long wait between carving and serving, the juices may not look very attractive.
• Pot-roasts keep perfectly moist and hot in their heavy pots, so there is no need to rush to the table when they are done. They can also be reheated on the stovetop if necessary.
• Pot-roasting is difficult to do for large numbers of people but is a surprisingly convenient means of cooking a mid-week supper.

Stewing

I remember eating an Irish stew cooked by a Lyonnais housewife, and it changed my stewing forever. The process is simple: long, slow cooking, using plenty of liquid and the steam from it as the cooking agents. 'Cooking all night over the heat of a candle,' sums it up. The result is incredibly tender meat, falling off the bone with a rich and sticky texture – so tender it can be eaten with a spoon – surrounded by a lightly thickened gravy. Sadly we all seem to have experienced at one time or another soggy bits of meat, fat and gristle floating in a watery broth with insidious limey flavour, but a real stew is delicious beyond belief, and you should choose your meat for stewing with as much care as you choose a special joint for roasting.

Best foods for stewing

Beef especially shin, oxtail, chuck.
Lamb neck fillet, neck chops, lamb shanks, boned shoulder cut into large cubes.
Veal breast, shoulder, middle neck, scrag, knuckle.
Poultry leg joints and thighs, on or off the bone, drumsticks.
Game including older pheasant, grouse and partridge, jointed or halved, haunch of venison, wild rabbit.
Fish with a very firm texture not prone to flaking. Molluscs can be added towards the end of cooking.
Vegetables such as aubergine [eggplant], courgette [zucchini], okra, onions, tomatoes.

Picture captions
1 Tuck a disc of buttered paper down around the sides of the pot to keep the stew closely covered.
2 Straining the stew gives you time to give the main components of the dish a makeover while the cooking liquid is reducing to a delicious sauce.

You need A heavy, flameproof stewpot or casserole with a well-fitting lid. The best are made of enamelled cast-iron.
• A wide pan for browning meat before stewing. It can be done in the stewpot, but if anything burns, the sauce will be bitter.
• Tongs and a fish slice [spatula].
• Two large baking trays on which to lay any meat.
• A disc of greaseproof or silicone paper, cut the same diameter as the inside of the stewpot.
• A straight-edged wooden spoon or bamboo rice paddle.
• A large, heavy chopping knife for bone trimming.
• A fine-meshed sieve and whisk.

To stew If using meat, cut it into neat, even chunks (not too small, as it will shrink) and trim away the fat. Place the meat or your joints of poultry on a tray, bring it to room temperature, and make sure all is dry. Chop the carefully-chosen vegetables and tie up the herbs and spices that will flavour the all-important gravy. You also need plenty of stock, ideally to match the stewing meat, and perhaps some wine or brandy.

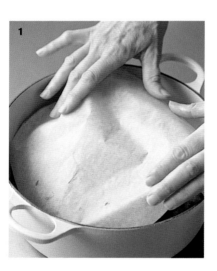

Heat a large frying pan. When 'jumping' hot, season the meat or poultry on both sides and brown it all over, pressing it down well and turning it as quickly as you can. Alternatively, if the meat has been coated in a moist, oniony spice paste, gently shallow fry it. Brown the vegetables, then drain and discard the fat. If the sediment in the pan is not bitter, deglaze it. When barely 2cm/¾in of the deglazing liquid is left in the pan, strain it through a fine mesh sieve into a jug and set aside to add later with the stock.

Heat the oven to 230°C/450°F/ Gas 8 and heat your stewpot on the stovetop. Lightly dust meat with 2-3 tbsp of flour and place in the open stew pot, in the very hot oven to toast the flour. Stir gently once or twice to ensure even browning.

Tuck the vegetables into and around the meat, add seasonings, herbs and spices. Add enough stock (plus deglazing liquid) to cover. Tuck all into place with the buttered paper, especially if the lid is a distance from the stew.

Reduce the oven temperature to 120°C-140°C/250°F-275°F/ Gas ½-1 or as directed in the recipe. Top up with stock or water just once or twice during cooking, and turn the stewpot occasionally so it cooks evenly.

When the meat or poultry is tender and cooked, strain the contents of the stewpot through a fine sieve, into a saucepan. Cover the meat with the paper to prevent drying. Now you have the time for a real makeover. Remove bones if you wish (they should fall out into your hand) or chop them close to the meat, with a quick, sharp blow from a cleaver. Discard spent herbs, bits of gristle and vegetables. Replace the vegetables with some that you have cooked freshly and briefly.

Start to boil the gravy, taking care to achieve the perfect consistency and flavour. If too salty, it is important you stop right away, as it only gets worse. When ready, the sauce should coat the back of a spoon when dipped in and raised. If you need to thicken the sauce at any stage, use a mixture of 2 tbsp cornflour

2

[cornstarch] and 2 tbsp water and add it to the pan slowly with the sauce at a rolling boil. Whisk briskly to give a shining, light sauce. If there are eyes of fat on top of the sauce, slide wide strips of paper towel over it until they've gone. Strain the sauce again, over the meat and vegetables.

Chill or freeze the stew at this stage if desired. Make sure you have enough sauce reserved to reheat the meat or poultry easily in the cleaned stewpot, or other pot suitable for serving. Take care to only serve enough sauce to coat the meat, and keep the remainder in the freezer or fridge to serve with a quick grill or pan-roast supper another day.

Fish stews are more like chunky soups and are highly versatile. The cooking time of fish and shellfish is gratifyingly short, apart from octopus, cuttlefish and large squid which require long cooking to become tender. Fish stock, fumet or salted water are used to form a soupy broth

that is not as unctuous as in a meat stew. Fish stews are best eaten as soon as they are made.

Vegetable stews usually take less than an hour, depending on the vegetables used. They often begin by cooking onions, garlic and aromatics until soft before adding other vegetables. Liquid is often supplied by tomatoes. Add quick-cooking vegetables towards the end of stewing to avoid a sludgey mush and keep their colour bright.

Advantages Meat and poultry stews taste better when made a day or so in advance.
• You have plenty of time to get the sauce the right flavour and consistency before serving.
• Stews are ideal buffet fare, and easy to eat when standing.
• They are made with inexpensive cuts of meat and vegetables.
• Stews can be cooked on top of the stove, or in the oven, whichever is most convenient.
• You can make a vast quantity, divide it into batches and freeze. The larger the quantity, the better the flavour.
• Twenty minutes either side of doneness is barely noticeable.

Points to remember Dark flat mushrooms give a rich flavour and plenty of tasty liquid.
• If you don't have stock to match your meat, chicken stock is a good alternative, even in a fish stew.
• Never use stock cubes for stewing. The flavour of the stock is paramount to the success of a stew and cubes make it too salty.
• Young meat stews badly, however careful your preparation.

Cooking en papillote

Best foods for cooking en papillote

Fish including red mullet, whole small trout, fillets of seabass, haddock, small tail pieces of cod, salmon and sea-trout
Shellfish such as large scallops, mussels and clams
Poultry including poussin, chicken breasts, boned quail
Pasta part-cooked then tossed with tomato sauce and shellfish
Vegetables including root vegetables, celery, leeks and broccoli
Fruit especially firm and tropical varieties, bananas, peaches, nectarines

Picture captions
1 Fold the sides of the parcel carefully and neatly to make an airtight seal.
2 With a little thought you can cook an entire meal of fish, pasta and vegetables in one bag.
3 Roasting bags are especially useful for dishes that need to be cooked longer than 40 minutes. After that length of time in the oven, paper papillotes turn brown and deteriorate.

Cooking en papillote is a rewarding process. Individual portions of food are smothered in butter, herbs and vegetables, then enclosed in a tightly sealed bag and cooked quickly and neatly in a hot oven. The bag is opened at the dining table, so that the tantalising aromas waft out as soon as it is opened, where they are most appreciated and don't disappear, as with other cooking methods, up the extractor.

You need A large sheet of greaseproof, silicone or parchment paper or aluminium foil per serving, or one roasting bag per serving.
• A stapler.
• An oven tray or baking sheet.

To cook en papillote Use lots of softened butter, the texture of face-cream, to lavishly grease a largish sheet of greaseproof or waxed paper, silicone or parchment paper, or foil. For attractive presentation, I cut the sheet in a heart-shape, which is traditional. Alternatively, you can use a roasting bag, which does not require buttering.

Place a fillet of fish or your chosen ingredient at the centre. Add some aromatic vegetables cut small and prettily, plus fresh herbs, and a few drops of stock or vermouth if available. You can include blanched and strained noodles if desired. If using fruit, cut it into neat cubes or slices, and sprinkle apples, pears and bananas with lemon juice to prevent discolouration. If you like, fruit can be macerated for 30 minutes in alcohol such as rum or liqueur, or a combination of sugar and alcohol. Dot it with butter before wrapping the parcel.

Gather up the paper, boat-shaped, so that the main ingredient lies in the middle. Fold the edges

tightly and neatly, from one end to the other, pinching each tiny fold to make an airtight seal, and then fold like this again. Staple the fold if necessary to secure it, but note this will make the parcel more difficult and less attractive to open at the table.

Put the pouches on a sturdy oven tray, which will protect your oven in case of leaks. Place in a very hot oven at 200°C-230°C/400°F-450°F/Gas 6-8 to generate steam quickly. Depending on the food used, the parcels will cook in 5-40 minutes. Bite-sized pieces of fish, and most seafood, will take around 5 minutes, fish fillets or small whole fish 15-20 minutes, pieces of fruit about 15 minutes, sliced root vegetables 30 minutes and whole poussin 40 minutes.

2

Serve the little parcels at the table, piping hot, in front of each person, so that they can open it themselves and enjoy the aromas.

Advantages En papillote is a clean, quick, tasty and fairly foolproof way to cook.
• Fish prepared this way is particularly juicy and delicious, and a clean light sauce is formed with no effort from the cook.
• Your oven stays pristine, there has been no smell of cooking, and a pleasant anticipatory element of surprise is added to the meal.
• The pouches can be prepared well in advance, and left in the fridge. Bring them to room temperature before cooking.
• The method is time-tolerant: the pouches can be left cooked out of the oven for about 10 minutes, without coming to harm or cooling very much.

Points to remember It is impossible to test if your main ingredient is cooked in a papillote, so you must make sure your oven is extremely hot before starting and follow the recommended timings given in your recipe.
• If you are combinging various ingredients in the same parcel, they must cook in the same time span. If the main ingredient or the vegetables generally take longer than 20 minutes to cook, fry them gently first. Examples include whole mushrooms, and quail. Pasta should be blanched before inclusion in the parcel.
• For cooking very tender, heat-shy items such as seafood, have your oven at its hottest temperature, and chill your paper bags until icy cold before use. They will be 'just-cooked' and steaming, when you take them out of the oven.
• This is not a method for feeding large numbers of people, unless you have a very large oven.
• Roasting bags do not require greasing before use.
• Greaseproof paper cooks to a rustic, shiny brown in about 20 minutes, parchment or silicone paper turns brown in

3

40 minutes, and then both tend to disintegrate. If you need to cook en papillote for longer, use a roasting bag or foil.
• Cooking papers such as greaseproof and silicone come in ever-smaller sheets, presumably to fit in the standard modern fitted kitchen drawer. As a result, it becomes more and more difficult, to my chagrin, to make large and roomy papillotes. Buy the largest rolls of cooking papers and foil you can find.
• Arrange the ingredients of your dish prettily inside the papillote and be sure to include herbs and other garnishes so that the meal looks as mouthwatering as possible when your guests open their parcels at the dining table.
• Place the parcels carefully on the baking tray and transfer them carefully to the plate after cooking so that the ingredients do not become too jumbled.
• This is a good method of producing a hot fresh fruit pudding in winter months.
• If using dark rum to flavour a dessert papillote of fruit such as pineapple, no further sugar is needed as the alcohol is sweet and packed with muscavado sugar flavours. Add vanilla bean, one or two allspice berries, and a clove for an evocative aroma.
• Fish fillets can also be cooked successfully in foil on a barbecue using this basic method.
• Fruit can be soaked in rum or a very thin fruit syrup and cooked in a foil bag on the barbecue too.
• Whole potatoes can be wrapped in foil and cooked in a barbecue's hot embers, where they will take about 40 minutes.

Stir-frying

Best foods for stir-frying

Seafood including tiger prawns, prawns or shrimps, reconstituted dried shrimp
Pork loin or rib chops, pork fillet
Veal loin or rib chops
Beef loin, rib, rump
Venison loin or haunch of venison
Chicken breast fillet
Vegetables including spring onions [scallions], bean sprouts, peppers, Cos, Webb or Iceberg lettuce, Chinese cabbage, mangetout [snowpeas], asparagus, mustard greens
Dried Chinese mushrooms reconstituted
Canned water chestnuts and bamboo shoots, drained
Tofu cut into cubes

Picture captions
1 All stir-fry ingredients should be neatly chopped and laid out ready to add to the wok before you start cooking.
2 Use your wok scoop to reach right down into the base of the pan and lift and toss the ingredients.

Although I have used the expression 'to stir-fry' in recipes in this book, meaning to cook food in fat in a saucepan or frying pan while stirring constantly or frequently, the special technique of stir-frying in a wok, as described below, is believed by the Chinese to be their unique contribution to world cooking. Only carefully chosen, tender, nicely cut or small ingredients are stir-fried. Cooking lightly and briskly, in very little oil over a very high heat, stimulates their natural fragrances and textures, so the resulting dish is an exciting and colourful combination of crunchy and slippery ingredients.

You need A wok, preferably made of iron or carbon steel.
• A fierce and responsive heat for cooking, ideally gas. Cooking on an electric hob doesn't produce the same results, and takes longer.
• A flat-ended wok scoop.
• A tray.
• A small oven glove to protect one hand as you tip and tilt the wok over a high heat.

Choice of wok If I had to buy a wok again, I would choose an enamelled carbon iron wok, which is easy to keep clean, not too heavy to lift and manoeuvre at speed, and consumes the heat of the flame efficiently for a good

stir-fry. Normal iron woks are cheap but need regular oiling to care for the surface.

If you are considering a non-stick model, realize it needs to be heavy enough to absorb heat, hold the heat evenly, and transfer it to the contents of the wok.

Electric woks have the advantage of not taking up space on the stovetop, and they are far better at mimicking the heat of a powerful gas flame than a conventional wok sitting on an electric ring. Providing your oil is smoking hot before you begin, you should enjoy good results.

Alternatively, try a shallow saucepan with rounded sides, at least 20cm/8in diameter if cooking for one, with superb conduction properties. If it is stainless steel, the saucepan will need a copper or aluminium lining sandwiched, not only on the base, but all the way up the sides of the pan.

To stir fry Prepare all the ingredients before you try to start cooking. Except for beansprouts, vegetables need to be uniformly cut into small cubes, thin slices or matchsticks, not bigger than 5-6cm/2-2½in long and 0.4cm/¼in thick. Mangetout [snowpeas] and baby sweetcorn may be sliced lengthways or left whole as desired. Meat and poultry must be trimmed of all fat and bone, and cut across the grain into strips or cubes. Line up your prepared ingredients on a tray in the order you will be cooking them, and place next to the stove.

Heat the wok or saucepan until you can see smoke rising from it. This prevents the food from sticking. Gently add 3-4 tbsp oil, such as grapeseed or groundnut – you need one that has a high smoke point. Run it down and around the sides of the wok by tipping and tilting the pan with your gloved hand.

Start by adding your aromatic ingredients first – onion, garlic and ginger – taking care they do not burn. Then add the remaining ingredients at high speed. Those with the densest texture or chunky stalks should go in first, followed by softer, leafier vegetables that cook in less time. Beansprouts are usually added at the end as they cook in just a few seconds. Slide the wok scoop to the bottom of the wok, turning and tossing, generally cooking for 3-5 minutes in total.

Advantages Stir-frying is fun, quick and easy to do, watching the vegetables shining and tumbling over each other and the steam hissing up the extractor.
• The food is lightly cooked (except for chicken and pork which must be cooked all the way through) and nutritious.
• It can be an all-in-one-meal, with a good splash of Chinese rice wine or medium-dry sherry around the sides of the wok, and

a tablespoon or so of soy sauce, oyster sauce, or sesame oil afterwards for flavouring.

Points to remember The preparation, the uniform slicing, chopping and cubing of ingredients, is fairly time-consuming, but integral to the success of stir-frying. It will also make the finished dish look more attractive.
• My Chinese friends add far, far more oil than you will ever find recommended in a recipe book. It is this that gives their dishes that outstanding crisp-crunchiness and wok aroma we love so much.
• Chill the meat to almost frozen to make it easier to cut into bite-sized pieces or thin strips.
• Add the aromatic ingredients first to flavour the oil and distribute the fragrance.
• Ingredients with high moisture content such as soft leafy vegetables and beansprouts are added near the end.
• Sesame oil is more a condiment or flavouring than a cooking medium. It is often sprinkled over

stir-fries right at the end to optimize its delicious aroma.
• Make sure the table is set and serving plates are hot and ready: like soufflés and salads, stir-fries need to be served immediately.
• Stir-frying is not restricted to Oriental and Southeast Asian recipes. Try crisp stir-fried cucumber with dill (page 114) as a partner to European dishes.
• While it may be tempting to use whatever utensil is closest to hand, a proper wok scoop produces the best results. Its unique shape corresponds to the sides and base of the wok, so that the food can be scooped and flipped most efficiently.
• Make sure your wok has a lid, and use one of your own, if you have to. Placing a lid over the wok for a short period at the end of stir-frying will trap the dense, moist heat generated in the pan and give the ingredients a powerful final blast to finish cooking.
• Woks can be used for more than stir-frying. They are also suitable for small deep-frying and simmering jobs, and especially for quick braises of fish.
• Although you never want a gas flame to surround a saucepan, only burn beneath it, the opposite is true for wok cooking. On the wok gas burners now fitted in many domestic kitchens, a powerful flame cradles the base and sides of the wok, which is held in place safely by a metal ring.
• Electric and induction hobs are not satisfactory sources of heat for stir-frying, as the area of contact between the rounded base and the hot plate it touches, is much too small for the job.

Shallow-frying

**Best foods for
shallow-frying**

Fish and shellfish such
as white fish fillets and
steaks, scallops, shelled
raw prawns
Meat including veal
fillet and escalopes,
sausages, fillet steak
medallions or thick
slices
Poultry such as chicken
breast fillets, turkey
escalopes and duck
breasts
Vegetables including
mushrooms, aubergines
[eggplant], onions and
ingredients for sauces
and stocks
Eggs
Bread items such as
croûtes and croûtons

Like many people, I have cut back on the amount of shallow-frying I do. It's not just a concern about the calories consumed when one eats a lot of fried food, but it is a fairly messy process for a small kitchen. Still, there's no doubt it produces delicious results, especially for white fish. In shallow-frying, only tender, small ingredients are cooked in a frying pan, over a gentle heat. The combination of fat or oil and heat accentuates and complements their flavour, and the process can be very quick or fairly lengthy, depending on the ingredients chosen.

You need A frying pan, preferably non-stick.
• A fish slice [spatula], perforated spoon, tongs or palette knife with which to turn and move the food.
• A fat screen (looks like a lightweight metal version of a tennis racquet) for frying chicken.
• A tray lined with crumpled paper towel.

Choice of fats for frying Choose from oils such as sunflower, safflower, groundnut or pale gold olive oil, but not cold-pressed. I never buy 'vegetable oil'. Sunflower has a delicate, neutral flavour but goes rancid quickly. Good quality olive oil has a terrific flavour and is considered good for you. Always use the best oil you can afford, as you will taste it in your dishes, and keep it in a cool, dark place to prolong its life.

Solid fats suitable for frying include butter, lard, bacon fat, duck fat, and goose fat. The better the butter, the more delicious the result, but it needs the lowest of all temperatures when frying. Lightly salted or unsalted dairy butter is ideal, if you can afford it. It has less milky white solids than other butters, and it is these that turn brown in the heat. Although the result will

still taste good at this stage, the toasted solids sometimes produce a speckled result – and just a few minutes inadvertently spent at too high a heat in the frying pan will result in them darkening to unpleasant black spots.

A combination of oil and butter is ideal for frying fish, meat and vegetables, and gives you a little more leeway on the browning of the butter, as the oil 'stretches' or raises the temperature at which the butter particles start to burn, also known as the 'smoke point'. Heat a tablespoon of oil in the frying pan before adding the butter.

Alternatively, use clarified butter – pure butter fat from which the milk solids have been removed. It stores well and is ideal for frying foods that are best seared, such as the surface of beef fillet before roasting. Ghee, from India, has similar qualities, and does not need to be stored in the refrigerator.

To shallow fry Meat and poultry fillets and escalopes, as well as pieces of fish, are often seasoned before frying. Place the oil or other fat in the pan and heat. You need a depth of 1cm/½in. To test the heat, drag a piece of food lightly across the oil: if it sizzles, the oil is ready. Place the pieces of food in it, one by one, arranging them like figures on a clock if appropriate, so you will remember which to turn over first. Brown the surface, and partially cook the interior. The fat conducts heat, some is absorbed by the food, giving it a delicious flavour.

Turn the food over and repeat on the other side until the food is cooked. Then place it gently on a baking tray lined with crumpled paper towel, which will absorb the excess fat from the food. Keep the tray of food in a low oven until ready to serve.

If the fat and crusty sediment in the pan are not burned (taste it and see) you can make a quick sauce to serve with your fried food. Pour off any excess fat, then add stock, cream, wine or other liquid to the pan, and boil until it is thick enough to coat the back of a spoon. Strain through a fine sieve and serve immediately.

Advantages Shallow-frying is a quick method of cooking, and gives bland and tender food such as mushrooms, escalopes of veal, crumb-coated chicken fillets, and eggs, a buttery taste and seductive feel in the mouth.

Points to remember Frying adds calories to the food, and saturated fats such as beef dripping and lard are high in cholesterol, which can be dangerous to good health. This is why I have not recommended frying everything that can be cooked this way, for example, cheese and fatty lamb cuts such as noisettes, in this

book. However, if you fry carefully following the guidelines given here, you reduce the problem. Non-stick pans and fat spritzers allow us to fry using very little fat and are readily available in kitchenware stores.
• Frying food with dry surfaces in hot fat will give an appetizing crisp coating and the food will absorb less fat.
• Cold food absorbs more fat, as does frying in cool oil or fat, so food must be at room temperature before cooking, and the fat heated to the correct temperature.
• The penetration of fat is kept at bay by the moisture in the food turning to steam; the escaping steam prevents fat seeping into the food and making it soggy and overly greasy.
• Watch the pan all the time! Never go away and leave it. Practise makes perfect.
• Thick pieces of food will burn on the outside before the interior is cooked. You must choose food that is tender and thin.
• The smaller and thinner the food, the more rapidly it cooks. Finely sliced liver takes less than a minute at a high temperature and is juicy and tender.
• Do not move the food round the pan if you want it to take on colour. Let it sit in one place, allow the steam to evaporate, and then it will start to brown.
• Choose the correct oil or fat, which reaches the temperature you require without burning.
• Butter has a unique way of telling you when it is hot enough to start to fry. Butter contains water, which foams and sizzles as it evaporates, after which the

temperature of the butter begins to rise. Fry then, when the butter has stopped foaming or 'singing'.
• Foods with high water content, such as aubergine [eggplant] and courgettes [zucchini], are sometimes salted, rinsed and dried before frying to get rid of excess moisture. Unfortunately this process leaves them very damp and they fry better if thoroughly blotted dry with paper towels. Aubergines are also notorious for soaking up oil. The trick to frying them is to heat your oil until almost smoking: don't be afraid, you will be thrilled with the results.
• Many foods today have water added during production. Unless your source of poultry is a top free range or organic supplier, you will find that frying chicken often results in tremendous spitting of hot fat as the injected water boils and escapes, so use a fat screen on the pan.
• Vegetables, some of which contain up to 90 per cent water, take ages to colour as they only brown once all the water has evaporated. Don't hurry this process. They sweeten as they cook, and this flavour is valuable.
• Fried eggs can be tricky to turn over, so spoon the fat over the eggs to cook them on the upper side. Alternatively, slip them under a hot preheated grill [broiler] to finish cooking, which will give a less fatty result.
• When preparing food that has been coated with egg and breadcrumbs, leave it to rest in the fridge for at least 30 minutes and up to several hours before frying, to help the coating settle.

Deep-frying

Deep-frying involves cooking in powerful heat, using hot oil or fat. It is the best way of cooking very crisp little morsels of fish and vegetables such as tempura, chips and vegetable crisps. In deep-frying, food is cooked by the heat from hot oil which totally surrounds it. It should be cooked right through, golden-brown in colour, crisp and dry on the outside, succulent and juicy within. The periods of actual frying are always short, the food must be removed when nicely coloured. This means that we can only fry foods that cook quickly, which usually means they must be tender to begin with. Once the oil is hot, cooking is brief – as little as 1 minute for game chips or 4-5 minutes for fritters and croquettes.

Best foods for deep-frying

Fish including small whole fish such as whitebait
Seafood especially baby squid
Vegetables such as sliced courgettes [zucchini], onions and aubergine [eggplant], and thinly sliced wafers of root vegetables
Potato chips cut long or round
Croquettes
Fritters

Best fats for deep-frying

Mild-flavoured oils such as groundnut, grapeseed, avocado and corn oil

Solid fat such as lard and pure beef dripping, especially for chips

Picture captions
1 Use a deep-frying thermometer to help you maintain the oil at the correct temperature.
2 For successful frying, the fat must bubble briskly around each piece of food.
3 A simple dusting of seasoned flour is all that is required to give a tasty coating to onion rings.

You need An electric deep-fryer, or a deep pot with a lid, such as the one you use for cooking pasta.
• A blanching basket, or a chip basket. Wide mesh wire is best.
• A large tray lined with crumpled paper towel to absorb excess oil after cooking.
• A baking tray lined with paper in an oven of 110°C/230°F/Gas ¼, for keeping the fried food hot if absolutely necessary. If you have a gas oven, forego the paper.
• A lidded container for storing the used fat.
• A funnel, to help you return cold used fat to the container.
• Tongs and a skimmer.
• A thermometer suitable for use when deep-frying.

The electric deep-fryer Some are built into the counter top, others stand on top of it. Their great advantage is that they are temperature-controlled. When the cold food hits the hot oil and the temperature drops dramatically, there is a surge of heat to return to the proper cooking temperature. Deep-fryers that operate only when covered by a clamp-on lid, I find a little strange, as I always judge when fried food is done by its colour and dying out of the bubbles. But the cover does prevent some of the smells and oily steam escaping into the kitchen. Read the fryer's instructions before purchasing. If, for example, you like to fry in solid fats and it only takes oil, you may decide it's not for you.

Coatings for deep-fried foods can be dry, such as a dusting of seasoned flour, or moist, as in a batter. They prevent the food's juices leaking out into the oil or fat and spoiling it. To some extent, such

coatings also prevent the food absorbing too much oil.

To deep-fry Turn on the extractor before you begin. Crumple some kitchen paper and place it on a tray. Test the temperature of the oil with a cube of bread – it should brown in 30 seconds. Alternatively, use a deep-frying thermometer. Most foods are fried at 180°-190°C/356-374°F but check the recipe, or the packet, before cooking.

First dip the basket briefly in the hot oil to prevent food sticking to the mesh. Ensure the food has been well dried, otherwise it will splatter when it meets the hot oil. Place a small batch of the food in the basket; ideally it should take up one-tenth of the basket.

Quickly plunge the basket into the hot oil – this element of 'surprise' is vital to successful frying. Maintain the heat if frying on the stovetop, so that the fat bubbles briskly around each piece of food. When it is the desired colour, or when the bubbles disperse, lift the food quickly from the oil, shake well, and distribute evenly over the crumpled paper. Fried food should rustle as you shake it. It should be crisp, not leathery or softly soggy with oil. Traditionally fried food was served on a white linen napkin, to show that there wasn't a trace of grease on it. Does yours pass this test?

Advantages Fried food is delicious. The crunchy outer coating, the juiciness of the filling, the sprinkling of salt or sugar, or both, over the top – all combine to give flavours to which most people love to succumb.

Points to remember Hot oil is highly volatile, especially when put in contact with moisture, and all food is naturally moist. Dry the food thoroughly before frying.
• Ensure the oil is as deep as possible. Use a pan large enough to hold at least 2 litres/3½ pints/ 8¾ cups without being more than half-full. This allows space for all the bubbling that will take place yet there is enough oil to surround the food completely, ensuring the pieces are all equally and evenly cooked. A good quantity of oil also ensures that the addition of food to the pan does not cause too great a drop in temperature, resulting in greasy, soggy food.
• As long as the oil bubbles, the moisture in the food, which has turned to steam in the heat, is keeping it at bay. Once the bubbling stops, it is a sure sign the food must be removed immediately from the pan.

• Without a temperature-controlled deep-fryer, it is tricky keeping the fat hot enough to fry, but not so hot that the food burns.
• Frying in batches takes time.
• Large pieces of uncooked food (for example big chips) need to be deep-fried twice for best results.
• Coatings and batters add to the preparation time, the washing up, and sadly pack on the calories.
• Fried food must be served as soon as it comes out of the fryer.
• Never leave the fryer unattended.
• If the oil begins to smoke and change its consistency it is a sign it could be about to burst into flames. Cover it with the lid, remove immediately from the heat, and be ready to cover it with a fire blanket.
• Hot oil has a penetrating smell, and seems to coat everything in the kitchen with a fine, sticky film.
• Take good care of your oil. Strain it through muslin or a fine sieve after each frying session. Change the oil or fat completely when it darkens and begins to have a taste and odour when cold.

Sweet baking

There is absolutely no mystique to baking, and creating the wonderful aromas that will pervade your home as you do so. But for instant and consistent success follow good recipes to the letter and measure out the ingredients exactly and accurately. Baking is similar to roasting, but does not employ fat as a cooking medium. It is a dry method of cooking, so items to be baked must have a high liquid content which, in the heat of the oven, will set enough to remain intact when taken out of the tin, and still be appetizingly and comfortingly moist.

Best foods for baking

Desserts including soufflés and roulades
Pastries such as tarts and pies
Biscuits and cookies including crackers
Cakes of all types and sizes, as well as traybakes and slices
Bread and quick-breads including scones and muffins

Picture captions
1 *Baking rice (stored in a jar and used only for baking) is used to hold up the sides of a pastry case during baking and prevent collapse. You could also use dried beans.*
2 *Test a cooked cake for doneness by pressing it in the centre. It should spring back immediately.*
3 *If dough or pastry gets sticky while you are working with it, even once you've started cutting, slide it onto an upturned baking tray and place in fridge or freezer to firm up.*

You need A good oven.
- Accurate weighing scales.
- Measuring spoons.
- 2-3 unbreakable measuring jugs.
- A few unbreakable bowls.
- A flour sieve.
- Heavyish metal baking sheets.
- Shallow fluted tart [pie] tins.
- Cake tins, ideally non-stick, in a variety of shapes and sizes.
- A large cool, roomy surface for rolling out.
- A wide rolling pin.
- A palette knife, large metal spoon, and rubber spatula [scraper].
- A flour dredger.
- A pastry or paint brush.
- Cookie cutters.
- A wire cooling rack.
- Hand-held electric mixer.
- Large electric mixer.
- Baking rice.
- Silicone or parchment paper.
- Teflon liners, mats or similar.
- Kitchen foil.

To bake a pastry shell 'blind', you need to line the pastry shell in its tin, with a generous sheet of foil so that it comes well up the sides, with plenty to spare. Stroke the foil vertically into the flutings.

Fill the centre with a generous amount of rice. Push it up the sides of the foil, so that the pastry

is anchored to the sides of the tin and prevented from sagging. You are not weighing the pastry base down as much as propping the sides up. If you have not done so earlier, chill the pastry shell for at least 30 minutes, or keep it overnight in the fridge.

For optimum crispness, cook the shell on a preheated baking tray, or on the floor of a 'falling' oven – that is, an oven decreasing in temperature. Start off at 200°C/400°F/Gas 6. After 15 minutes, turn down to 180°C/350°C/Gas 4. Feel the pastry. If it is firm and dry, but not crisp, remove the foil and rice. Take the pastry shell out of the oven to do this.

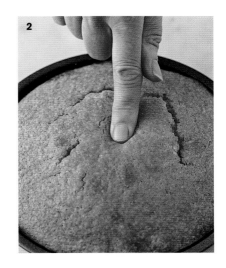

Return the shell to the oven to dry out, watching the colour of the pastry carefully, keeping it blonde. Try covering it loosely with foil, (not easy in a fan oven). If the top edges are darkening significantly, crimp a ribbon of foil over them. The pastry shell is done when it feels and looks crisp, and has started to shrink inwards from the edges of the tin.

To bake cakes, line the base of the tin neatly with a disc of buttered silicone paper, buttering the tin first to make it stick. The bottom of the cake becomes the top, which should end up neat and trim. Place a roasting pan of water in the bottom of the oven to moisten the oven. This prevents the sugars caramelizing and firming up too early. The cake is able to rise to its maximum expansion before setting. If the cake is to be cooked for longer than 50 minutes, line the sides of the tin with several layers of paper, otherwise the tin burns the sides of the cake, making it crusty, dark and scorched.

Advantages Home baking allows you to choose the best ingredients for your cake or pastry, which mass manufacturers tend not to use.
• It is easier than you probably think. Pastries freeze beautifully with no loss of quality and, with a bit of forethought, they can always be on hand when you need them.
• Baking also makes you feel good and alleviates stress. When you come in from work and start baking cookies or a quick bread, you'll find a great deal of pleasure, and have the lovely results to eat.

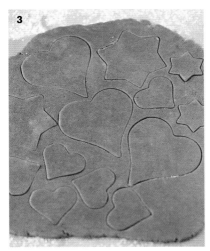

Points to remember The size of tin is crucial to success. Place a cake batter or sponge mix in too large a tin, and it will come out like a pancake. Good recipes will specify the right tin, giving you the correct diameter and depth for each cake. All soufflé dishes and cake tins need to be filled to within 1cm/½in of the top to help them rise properly. You won't need a lot, but four or five tins of different sizes will ensure success each time.

• For quick conduction of heat, tart tins should be light and thin.
• To cool tarts or cakes effectively, always place them on a wire rack immediately after baking.
• Butter all tins well. Whatever goes in, has to come out. Winkle stuck-on pastry or cake loose with patience and perseverance, using the tip of a thin pointed knife or a skewer.
• Line every cake tin with a disc of well-buttered silicone paper. Soften the butter in a microwave first, and apply liberally. Use a brush to reach into the corners.
• Wash your tins then dry them in the oven as it cools, to prevent them going rusty.
• Cakes and soufflés are best made in warm kitchens: 35°C/95°F, about blood temperature. This warms all your ingredients, equipment and tins equally. Any colder than this (my kitchen is 24°C/75°F most days) means you have to warm the eggs and equipment, by placing them in a bowl of hot water.
• It is a nightmare making pastry in a warm kitchen, but in an uncomfortably chilly kitchen you will find it incredibly easy. To help the process on a hot day, turn your fridge down to the coldest setting, empty a shelf for the rolled out pastry, and store your rolling pin, flour, sugar and water in the fridge or freezer until icy cold. If you have warm hands, cool them by holding a small plastic bag of ice-cubes.
• Give sweet pastry a little extra attention when you bake. It needs a slightly cooler oven due to its higher butter and sugar content, and can brown and burn quickly.

PART TWO

Recipes

"It was Lyn who enabled me to become the kitchen equivalent of a couturier." Bruce Oldfield

Fish and shellfish

**Fast ways with fish
and shellfish**
Make ceviche by
marinating exquisitely
fresh scallops in lime or
lemon juice for 30
minutes. Or serve fresh
fish as sashimi, fish
carpaccio or tartare.
Marinate salmon in
equal quantities of soy
sauce and runny honey
for 30 minutes, then
cook en papillote in foil
parcels using no butter
or other liquid.
Steam squares of white
fish fillets. Serve with
boiled jasmine rice and
drizzle with a sauce
made from 3 tbsp soy
sauce, 1 tbsp rice
vinegar, and ½ tbsp
finely grated ginger.
Steam white fish fillets
and serve with ready-
made sweet chilli jam.
Bake swordfish steaks
in the oven and serve
with lime butter and
green salad.
Pan-roast salmon fillets
and serve with pickled
cucumber sauce.
Char-grill tuna steaks
and serve with
watermelon salsa.

Born within earshot of the breakers of the Indian ocean, I was lucky
my father was a keen fisherman; rarely have I seen such whiteness in
the flake of sea fish. I preferred the elegance of casting for brown trout
in cool, upland streams. The fish, cooked in butter over an open fire,
was succulent with a crisp, tasty skin, so I learned while still a child
the first lesson: the fresher the fish, the simpler the cooking method.

The nomenclature of fish and its
preparation is confusing to expert
and beginner alike. Be very
specific with your fishmonger and
hold out for what you really
want. Two minutes of
embarrassment at the fish counter
is worth half an hour of flailing
about at home with a slippery
fish you knew you didn't want.

If buying from large stores,
choose the one with the smallest
fish counter to ensure a quick
turnover. Avoid any counter with
a strong fishy smell. Buy early if
you want a particular fish, buy
late and you will have to take what
is left. Try to cook it that day.

When just starting out as a
cook, it is a good idea to buy fish
ready-filletted for a better yield.
Fillets and steaks are also the
easiest to cook. The fishmonger
will be happy to fillet the fish for
you. Ask him to remove all
scales, fins and spines. When
buying white fish, ask for the
bones to make broths or stock.
You can freeze the bones if you
don't require them immediately.

What to look for, what to avoid
• In fresh whole fish, eyes should
be bright, full and transparent.
• Gills should be red, pink or
burgundy in colour, and moist.
• Scales should be moist, shining
and plentiful and should lie flat,
firmly attached to the skin.

• Flesh should be firm, undamaged
(no splits) and resilient, so that
when pressed with a finger, the
impression goes quickly. Also, the
flesh should shine, not appear dry.
• Skin can be slimy, but not sticky.
• The smell should be pleasant: of
iodine or the sea. Sometimes a
quick rinse under cold running
water will freshen up the smell. In
fact, it is always good to do this
before cooking fish, but never soak
fish in water, unless you are trying
to eliminate a muddy flavour.
• When buying packaged fish, it
should be plump, firm and moist,
but not sitting in a pool of liquid.

Storing and freezing fish
• If you have to keep fish overnight
in a domestic fridge, remove it
from its original packaging. Give
it a quick rinse, then dry and wrap
in foil. Place a chiller pack on top
of the fish to keep its temperature
at 1°-2°C/33-36°F.
• Freeze only fish caught that day,
with the innards intact. It is best
to have a word with your
fishmonger and ask him if the
fish is fresh enough to freeze.
• Prepare your freezer in advance.
Turn it down to its lowest setting
before placing the fish in it. Whole
fish will retain a better flavour
than fillets. Keep it wrapped and
eat within three months.
• Defrost fish, still covered, in a
dish overnight in the fridge.

The principles of cooking fish Our aim in cooking fish is to:
• Conserve and add to the natural flavour of the fish.
• Prevent it falling apart.
• Keep it moist and succulent. Fish in the main has delicate flesh. It never needs long cooking, but some methods are faster and, in my opinion, better than others. When using high temperatures, as when grilling, the heat has to be extreme to cook the fish as fast as possible before it dries out. Overcooked fish is similar to a curdled sauce. When the protein elements lose their ability to hold the water dispersed through the flesh, the proteins and juices separate. The flesh then becomes hard and dry and will be surrounded by the fish juices.

How to tell when fish is cooked The protein (flakes of fish) begins to coagulate or firm up at 55°C/131°F. Get ready to take fish off the heat at this point. At 60°-65°C/140°-150°F the fish is perfectly cooked.

The tip of a knife inserted deep into the flesh feels hot when pressed flat to the wrist. At this stage, the flesh comes easily off the bone, and the translucent flesh turns opaque all the way down to the bone and in the deepest part of the fillet.

Test and look, opening the fillet with a small, fine knife in the thickest part of the fish. Hide the hole with a garnish when serving.

Above 71°C/160°F the juices begin to squeeze out. The flakes become dry and tough and the fish breaks up cleanly when you try to pick it up.

You can actually see fish cooking when using a frying pan or char-grill. Watch the translucency disappear from the bottom of the fillet, next to the base of the pan. When the opaqueness reaches the centre, it is time to turn the fish over and cook the other side. In small fish, the eyes go white when the fish is cooked. In large, whole fish the fins, or their remains, come out easily when tugged.

Rule of thumb For whole fish, steaks and fillets, for baking, grilling, poaching and frying, measure the fish at its thickest point and for every 2.5cm/1in allow a total of 10 minutes cooking time. Add on a few minutes if:
• The fish is very cold.
• You have filled your pan, griddle plate or oven full of fish or any other cold ingredient.
• The fish is wrapped, for example in foil or leaves.
• The cooking vessel is very heavy (cast-iron for example) and the weight of the pan is not specifically mentioned in the recipe. For this allow 15-20 minutes extra.

The best advice I can give
• Take care not to overcook it. Cook fish lightly. It really is easy.
• Cook with feeling. Try to imagine what is happening during the cooking process. You will be surprised how quickly your timing will improve.
• Remember it is the thickness of the fillet, not the length, that determines the cooking time.
• Remember that fish continues to cook as it waits to be served, especially small fish and fillets. Eat it as soon as you can.

• Use your common sense and you will soon be proud of your results.

The best cooking methods My favourite methods for fish are:
Pan-roasting. It's easy and quick, especially for 1-4 people, and produces a delectably crunchy skin. Try it with fillets of sea bass and salmon, skin on, also for thick cod and salmon cutlets.
Char-grilling. It gives optimum flavour but is best suited to steaks and fillets of oily fish. Try it too with whole small fish such as bream, red mullet and sardines. Don't use anything larger as the heat will not penetrate.
Steaming. It's simple and healthy, perfect for fillets of white and oily fish. Knots and rolls of white fish fillets look attractive. You can also steam whole fish. Avoid steaming cod as it falls apart into large, tender flakes.
Shallow-frying. This brings out the flavour of delicate white fish.
En papillote. Excellent when you want to prepare the fish, vegetables and sauce well in advance.

Tips for shellfish
• All shellfish have the potential to become toxic.
• Keep them chilled at all times, even during car journeys.
• Faced with two specimens of equal size, choose the heavier.
• It is best to buy, cook and eat shellfish within the day. However, if on your fishmonger's advice you can cook them the next day, store the shellfish in the fridge in a clean basin covered with wet, folded newspaper.
• Try purchasing fish and shellfish by mail order.

Smoked trout with radishes, cucumber, wasabi and yogurt
Serves 4

150ml/5floz/²⁄₃ cup Greek set yogurt
½ cucumber, unpeeled, plus
*   75g/2½oz/½ cup cucumber, peeled,*
*   deseeded, and cut into fine strips*
75g/2½oz smoked trout or smoked
*   salmon, cut into fine strips*
75g/2½oz/½ cup red radishes, cut into
*   fine strips*
3 tbsp double [heavy] or whipping
*   cream, whipped*
1 tsp wasabi paste or hot horseradish
*   sauce*
1 tbsp chopped dill, plus 4 sprigs extra,
*   to garnish*
4 tsp salmon or Sevruga caviar
salt and freshly milled pepper

You will also need

a salad ring or cookie cutter about
*   6.5cm/2½in diameter*

Line a sieve with a sheet of paper towel and set it over a bowl. Place the yogurt in the sieve to drain for approximately 1 hour. Meanwhile, run a canelle knife down the side of the unpeeled cucumber to decorate, then cut it into thin discs.

When ready to serve, arrange the cucumber slices in a circle in the centre of four serving plates. In a mixing bowl, combine the drained yogurt, smoked trout, cucumber strips, radishes, whipped cream, wasabi or horseradish and chopped dill and season thoroughly.

Place the salad ring or cookie cutter in the centre of each circle of cucumber, fill with the fish mixture, spread the surface flat, then lift the mold away vertically. Garnish each portion with the dill sprigs and caviar and serve immediately.

Recipe notes During my time working with Anton Mosimann on his healthy eating cookbook *Cuisine Naturelle*, I prepared this elegant, light, summery starter for guests in some of the world's finest hotels. Over the years I have come to love its reliability.

It can be prepared hours before serving, as long as you keep all the elements separate and assemble them at the last minute, otherwise the salt in the fish will draw out the moisture in the other ingredients. Keep the prepared ingredients in plastic boxes or wrapped in damp paper towel.

If you are preparing this dish for large numbers, slice the vegetables on a mandoline before cutting them into strips. The mandoline is a specialized cutting gadget with an exceptionally keen set of blades that cut vegetables easily, evenly, beautifully and swiftly. The results look as if they were produced by an experienced chef. Avoid wooden models, which warp too easily, and instead choose a sturdy Japanese plastic mandoline, or the larger stainless steel type. Although more expensive, I prefer the stainless steel versions because they feel safer to use.

Little smoked haddock custards
Serves 6

170g/6oz smoked haddock fillet
1 bay leaf
1 sprig parsley
6 peppercorns
about 150ml/5floz/²⁄₃ cup whipping
*   cream [heavy cream]*
about 150ml/5floz/²⁄₃ cup milk
juice of ½ lemon
4 small eggs
4 tbsp chives, finely cut (optional)
softened butter, for greasing
salt and freshly milled white pepper

To serve

a little Saffron Shrimp Sauce (page 172)
6 sprigs dill or mizuna

You will also need

a roasting tray bain-marie
6 small timbale molds 7cm/2¾in
*   diameter of 150ml/5floz/²⁄₃ cup*
*   capacity*

Brush the molds with softened butter, ideally twice, chilling between each buttering. Preheat the oven to 160°C/310°F/Gas 2-3.

Rinse the smoked haddock briefly in cold water. Place in a shallow saucepan or frying pan with the bay leaf, parsley, peppercorns, cream and milk. Bring to a boil and simmer for 1 minute or so, cooking until the haddock flakes are creamy-white and slide off the skin easily.

Lift the haddock from the poaching liquor. Separate the flesh into large flakes and remove and discard the skin and flavourings. Strain the liquor into a measuring jug and, if necessary, add extra cream or milk to make the quantity up to 425ml/14floz/1¾ cups. Set aside to cool. >

Sprinkle a little lemon juice over the fish and leave to marinate while the liquor is cooling.

Whisk the eggs together in a jug. When the poaching liquor is tepid, add the eggs and chives, if using. Season with pepper and a little salt.

Prepare the bain-marie by filling a roasting tray with steaming water (see page 24). Place a buttered silicone disc in the base of each mold. Divide the flaked haddock between the molds. Pour the custard mixture over and cover each custard with a square of buttered paper.

Arrange the molds in the bain-marie in the centre of the oven and cook for 35-40 minutes. They are done when they feel spongy yet set when pressed in the centre with a finger. Remove from the oven and leave to stand in the bain-marie for about 10 minutes before turning them out. Serve with the saffron shrimp sauce, garnished with the herbs.

Recipe notes This makes a luxurious starter or lunch dish when followed by salad. Although it works well with semi-skimmed milk, I always use full cream or Guernsey milk for cooking, because the recipes work better and the taste is improved. Fillet of undyed haddock, on its skin, gives the best flavour.

Leaving the custards to stand in the bain-marie for 10 minutes after cooking is the secret of turning them out successfully. If you have to wait longer before serving, top up the bain-marie with boiling water to keep them hot, and make sure your sauce and plates are hot before serving.

Salt roast salmon
Serves 6-8

1 side fresh salmon, about 1kg/2¼lb, scaled and pin-boned, skin intact

For the marinade
4 tbsp coarse sea salt crystals [kosher salt]
4 tbsp caster sugar [superfine granulated]
1 tsp whole white peppercorns, crushed
15g/½oz/⅓ cup dill, chopped

To serve
Warm Tomato and Herb Vinaigrette (page 165) or Pickled Cucumber Sauce (page 166)

Lay the side of salmon on a large, long piece of foil. Mix all the ingredients for the marinade together and spread over the flesh-side of the salmon. Wrap the fish up well and store in a cool place for about 2 hours, but not much longer.

Remove the side of fish from the marinade and rinse well under lots of running water. Pat dry with a cloth. Cut the salmon into 6-8 equal portions and chill until required.

When ready to cook, preheat the oven to 200°C/400°F/Gas 6. Heat a large non-stick pan on the cooker. Add the salmon portions, skin-side down, then after 1 minute or so, transfer the pan to the oven for 8-10 minutes. Serve with the warm tomato and herb vinaigrette, or pickled cucumber sauce.

Recipe notes Pre-salting concentrates the flavour, brightens the colour and gives an intriguing impact when the fish is cooked. This is best made with farmed salmon and can be served with mashed potatoes and green vegetables, boiled or steamed.

Fillets of fish with tarragon crust
Serves 6

30g/1oz/½ cup tarragon leaves
110g/4oz/2 cups fresh breadcrumbs
80g/3oz/¼ stick butter
6 fillets of turbot, brill or halibut, about 140g/5oz each, skinned
3 tbsp sunflower oil
flour, for dusting
salt and freshly milled white pepper

In a food processor, combine the herbs, breadcrumbs and 30g/1oz/¼ stick of the butter and blend until the mixture is green. Season to taste.

Pat the fish fillets dry, then season them and dust with flour, gently shaking off as much of the excess flour as you can so that only the finest coating remains.

Heat the remaining butter and the oil in a large frying pan until the mixture froths in golden bubbles. Fry the fish for 2-3 minutes each side until just cooked. Remove the fish from the pan and place on a heavy non-stick baking tray. Cover each fillet with some of the herb topping, patting it into position. Set aside until ready to cook – the fish can wait for several hours at this stage.

To finish cooking, preheat an overhead grill [broiler]. Place the prepared fish under the grill and cook until the crust is lightly toasted and the fish is hot all the way through. To test it, insert a skewer in one of the fillets for 2 seconds, then hold it against the inside of your wrist – if it feels hot the fish is ready. Serve immediately.

Recipe notes We use this often in my classes at Anton Mosimann's Culinary Academy in London, and like most of his recipes, it is ideal for serving to a crowd.

Frying the fish in advance in a mixture of oil and butter will bring out the best of the subtle, delicate flavours that make brill, turbot and halibut so expensive. Your fillets need to be evenly shaped and flat, otherwise the topping can fall off in an undignified manner. You should also avoid fish that tend to separate into large flakes, such as thick cod fillets, as the topping will fall from them too. If you are not sure, ask your fishmonger which variety is best.

If you chill the fish after preparing it, you may need to place it in a very hot oven first for a few minutes, before finishing it under the grill.

Herbs other than tarragon may be used, but go down the road of soft varieties such as parsley and dill.

If you would like to include a sauce with this dish, choose white wine and dill sauce (page 170), warm tomato and herb vinaigrette (page 163), hollandaise sauce (page 168) or sauce shoron (page 168).

Grilled monkfish with vanilla and orange sauce
Serves 4

3 tbsp olive oil
3 cardamom pods, lightly crushed
½ tsp Chinese five-spice powder
200ml/7floz/scant 1 cup sweet white wine
300ml/10floz/1¼ cups fresh orange juice
grated zest of 1 orange
2-3 bay leaves
½ tsp ground coriander
1 vanilla bean, quartered
about 2 tsp arrowroot
70g/2½oz/⅔ stick butter
675g/1½lb monkfish fillet, skinned and trimmed
250g/9oz carrots
250g/9oz sugar snaps or mangetout
250g/9oz fine green beans
salt and freshly milled white pepper

Peel the carrots, run a canelle knife down the side of each to give a star shape and cut into slices.

In a large pan fitted with a blanching basket, bring a generous quantity of well-salted water to the boil. Blanch the carrots, sugar snaps or mangetout, and the fine green beans separately, plunging each batch into cold water to stop the cooking process. They should be brightly coloured and very crisp. Reserve a little of the cooking water and set aside for serving later.

In a saucepan, heat 1 tbsp of the oil and fry the cardamom and Chinese five-spice powder for 2-3 minutes. Add the wine and boil until reduced by half. Pour in the orange juice, then add the zest, bay leaves, coriander and vanilla bean and mix well. Bring to a boil and simmer for 2 minutes.

Strain the sauce through a fine-mesh stainless steel sieve and return the sauce to the cleaned out pan, together with the pieces of vanilla bean. In a small bowl, combine the arrowroot with 2 tbsp cold water and blend to a paste. Stir this mixture into the sauce and add 1 tbsp of the butter. Bring to a boil, stirring constantly until the sauce has thickened. Remove the pieces of vanilla bean and set the sauce aside until ready to serve.

Cut the monkfish into large, even chunks and brush them liberally with 2 tbsp olive oil. Season well. Place them in a sturdy grill-pan [broiler pan] or shallow baking tray.

Preheat an overhead grill [broiler] and cook the fish for 4-5 minutes. The smaller pieces will be fully cooked and tender within this time so remove them from the heat as soon as they are done.

Meanwhile, reheat the blanched vegetables in the reserved cooking water, adding 55g/2oz/½ stick butter.

To serve, pour some of the hot orange sauce onto a serving dish and arrange the vegetables and monkfish on top. Drizzle with the remaining sauce and serve immediately.

Recipe notes This is a warmly spiced, fragrant and colourful dish from chef Jean-Christophe Novelli, from the days when he was at The Four Seasons in London. It is almost a complete meal in itself – all you need to serve it are some boiled new potatoes.

Ask the fishmonger to remove the slippery membrane that surrounds the monkfish or a brown skin will appear after cooking. You can use any firm white fish in place of monkfish in this recipe.

Never cook orange juice a fraction longer than you have to because the flavour can change from citrus to metallic very quickly.

Fish baked with potatoes, olives, tomato and Mediterranean herbs
Serves 4-6

4 bay leaves
2 large sweet onions, finely sliced
2 large potatoes, peeled and sliced into
  rounds 3mm/⅛in thick
about 150ml/5floz/⅔ cup olive oil
10g/⅓oz/¼ cup thyme sprigs
900g/2lb large ripe vine tomatoes
900g/2lb fish such as snapper, red
  bream, salmon trout or sea bass,
  gutted, scaled and trimmed
4 slices lemon
4 cloves garlic, lightly crushed
15g/½oz/⅓ cup fresh oregano
70g/2½oz/scant ½ cup black olives,
  pitted
5 tbsp white wine
15g/½oz/⅓ cup basil, cut into strips
1 lemon, thickly sliced
salt and freshly milled black pepper

Heat the oven to 220°C/425°F/Gas 7.
Lay the bay leaves at the base of the
baking dish. Add the onion and
potatoes in alternate layers, sprinkling
them as you go with 5 tbsp of the
olive oil, plus the thyme, salt and
pepper. Bake in the oven uncovered
for 45-50 minutes, basting with the
oil twice during cooking.

Meanwhile, blanch and skin the
tomatoes. Then cut them into
quarters and deseed.

Rub the cavity of the fish with
lemon, and season with salt and
pepper. Place 2-3 slices of lemon, the
garlic cloves, some oregano leaves
and 1 tbsp olive oil inside the cavity.

Set the fish on the hot potatoes,
season well and cover with layers of
tomato, the remaining oregano and
the olives, seasoning again as you go.
Baste well with the pan juices,
sprinkle with white wine and the
remaining 60ml/2floz/¼ cup olive
oil. Cover and return the baking dish
to the oven for 35 minutes.

Char-grill the remaining lemon
slices. When the fish is ready, scatter
with the char-grilled lemon and basil
strips. Take to the table and serve
the fish from the dish, spooning the
cooking juices over each serving.

Recipe notes A whole meal in one
dish, here all the flavours are melded
and baked together, with the olive
oil, wine and juices trickling through
to help. Pot-roast it using a large,
deepish cocotte [Dutch oven] with a
heavy lid, if you have one. Otherwise,
use a roasting pan covered with foil.

A little more, or less, of the
vegetables and herbs does not matter,
simply choose the ripest and the best
available on the day.

When cooked, the fish will lift
easily off the bones. Use a sharp
spoon, a lasagne lifter, or a custom
designed fish serving knife and fork.

To help get ahead, you can bake
the potatoes hours in advance and
then cool and chill them. Add about
20 minutes to the final cooking time
to compensate for the coldness of the
pre-cooked potatoes.

North African fish bake with fennel and pickled lemons
Serves 4

2 large fennel bulbs, cored and thinly
  sliced
1 large stick celery, cut into matchsticks
5 tbsp extra virgin olive oil
a pinch of chilli pepper or cayenne
1 large tomato, deseeded and diced
8 black olives, stoned and diced
½ preserved lemon, finely diced
3 tbsp chopped flat-leaf parsley,
  plus 8 sprigs to garnish
4 fillets of red snapper, bream, halibut
  or pollack, about 200g/7oz each, or
  800g/1¼lb smaller fish fillets, boned
  and skinned
2 tbsp fish stock
2 tbsp white wine
8 coriander seeds, crushed
1 tsp cumin seeds
½ tsp cracked black peppercorns
salt and freshly milled black pepper

In a pan of boiling salted water, blanch
the fennel for 1-2 minutes, then add
the celery and blanch for another
minute. Drain the vegetables, refresh
in iced water, then drain and dry.

In a small bowl, combine the olive
oil and chilli pepper. Grease the
bottom of an ovenproof baking dish
with 4 tbsp of the chilli-flavoured oil.
Add the fennel, celery, tomato, olives,
pickled lemon and chopped parsley
and toss to coat with the oil. Season
the fish fillets with salt and pepper,
and place them in the baking dish on
top of the vegetables.

Brush the fish fillets liberally with
the remaining chilli oil. Sprinkle the
stock and wine over the fish.

Heat the oven to 200°C/400°F/
Gas 6. Place the dish of fish and
vegetables in the oven and bake for
about 20-30 minutes or until the >

fish is firm and just starting to flake when pierced with the tip of a small thin pointed knife.

Divide the fish amongst four warmed serving plates and surround with the vegetables. Sprinkle each fillet with crushed coriander, cumin seeds and cracked pepper, then garnish with the parsley sprigs and serve immediately.

Recipe notes If you can find an earthenware dish in which to bake this wonderful Moroccan recipe, so much the better, as it will enhance the flavours of the ingredients.

Preserved lemons are an indispensable part of Moroccan cooking and now available from a number of fine food stores and supermarkets. They are also fairly easy to make at home. Preserved lemons have a vivid citrus flavour and soft, silky texture, created by steeping the slashed fruit in salted lemon juice for at least a month. Rinse off the salt thoroughly before using them in any recipe.

Rouget en papillote with pappardelle, carrot and leek
Serves 4

1 large carrot, cut into long thin strips
1 leek, cut into long thin strips
1 small daikon [white radish], cut into
*   long thin strips*
200g/7oz papardelle or linguine
8 tbsp sunflower or groundnut oil, or
*   60g/2oz/½ stick softened butter*
4 large shallots, finely sliced
4 small red mullet or trout, gutted and
*   scaled*
4 sprigs thyme
4 sprigs tarragon
8 tbsp white wine
salt and freshly milled black pepper

You will also need
4 large sheets of greaseproof, silicone
*   paper or foil, or 4 roasting bags*

Bring a large pot of salted water to the boil. Blanch the strips of carrot, leek and daikon, then refresh in cold water. Cook the pasta lightly, then drain. Immediately transfer the noodles to a bowl of cold water, to stop them sticking together, and set aside until ready to use.

Heat the oil or butter in a frying pan and fry the shallots, stirring from time to time, until they are transparent but not coloured. Add the carrot, leek, daikon and drained pasta and turn briefly and gently in the oil or butter until coated and shining.

Trim the fish with scissors, removing any fins. Rub the backbone inside the fish with the point of a teaspoon to dislodge any blood and give it a final quick rinse in cold water. Measure the fish at the thickest part and make a note of the measurement.

If using greaseproof or silicone paper for the papillotes, cut them

into large heart shapes. Distribute the oil or butter generously between the papillotes and season the paper.

Divide the vegetable and pasta mixture among the papillotes, keeping back some of the vegetable strips, then lay the fish on top of each pile, making sure the head and tail are well clear of the edges of the paper, where they are inclined to stick.

Place the remaining vegetables and the herbs on the fish and sprinkle with the wine. Sprinkle salt and pepper over everything. Seal by folding and crimping the edges of the paper two or three times to prevent the juices escaping. Use a stapler if you wish.

Preheat the oven to 200-230°C/ 400-450°F/Gas 6-8. Place large oven trays in the oven to heat. Sit the papillotes on the trays and bake for 10 minutes per 2cm/¾in thickness of fish. Do not bake the parcels for less than 6 minutes.

Remove from the oven and place each papillote on a hot serving plate, to slit open at table.

Recipe notes Use oil if serving the fish at room temperature and butter if serving it hot. There is no need to serve anything else with this as you have a complete meal in the bag.

Remember to cook the pasta very lightly, as it will be cooked further when it is in the oven.

Four 180g/6oz fillets of salmon, sea bass, cod, snapper or bream, boned and skinned, can be used in place of the whole fish.

Alternatively, marinate salmon for 30 minutes or so in equal quantities of dark soy sauce or Japanese tamari and runny honey. Enclose the fish and marinade in the pouch before baking and, when cooked, lift the salmon off its skin to serve.

Sea bass Bois Boudran
Serves 4-8

4-8 sea bass fillets, about 170g/6oz
   each, or one large side of sea bass,
   skinned and boned
2 small onions, finely chopped
2 bay leaves
3 sprigs parsley
3 sprigs thyme
about 300ml/10floz/1¼ cups fish stock
   or water
1 tbsp chives, finely cut
1 tbsp tarragon, finely chopped, or
   30g/1oz/½ cup fresh coriander
   [cilantro] leaves
salt and freshly milled white pepper

For the marinade
150ml/5floz/⅔ cup sunflower oil
50ml/1¾floz/scant ¼ cup white wine
   vinegar
85g/3oz/¼ cup tomato ketchup
1 tsp Worcestershire sauce
5 drops Tabasco sauce
100g/4oz/1 cup shallots, finely chopped

Line a shallow roasting pan with a large sheet of Bake-O-Glide or a Teflon liner. Season the fish and lay it in the dish. Strew with the onions, then add the bay leaf, parsley and thyme, tucking some beneath the fish.

To make the marinade, combine the oil and vinegar in a jug. Add a pinch of salt and a grinding of pepper, then the tomato ketchup, Worcestershire and Tabasco sauces. Whisk until well-blended. Stir in the chopped onion. Season to taste with more salt and pepper and set aside for at least 30 minutes, so that the raw shallots 'cook' in the acid and the flavour mellows.

Heat the oven to 200°C/400°F/Gas 6. Place the fish in a clean roasting pan and pour in just enough stock or

water so that the liquid comes halfway up the sides of the fish, no more. Spoon a little of the liquid over the fish, then cover with foil and braise in the oven for about 30 minutes. It does not matter if the fish is not cooked through at this point, because the acidity of the marinade will complete the cooking.

Lift the fish from the roasting pan and transfer to a china, ceramic or enamelled serving dish. Set aside in a warm place. Strain the cooking liquor into a saucepan, then boil it rapidly until the volume of liquid has reduced by two-thirds. Add this to the jug of marinade.

Pour the marinade over the still-warm fish and submerge. Keep the fish in a cool place (not the fridge) for a few hours. Shortly before serving, sprinkle the chives and tarragon or coriander [cilantro] over the dish, gently mixing them into the marinade.

Recipe notes A favourite picnic dish of the Rothschilds, and originally made with chicken, this recipe was first given to me by Michel Roux. It was Jacqui Pickles, a top teacher at my old cooking school, who introduced the fish to the recipe. Impressed, Michel promptly put our version, made with salmon, on the menu at The Waterside Inn, his three-star Michelin restaurant. We were most flattered, as you can imagine.

You too can use salmon instead of sea bass in this recipe. To prepare in advance, the fish may stay in the fridge all day in the roasting dish with the herbs and onion. Just add the fish stock or water before cooking. The marinade can be made the day before too, except for the chopped shallots, which should be mixed in on the day of cooking.

Lemon sole with toasted hollandaise
Serves 6

1 quantity Hollandaise Sauce (page 168)
150ml/5floz/⅔ cup double [heavy] or
   whipping cream
6 fillets of lemon sole or plaice, skinned
1 tbsp sunflower oil (optional)
6 wedges of lemon
salt and freshly milled white pepper

Make the hollandaise sauce and allow to cool to room temperature. Whip the cream until it is the same consistency as the hollandaise, then fold it into the sauce carefully. Adjust the seasoning to taste and set aside.

Preheat an overhead grill [broiler]. Working with the skin-side down, fold the ends of the fish fillets under the central part, so that the ends are just touching underneath. Place the fish on a small, non-stick, heavy baking tray (or one lined with oiled foil), sitting the largest of the fillets in the centre and the smallest towards the edges. Season, then grill [broil] for 4-5 minutes, until the fish is firm to the touch. Transfer to a plate and set aside to cool, but do not chill.

To finish the dish, clean the baking tray and place it under the grill to reheat. Slather the hollandaise sauce all over the grilled fish. Using a fish slice or spatula, transfer the coated fish to the hot tray and grill for 2-3 minutes, or until the hollandaise is toasted to a golden brown and the fish is piping hot. Serve immediately with lemon wedges.

Recipe notes I like to serve this with English asparagus and baby new potatoes. Ask the fishmonger for half fillets, rather than quarter fillets, so each person has half a fish.

Tiger prawns with lemon, garlic and chilli
Serves 2-4

24 raw tiger prawns, about 15g/½oz
  each, shelled
extra virgin olive oil, for frying
4 cloves garlic, squashed
2-3 large red chillies, deseeded and diced
juice of ½ lemon
10g/⅓oz/¼ cup parsley or basil leaves
salt and freshly milled black pepper

Devein the prawns if necessary. Run the tip of a sharp pointed knife around the larger C-curve of each prawn and remove the black thread. Pour just enough oil into the base of a wide frying pan so that it is about 3mm/⅛in deep and heat gently.

Add the garlic and chillies and allow them to infuse the oil for 1-2 minutes. Add the prawns, stir and watch them turn pink.

Season with salt and pepper, add the lemon juice, discard the garlic cloves and serve immediately.

Recipe notes There are some ingredients that are so good, they need very little cooking and the fewest possible ingredients to make them taste their best – tiger prawns are one of them. The key is not to leave the pan for the minute or two they need to cook, and to have everything ready at the table, so you can eat them at their juiciest and most appetising.

Apart from the olive oil, you can leave out any of the ingredients if they are not available. Serve this dish with a basmati and herb pilaf or plain boiled rice as a main course, or with some soft, olive oil-flavoured bread as a starter.

Baby clams with chilli, white wine and garlic
Serves 4

1kg/2lb 4oz small clams
5 tbsp extra virgin olive oil
1 shallot, finely chopped
2-3 fresh red chillies, deseeded and
  finely chopped
2 garlic cloves, chopped
30g/1oz/ ¼ cup pancetta or bacon, diced
  (optional)
100ml/3½floz/½ cup dry white wine
15g/½oz/⅓ cup flat-leaf parsley or basil,
  cut in strips
salt and pepper

Wash the clams in plenty of cold water, discarding any with damaged shells or that refuse to close when tapped. Soak under cold running water for a few minutes, then drain well and set aside in a cool place.

In a wide frying pan with a lid, heat the oil and gently fry the shallot, chillies, garlic and pancetta or bacon, if using. Raise the heat to high, add the clams and wine, cover and cook for 2 minutes or until the clams open.

Season to taste, adding the fresh parsley or basil, and serve immediately.

Recipe notes This is a favourite midweek meal or starter. Doubling the ingredients will give a simple main course for four that is lovely served with pan-roasted cod.

Deliciously sweet clams are now farmed in Italy and New Zealand; ask your fishmonger to get them if you do not see them on display. Keep live clams in your fridge in a bowl under a wet tea towel or folded newspaper. Try your best to cook and eat them within one day.

Moules grillée
Serves 4

1kg/2lb 4oz large mussels
200g/7oz/2¾ sticks unsalted butter,
  softened
15g/½oz/⅓ cup parsley, chopped
1 small shallot, finely chopped
1-2 cloves garlic, chopped
about 45g/1½oz/¾ cup fresh breadcrumbs
salt and freshly milled black pepper

Rinse the mussels under running water, and remove any grit or little beards with a sharp knife. Soak in cold water for 15 minutes, then rinse and drain.

Place the mussels in a single layer in a wide, shallow pan. Cover and set over a high heat. Stir after 1 minute, and stop cooking as soon as the mussels open. Discard any that don't.

Lift one shell from each mussel, leaving the meat attached to the other. Arrange the mussels in gratin dishes.

Strain the cooking liquor into a small saucepan. Bring to a boil and boil rapidly until the volume of liquid has reduced by at least half.

Place the butter in a mixing bowl with the parsley, shallot, garlic and some salt and pepper. Mix well to make a paste. At the last moment, add the reduced mussel juices. Divide the butter mixture between the mussels and sprinkle with the breadcrumbs.

When almost ready to serve, preheat the grill [broiler]. Place the gratin dishes under it and cook for 4-5 minutes until bubbling and golden. Serve the mussels straight from the dishes to keep them piping hot.

Recipe notes Mussels are wonderfully inexpensive. Here you can prepare them to the half-shell stage in advance, but ideally should eat them within a day of purchase.

Red meat

Much as I adore the convenience of shopping in a large food store, when it comes to meat I prefer my local butcher, who is now a protected species. He tells me where the meat comes from, the type of farm and the age of the animal. He cuts it beautifully, French-style or English, so I can follow recipes easily, and he gives me bones and trimmings to make the sauce. The meat is safe, healthy and matured, and I enjoy the short ritual of speaking to an expert, watching a craftsman, and getting exactly what I want.

Fast ways with meat
Char-grill lamb leg steaks and serve with anchovy dressing or green coriander and coconut chutney.
Shallow-fry pork or beef steak then pour off any excess fat and deglaze the frying pan with cream. Add a little mustard to taste and simmer to thicken the sauce.
Roast racks of lamb. Begin at least 50 minutes before you need to eat. The little racks will require 20-25 minutes cooking time and 20-25 minutes resting.
Pan-roast single ribs of beef on the bone, pork loin chops, or loin of lamb and serve with chilli jam.
Char-grill venison steaks and serve drizzled with walnut or hazelnut oil.

How can you find a good butcher? Choose one whose shop looks and smells clean. Don't be put off if you do not see plenty of cuts of meat displayed, just allow extra time in the shop. The butcher may cut and joint especially for you. Choose a butcher with helpful, enthusiastic staff who know the source of the meat. Avoid shops with meat displays lit by a red light, which is designed to make the meat look bright and red. In any case, vivid red meat is too fresh and too young – avoid it.

What to look for, what to avoid It is important to select the right cut of meat for the cooking method you plan to use. You cannot change nature entirely, though some parts of the food industry are trying to do so.
• Expect to pay more for tender cuts and less for tougher cuts.
• All meat should have some fat. It lubrictaes the flesh and gives flavour. Choose meat with fat that is firm, white or pale gold, or yellow on grass-fed mature beef.
• Tenderness is always found in young animals, such as veal, lamb and suckling pig.
• Meat is composed of muscle. Those used most often during the animal's life will be tough and those used least will be tender. In naturally farmed meat, where animals walk about, you will find tender meat mostly in the hindquarter, with just a little in the forequarter. The meat in the forequarter is usually tougher, but juicier if cooked correctly.

Storing and freezing meat
• Take a chiller bag when you set out to buy meat.
• Unwrap the meat from its plastic as soon as you get home. Pat it dry with paper towel and place on trays or plates, covered, in the coldest part of the fridge.
• Keep meat dry at all times. Replace any damp kitchen paper, keep the plate or tray bone-dry. Moisture causes meat to spoil.
• Raw meat juices can be dangerous, especially if they drip onto foods eaten raw, such as dairy produce or mayonnaise.
• Some of the biggest culprits of food poisoning are cooked meat dishes, stocks and gravies. Bacteria proliferate at 10-65°C/ 50-150°F, so always chill meat dishes fast and heat them fast. Do not store meat dishes for more than 48 hours in the fridge, and simmer them for 15-20 minutes before eating. Longer storage should take place in the freezer.
• If you have purchased meat in vacuum packs, follow the storage

instructions on the packet. Once you see bubbles in a vacuum pack, the meat is off.

• During freezing, the moisture in meat forms ice which expands, breaking down the muscle tissues and tenderizing the flesh. Use frozen meat within six months and defrost it in the fridge.

The principles of cooking meat Our aim in cooking meat is to:
• Cook it until it is tender.
• Conserve its natural juices, keeping it moist and succulent.
• Kill any resident bacteria. Cooking meat is a compromise or balancing act – and a knack. Doing it successfully relies largely on finding the right temperature and cooking it for the correct amount of time. Too much heat and cooking for too long makes meat tough, grey, dry, opaque and chewy. Too little heat and it is tough, translucent and chewy. The result is exacerbated if the pieces of meat are small, not hung properly, or badly farmed.

How to tell when meat is cooked
Meat cooks from the heat source inwards, driving the juices towards the centre. The wobbly protein firms up in the heat, the cut surfaces stick together, the heat squeezes out the juices in the meat, and it shrinks.

When meat is cooked 'blue', the outside is browned and the inside is barely warm. Blue meat contains the most juices and is most suitable for tender cuts of beef and venison, such as fillet, sirloin and beef rump steak.

'Rare' or 'underdone' is when the colour of the meat is pink and

the temperature is almost hot. The juices will run very bloody and pink while the meat rests – don't be alarmed, the meat is cooked. Rare cooking is suitable for tender cuts of lamb such as the saddle, rib fillet, cuts of beef such as rib-eye fillet, fillet, sirloin and rump steaks, and venison sirloin and haunch steaks.

'Medium' meat is a bit firmer, pale pink just in the very centre, with an appetising brown exterior. The juices run pale caramel with a barely perceptible hint of rose. All the tender cuts listed above may be cooked to medium, it just takes a bit longer.

Veal and pork (and breast of chicken) must be cooked until there is only the faintest tinge of pearl-pink and the meat is opaque all the way through. This is just past medium, but the meat is still spongy to the touch. When pierced with a skewer, the juices run clear.

All meat can be cooked to the well-done stage, but you will get one of two different results. Naturally tough meat cooked by a moist cooking method (for example, stewed oxtail, poached brisket of beef, poached ham or shin of veal) will be tender and juicy when well-done. The collagen will melt and become delightfully sticky. Indeed, this meat should never be served rare.

Alternatively, well-done tender meat cooked by a dry cooking method loses its translucency and becomes stiff, hard, grey and dry. There will be no juices at all. When cooked by a moist cooking method, when it has just reached the grey state, the meat will be tough. However, if you continue

to cook it, the meat will eventually become tender again. This is particularly true of veal.

Rule of thumb
• The smaller and more tender the meat, the higher the cooking temperature, the shorter the cooking time.
• Long thin pieces of meat cook quicker than thick dense cuts, such as boned and rolled meat. The length of a roll of meat does not increase its cooking time.
• Meat with the bone in cooks faster than boned and rolled cuts.
• Meat continues to cook in its residual heat and the temperature of some cuts of meat will rise 5°C/41°F while resting.
• All cooking times in this book are based on meat being at a cool room temperature, 20°C/68°F, before cooking.

The best advice I can give
• Choose the right method for the cut you have bought. Cook it often, get a perfect result, then master another cut.
• While cooking, try to imagine what is happening inside the meat.
• Adjust the temperature to get the result want. Be confident.

The best cooking methods My favourite methods for meat are:
Barbecuing. This is perhaps the ideal way to cook meat.
Roasting. It brings out the real flavour of the joint.
Grilling [broiling]. Maximises the flavour of small thin cuts.
Shallow-frying. Use a minimum of oil in a non-stick pan.
Pan-roasting. The perfect way of achieving a small, tender roast.

Roast sirloin of beef in its own gravy
Serves 10-12

2.5kg/5lb 8oz rolled beef sirloin [short loin], fat trimmed to less than 1cm/½in
olive oil
90g/3oz/scant ½ cup onion, finely chopped
45g/1½oz/¼ cup carrot, finely chopped
45g/1½oz/¼ cup celery, finely chopped
45g/1½oz/½ cup dark mushrooms, finely chopped
850ml/1½ pints/1 quart strong beef stock
15g/½oz/⅓ cup rosemary or thyme
salt and freshly milled black pepper

Take the meat out the fridge well in advance, and keep it in a cool place until it is quite dry and at room temperature. Preheat the oven to 450°C/230°F/Gas 8.

Put a thin film of oil in the roasting tin and place it in the oven to heat while you chop the vegetables. Before the oil starts to smoke, strew the vegetables over the base of the tin and leave to roast until browned. Pour in the stock and add the herbs.

Meanwhile, heat a frying pan on top of the stove. Brush the meat all over with olive oil, then quickly brown it all over, pressing the meat down well to help it sear. Transfer the meat to a roasting rack and set over the vegetables.

Roast for 15 minutes, then reduce the oven temperature to 180-190°C/ 350-375°F/Gas 4-5, and continue roasting for 1½ hours. At the end of this time the meat should still be pink. Remove the roasting pan from the oven. Wrap the meat in foil and set aside to rest for 30 minutes while you make the gravy.

Strain the vegetable and stock mixture through a fine-meshed sieve into a clean saucepan. Remove the fat by laying wide strips of paper towel across the surface. When the sauce has no eyes of fat left on the surface, boil it hard for 5-10 minutes until the flavour is strong and meaty. Turn off the heat and leave the gravy in the pan until you are ready to serve.

Carve the rested meat and, just before serving, bring the gravy to the boil again and serve it piping hot in a heated gravy boat, or over the meat.

Recipe notes Rolled beef sirloin is a luxurious cut of beef, ideal for roasting. Choose a larger piece than you need, so that on another occasion you can serve the cold beef with horseradish or a mustard mayonnaise and salad. Or make thick chunky sandwiches with soft brown bread.

A large piece does not require much more cooking than a smaller one, as the joint is longer, not thicker. Check on the roasting chart (page 218) for the cooking times, and allow 30 minutes resting time. The meat can be browned hours in advance of serving, in which case it may need just a little longer to roast.

The gravy will take 1½ hours from start to finish. For a smaller joint, which cooks to rare in less than an hour, start cooking the gravy first, without the meat. If you prefer to have the gravy made well in advance, try clear brown gravy (page 172), which can be reheated from frozen. To thicken the gravy, add some slaked cornflour [cornstarch] if desired.

Serve with roast potatoes and boiled and buttered vegetables. In winter include a root mash, such as carrot and swede purée with mustard seeds and ginger (page 118).

Roast fillet of spiced beef
Serves 8-10

1 whole beef fillet, fully trimmed
about 7 tbsp Thyme, Shallot and Garlic Aromatic Oil (page 166)
45g/1½oz/1 cup fresh coriander [cilantro] leaves

For the marinade
2 tbsp coriander seeds
2 tbsp allspice berries
1 tbsp dried chilli flakes
6 large cloves garlic, unpeeled
170ml/6floz/¼ cup mushroom ketchup
4 tbsp Worcestershire sauce
5 tbsp runny honey
375ml/13floz/1⅓ cups soy sauce
120ml/4floz/½ cup extra virgin olive oil

Make the marinade. Lightly crush the coriander, allspice berries and dried chilli using a pestle and mortar, or place them in a plastic bag and bash with the base of a saucepan. Smash the garlic cloves with the side of a knife. Combine the crushed spices, garlic, mushroom ketchup, Worcestershire sauce, honey, soy sauce and olive oil in a deep non-corrosive ceramic or glass dish, or in a Ziploc bag.

Place the beef in the marinade and leave overnight or for several days, turning from time to time.

When ready to cook, preheat the oven to 220°C/425°/Gas 7. Heat a heavy roasting tin on top of the stove. Wipe the beef dry with your hands. Add a light film of aromatic oil to the pan and sear the fillet on all sides, then place it in the oven to roast for 10 minutes.

Meanwhile, strain about 450ml/ 16floz/2 cups of the marinade into a jug. When the beef is cooked, remove it from the oven and set aside to >

cool. Deglaze the hot roasting pan with the marinade and 4 tbsp of the aromatic oil, and simmer gently for about 10 minutes, stirring often.

When the beef is cooler, chop the coriander leaves roughly and add to the sauce. Slice the beef as thinly as you can and arrange on a long serving dish. Serve with the sauce.

Recipe notes Originally from The Castle Hotel in Taunton, this dish can be served hot or cold and is ideal for buffets. The beef may be prepared days ahead, and left safely in a cool place if there is no room in the fridge. The marinade cures the fillet, taking away excess juices, so the result is an intense flavour and beautifully pink slices of meat, which remain so for hours on the party table.

I like to serve it with parsnip crisps (page 121), onion rings (page 121), deep-fried wonton wrappers, and Chinese rainbow salad with sesame and soy dressing (page 127). It also makes an excellent carpaccio when chilled, thinly sliced and topped with shavings of parmesan cheese.

Bobotie in iceberg lettuce with bay leaf skewer
Serves 6

1 large slice brown or white bread
a little milk
3 tbsp sunflower or groundnut oil
1 large onion, finely chopped
500g/17oz lean minced beef or lamb
1 tbsp mild Madras curry powder
1 tbsp ground turmeric
2 tbsp white wine vinegar
100ml/3½floz/scant ½ cup beef or lamb
   stock, to match the mince
1 large tomato, skinned, deseeded and
   chopped
30g/1oz/¼ cup toasted flaked almonds
1 heaped tbsp dark brown sugar
50g/1½oz/¼ cup mango or peach
   chutney
softened butter, for greasing
salt and freshly milled pepper

For the topping

1 egg
200ml/7floz/¾ cup milk
4 thin slices lemon, cut in half
6 bay leaves

To serve

1 small iceberg or similar crisp lettuce
6 bay leaves

Heat the oven to 180°C/350°F/Gas 4. Place the bread in a small dish, cover with milk and leave to soak for about 20 minutes.

Meanwhile, heat the oil in a large frying pan and fry the onions until golden, stirring frequently. Add the meat and cook, stirring until the meat is just beginning to turn brown.

In a small cup, combine the curry powder, turmeric and vinegar, and stir this mixture into the meat. Add the stock, tomatoes and some salt and pepper and cook for 10 minutes.

Squeeze the milk from the bread. Break the bread into small pieces and stir them into the meat, adding the almonds, sugar and chutney. Spoon into a shallow, buttered gratin dish and bake in the oven for 20 minutes.

Remove the gratin dish from the oven and, if any fat has formed in shallow pools on top of the meat, mop it away with a paper towel.

Make the topping. Whisk the egg and milk together in a jug, adding a little salt. Strain this mixture over the meat, then decorate the bobotie with the lemon slices and bay leaves. Return it to the oven for a further 15-20 minutes or until the custard has set – bake it a little longer if you are cooking it from chilled.

Serve in the dish, wiping the edges clean before taking it to the table. Alternatively, remove the sliced lemons and bay leaves from the top of the bobotie. Trim off the base of the lettuce and cut it in half to give large lettuce leaf cups. Place each portion of meat in a large, crisp leaf, fold the edges together and secure by skewering with the extra bay leaves.

Recipe notes South Africa's famous meat and custard pie, bobotie, is simple to prepare in advance and, in fact, will taste better if you do so. Bake it without the topping a day or so in advance, then cool, cover and chill. Reheat the bobotie in the oven for 10 minutes, then pour the custard mixture over it for the final 20 minutes of baking.

Bobotie should never be dry. The soaked and squeezed breadcrumbs are a great means of absorbing runny juices while keeping the result moist.

For the chutney, I like to use Geeta's medium mango chutney, or Mrs Ball's peach chutney.

Vitello tonnato
Serves 6

900g/2lb fatless, boneless veal, from the
top of the leg, rolled and tied,
9cm/3½in in diameter
3-4 anchovy fillets, rinsed and drained
2 garlic cloves, cut into thin splinters
435ml/15floz/1¾ cups chicken stock
200ml/7floz/¾ cup dry white wine
1 onion, quartered
2 sticks celery, cut into large pieces
1 bouquet garni made from 1 bay leaf,
5 peppercorns, 5 juniper berries,
2 cloves, a few parsley stalks, a few
sprigs of tarragon and thyme

For the tuna mayonnaise
90g/3½oz canned tuna in olive oil
175ml/6floz/¾ cup sunflower oil
120ml/4floz/½ cup extra virgin olive oil
1 egg
½ tsp Dijon mustard
a pinch of salt
4 tbsp lemon juice
14 anchovy fillets, rinsed and dried
4 tbsp double [heavy] cream
4-8 tbsp strained veal poaching liquid
4 tbsp capers, rinsed and drained

To serve
1 lemon, finely sliced
1 tbsp capers, rinsed and drained
6-8 black olives
a few sprigs of flat-leaf parsley

Using a skewer, make deep incisions along the length of the veal fillet and insert a piece of anchovy fillet and a splinter of garlic in each hole. Season the veal and place it in a heavy saucepan just large enough to hold the meat comfortably. Add the stock, wine, vegetables, bouquet garni and water to cover.

Bring to a brisk simmer, skim the froth from the top, and immediately reduce the heat. Half-cover with the lid and simmer the veal very, very slowly, for about 1 hour or until a meat thermometer registers an internal temperature of 79°C/165°F.

Remove the pan from the heat and let the veal cool in the poaching liquid. Ladle out 600ml/1 pint/2½ cups of the poaching liquid and strain through a fine sieve into a saucepan. Bring to a boil and boil until the volume of liquid has reduced to 120ml/4floz/½ cup. Set aside to cool.

Make the mayonnaise. Open the can of tuna and pour the oil into a measuring jug. Add enough of the sunflower and olive oils to give 285ml/10floz/1½ cups of oil in total.

Break the egg into a small food processor and add the mustard and salt. Whizz for 30 seconds. Add 2 tbsp of the lemon juice and whizz for 10 seconds, then add the oils in a thin stream. Stop the machine and scrape down the sides of the bowl. Add the tuna, the remaining 2 tbsp lemon juice, the anchovy fillets and cream. Blend until smooth. Adjust the flavour of the sauce with 4-8 tbsp of the reduced poaching liquid, lemon juice, and salt and pepper. The mayonnaise should taste lively.

When the veal is cool, trim off any gristle or fat, and cut into thin, even slices. Spread a light film of tuna mayonnaise in the bottom of a large gratin dish and arrange the veal in even layers, each spread with some of the sauce. Cover with plastic wrap and refrigerate for at least 2-3 hours, overnight, or longer if desired. Chill the rest of the mayonnaise separately.

About an hour before serving, remove the veal from the fridge. On a serving dish, arrange the slices so they overlap as neatly as possible. Spoon the remainder of the tuna mayonnaise over them, and garnish the dish with lemon slices, capers, black olives and sprigs of parsley.

Recipe notes It was my first encounter with this luxurious Italian dish of veal with tuna mayonnaise, on the banks of Lake Como at Villa d'Este, that inspired me to open a cookery school. The mild, mingled flavours of the veal, tuna and olive oil were so subtle and intriguing, that I realised I wanted to teach people the most flavourful dishes of Italy and France, cooking to the highest standards and using only the best ingredients.

Vitello tonnato is one of the best meat recipes to prepare in advance because it improves the longer you leave it in the fridge. Serve it as a starter, antipasto or summertime main course or lunch dish. In Milan it is traditionally served during the Assumption Day feast, in the intense heat of August. However, you should never leave a mayonnaise dish such as this one out in the warm sunshine for any length of time.

Vitello tonnato is characteristically very pale and needs to be garnished brightly with black olives, yellow lemons and green parsley, each of which contrast beautifully with the subtle flavours beneath. It's important that the result is very delicate, so slice the meat thinly and coat it with a minimum of mayonnaise. Remember to keep the dishes served alongside the vitello tonnato light in flavour and texture too, so that they don't overwhelm it. A green salad is ideal.

Chicken may be used in the same way as the veal for a delicious variation. Ask your butcher to bone, roll, and tie a whole chicken, then poach it until it reaches an internal temperature of 80°C/175°F.

Ossobuco with white wine, garlic and parsley
Serves 4

4 pieces shin of veal, 4cm/1½in thick,
*   tied around the middle*
90g/3oz/12 tbsp plain [all purpose] flour
8 tbsp olive oil
30g/1oz/¼ stick butter, plus extra for
*   greasing*
2 large onions, finely sliced
2 cloves garlic, crushed, plus 1 small
*   clove garlic, finely chopped*
6 tbsp white wine
6 anchovy fillets
about 350ml/12floz/1½ cups chicken stock
1 tsp grated lemon zest (optional)
4 tbsp chopped flat-leaf parsley
salt and freshly milled white pepper

Heat the oven to 180°C/350°F/Gas 4. Turn the pieces of veal in the flour, then gently slap off the excess until only the finest dusting remains. Repeat the flour dusting process, and season with salt and pepper.

Heat 5 tbsp of the oil in a large frying pan over a high heat and brown the veal quickly on both sides. Remove from the pan and set aside to drain on paper towel.

In a large, heavy ovenproof pan with lid, such as a cocotte [Dutch oven], wide enough to take the veal in a single layer, heat the remaining 3 tbsp olive oil with the butter and gently fry the onions until pale golden. Add the veal, crushed garlic, wine, and salt and pepper and simmer for a few minutes.

Add the anchovies and chicken stock. The liquid should cover the veal – if not, add more stock. Bring to the boil, cover with a disc of buttered paper and the lid. Transfer to the oven and cook for about 2 hours, turning once during cooking.

Meanwhile, combine the chopped garlic, flat-leaf parsley, and lemon zest (if using). Sprinkle this mixture over the veal just 15 minutes before the end of cooking. When done, the veal should be very tender when pierced with a skewer. If the juices are too thin to serve as a sauce when the veal has finished cooking, remove the shins from the pot, then bring the sauce to a boil on the stovetop and simmer until reduced and thickened.

Snip the trussing strings from the meat, then pour the sauce over the veal and serve, giving everyone a teaspoon to eat the marrow.

Recipe notes Bone-with-a-hole is the Milanese origin of the name ossobucco, and this is what you need from a good veal butcher for this dish. The shins are tender and sticky when slowly cooked and can be eaten with a fork.

Serve the veal shins on risotto, mashed potato or with large buttered noodles, accompanied by fennel gratin and slow roast tomatoes.

This recipe can be prepared in advance, kept chilled, and reheated shortly before serving.

Lamb shanks with mustard, rosemary, chickpeas and caramelized onion
Serves 4

4 tbsp olive, sunflower or groundnut oil
2 very large onions, sliced
4 cloves garlic, crushed
1 tbsp sugar
4 lamb shanks
4 tsp Dijon mustard
600ml/1 pint/2½ cups lamb or vegetable
*   stock*
2 tsp rosemary leaves, or 2 tsp cumin
*   seeds*
1 x 400g/14oz can chickpeas
*   [garbanzos], rinsed and drained, or*
*   250g/9oz/1½ cups cooked*
salt and freshly milled black pepper

Heat 2 tbsp oil in a frying pan and gently fry the onions and garlic over a gentle heat until softened. Sprinkle over the sugar, and continue cooking until some of the onions are dark brown but not burned. Transfer the onion to a large, deep stewing pot or casserole [Dutch oven].

Add the remaining oil to the frying pan and brown the lamb shanks all over, pressing them down well so they take on a good colour. Spread each lamb shank with 1 tsp mustard and place in the stewpot with the bones pointing upwards. Pour in the stock and add the rosemary or cumin.

Bring the stew to a simmer on the stovetop. Cover with a large disc of greaseproof paper, tucking it well down the sides of the pot, add the lid, then adjust the heat to a simmer and cook for 1½ hours, or until the meat is almost falling off the bone.

Remove the lid from the pot and add the chickpeas. Boil to reduce the sauce a little more and heat the chickpeas. Season with salt and >

pepper to taste, then place the lamb shanks in deep serving dishes and spoon the chickpeas and sauce over.

Recipe notes This is the simplest stew I know. It takes very little time to assemble, can be made days in advance of serving, and reheats perfectly in the microwave.

I love it with couscous, and make a variation of the recipe on page 138, adding 4 bay leaves to the stock before bringing it to the boil, and using dill instead of parsley. This stew is also good served with velvet mash (page 152), and courgettes [zucchini] cooked with plenty of mint in the final stages. It is important that a rich pulse stew such as this is eaten with herbs such as mint or dill as they help with the digestion.

My other favourite cuts for stewing lamb is neck fillet and that could be used in this dish, trimmed free of all fat, it will only take an hour to cook. You could try it with chicken thighs, browned first as per the lamb, then stewed for 45 minutes.

Roast racks of lamb with Provençale white beans, tomatoes and rosemary
Serves 6-8

2 racks lamb, fully trimmed and chined
2 x 400g/14oz cans cannellini beans, drained and rinsed
2 x 400g/14oz cans chopped tomatoes
6-8 sprigs rosemary, or a large pinch of herbes de Provence, plus 6 sprigs rosemary to garnish
3-4 tbsp extra virgin olive oil
300ml/10floz/1¼ cups lamb or chicken stock
salt and freshly milled black pepper

Preheat the oven to 180°/350°F/Gas 4. Using a sharp knife, score the lamb fat lightly in a criss-cross pattern. Rub in salt and pepper.

Heat a non-stick frying pan on the stovetop and brown the racks of lamb all over, starting with the fat side first. Pour off the burned fat from time to time during browning. Set the lamb aside in a cool place.

In a small-medium roasting tin, combine the beans, tomatoes, herbs, olive oil and stock. Stir and season to taste. Place in the oven for about 20 minutes to mingle the flavours.

Raise the oven temperature to 220°C/430F°/Gas 7-8 – allow about 20 minutes for this, especially if using a non-fan oven.

Place the lamb, fat-side uppermost, in the roasting pan with the cannellini beans and tomatoes and roast for 20-25 minutes. Remove the lamb from the beans and set aside to rest in a warm place for 20 minutes.

Check the beans and if they seem too watery, transfer them to the stovetop and boil gently to drive off some of the liquid. Bare in mind, however, that the beans must remain moist enough to serve as a sauce. Otherwise, put them back in the oven until ready to serve.

Carve the lamb into cutlets. Remove the spent rosemary from the bean mixture and discard. Serve the lamb with the beans, adding sprigs of fresh rosemary to garnish.

Recipe notes Robyn Roux, a fantastic cook of the relaxed genre, gave this recipe to me. Each time I visit the home she shares with husband Michel Roux, the pages of yet another cookbook are open, and she is trying out a new recipe for her friends and family.

The lamb can be browned hours in advance and kept in a cool place, but preferably not refrigerated. The remainder of the cooking needs almost no attention at all. An hour before serving, preheat the oven to 220°C/425°F/Gas 7, allowing 20 minutes for the oven to heat, then roast the lamb and vegetables for 20-25 minutes and finish as above. Accompany it with a salad or crisp green vegetables.

When shopping, ask your butcher to fully trim and chine the racks of lamb – that is, to remove the backbone – to make cutting easier.

Slow-cooked lamb with Baharat spices
Serves 6-8

1 shoulder of lamb, boned and tied
1 parsnip, sliced diagonally
2 carrots, sliced diagonally
1 onion or leek, sliced diagonally
salt crystals

For the Baharat spice paste
2 tbsp green cardamom pods
4 tbsp black peppercorns
2 tbsp coriander seeds
2 tbsp cloves
2 tbsp cumin seeds
1 whole nutmeg, grated
2 tbsp paprika
2 tbsp sunflower or groundnut oil, plus
    extra for storing the spice paste
1 large onion, chopped
2 cloves garlic, crushed

Make the spice paste. Remove the tiny black seeds from the cardamom pods and place in a grinder with the peppercorns, coriander, cloves and cumin. Grind to a fine powder, then stir in the grated nutmeg and paprika.

Heat 2 tbsp of the oil in a pan and gently fry the onion and garlic until softened. Stir in the spice mixture and cook for another 1-2 minutes. Set aside to cool, then spoon the mixture into a clean jar and cover with a thin layer of oil. Store in the fridge until ready to use.

Weigh the lamb and make a note of it. Smear about a quarter of the spice paste over the meat, rubbing it in well all over. Place inside two roasting bags and leave in the fridge overnight to marinate.

Heat the oven to 170°C/325°F/Gas 3. Add the parsnip, carrots and onion or leek to the bag, placing them under the lamb. Tie the bag, pierce it twice with the point of a knife and roast in a shallow roasting pan for about 35 minutes per 450g/1lb, or until the meat is meltingly tender. Allow at least 3 hours for roasting, bearing in mind that a little longer in the oven won't do the lamb any harm.

Carve the meat and arrange on a serving platter with the vegetables, sprinkling the spicy cooking juices and salt crystals over the dish before taking it to the table.

Recipe notes Baharat spice mix is a blend of aromatic spices, without the heat of chillies, popular in the Yemen and Gulf States, and marvellous for lamb and chicken. My friend Roz Denny, who lived in the Yemen as a child, introduced this dish to me. She has always been a great source of encouragement, and we taught the Bachelor Cook's course together.

This dish is perhaps the ultimate example of no-hands cooking. You just put the lamb, tied in its fragrant bath, in the oven. Use your oven's automatic timer and you can go out for the day, returning to find your home filled with the most intoxicating aroma. Serve with a crunchy, peppery green salad and fragrant basmati rice.

The lamb and vegetables can be kept marinating in the roasting bag for up to 4 days before cooking. Make a big batch of the spice paste, ready to use at any time, as it keeps indefinitely in the fridge.

Pork fillet mignons with roquefort sauce
Serves 4

8 pork fillet mignons, well-trimmed
2 tbsp olive oil
6 tbsp butter
2 garlic cloves, peeled
2 sprigs rosemary
400ml/14floz/1¾ cups chicken stock
1 small shallot, finely chopped
6 tbsp medium dry white wine
4 tbsp cider
2 tbsp plain [all-purpose] flour
120ml/4floz/½ cup crème fraîche
100g/3½oz/1 cup roquefort cheese, diced
salt and freshly milled white pepper

Bring the pork to room temperature and season with salt and pepper. Heat the olive oil and 2 tbsp of the butter in a wide shallow pan, adding the garlic cloves and rosemary sprigs. Carefully brown the meat on both sides over a high heat, then reduce the temperature to a moderate level and continue cooking for about 8 minutes or until the meat is done. Be careful not to overcook it.

Meanwhile, in a saucepan, bring the stock to a boil and boil rapidly until the volume of liquid has reduced to 200ml/7floz/¾-1 cup.

Remove the pork to a dish and set aside in a warm place. Pour the fat from the pan, discard the rosemary and garlic, and blot the pan lightly with kitchen paper.

Return the pan to the heat and add another 2 tbsp butter. Add the shallot and cook gently, scraping the base of the pan to incorporate the caramelized cooking juices from the pork.

When the shallot is tender, add the wine and cider and boil vigorously to for 1-2 minutes. Add the reduced chicken stock and return to the >

boil. Boil hard until the volume of sauce has reduced to approximately 170ml/6floz/¾ cup.

Meanwhile, combine the remaining 2 tbsp butter with the flour and knead them together with a round-bladed knife to make a beurre manie. Place the butter paste in a jar in the fridge and chill.

Strain the sauce into a clean saucepan, return to a simmer and add the crème fraîche. Stir in the diced cheese, then season to taste with salt and pepper. Be careful not to overheat the sauce at this stage.

To thicken the sauce, whisk little pieces of the beurre manie into the sauce, one or two at a time, allowing the sauce to bubble again after each addition. When it is the consistency of runny honey, place the pork on hot serving plates, cover with the sauce and serve immediately.

Recipe notes If the butcher cannot supply you with fillet mignons of pork, make them yourself – it is really easy. One pork fillet tenderloin, trimmed of fat, will make two or three equal-sized mignons, each weighing 70g/2½oz each, with the tapering tail of the fillet left over. Stand each log-shaped portion upright, and with a clenched fist, give each a light bash, so it flattens evenly into a mignon.

You will most likely have some beurre manie left over. Keep it in a jar in the fridge and use to thicken other sauces, including those of casseroles, instead of slaked cornflour [cornstarch].

Thai spiced pork with coriander and coconut dipping sauce
Serves 4-6

1kg/2lb 4oz pork tenderloin, trimmed
400ml/14floz/1¼ cups coconut milk
½ large red chilli, finely sliced
2-3 lime leaves, finely sliced

For the marinade

60g/2oz/1 cup fresh coriander [cilantro]
3 cloves garlic, crushed
3cm/1¼in fresh ginger, peeled and sliced
grated zest of 1 lime, or 4 lime leaves
7 spring onions [scallions], roughly
* chopped*
2½ large red chillies, deseeded
1 stalk lemongrass, outer leaves
* removed*
2 tbsp soy sauce
2 tbsp runny honey
2 tbsp white wine vinegar
2 tbsp fish sauce (nam pla)
2 tbsp sunflower oil

You will also need

18 bamboo skewers, soaked in water for
* 1 hour*

Cut the pork into 12 thin strips weighing approximately 60g/2oz each and set aside. To make the marinade, place half the coriander in a food processor with the garlic, ginger, grated lime peel or lime leaves, spring onions and chillies. Add 3cm/1¼in of the lemongrass, reserving the remainder of the stalk for finishing the dish. Whizz the ingredients until finely chopped.

Scrape the paste into a wide shallow porcelain dish, then stir in the soy sauce, honey, vinegar, fish sauce and sunflower oil. Slather the pork in the marinade and leave to marinate in the dish overnight, or for at least a few hours.

Place the marinade in a large jug. Thread the pork strips onto the soaked bamboo skewers and place in the jug of marinade. Cover with plastic wrap, and store in the fridge until ready to cook.

Heat a wide non-stick frying pan or ridged griddle on the stovetop. The pan must be wide enough that the pork skewers lie flat on the bottom of the pan. Working in batches, lay the pork skewers in the pan, and cook over a moderately high heat until dark brown on all sides. Take care, as they can change colour very quickly. Then, turn down the heat and continue cooking until the pork is done, about 15 minutes in all. A fine knife inserted into the thickest part of the pork should be piping hot when placed on the inside of your wrist.

Meanwhile, scrape the rest of the marinade into a saucepan. Add the coconut milk and the remaining lemongrass. Bring the mixture to the boil and simmer briskly until it is thick, stirring occasionally. Remove the saucepan from the heat and discard the lemongrass.

Finely chop the remaining coriander and stir it into the sauce. Transfer to a small serving bowl and garnish with the sliced red chilli and lime leaves. Arrange the skewers on a plate and offer the dipping sauce alongside.

Recipe notes I learned this working in the kitchen of my friend the celebrated caterer Lorna Wing, when she was the darling of London's party world. It works equally well as cocktail canapé or appetiser. To make a more substantial meal, serve the skewers straight from the pan, when the meat is at its juiciest, and offer plenty of jasmine rice to mop up the sauce.

Pork chops baked in spices, herbs and garlic
Serves 6

6 thick pork chops, trimmed of fat
1 clove garlic, halved, plus 3 cloves
garlic, peeled and finely sliced
10g/⅓oz/¼ cup thyme sprigs
10g/⅓oz/¼ cup rosemary sprigs
1 tbsp fennel seeds
6 bay leaves
a little extra virgin olive oil
salt and freshly milled black pepper

Lightly score the pork chops with a sharp, thin knife. Rub the cut surfaces of the halved garlic clove all over the pork. Remove some of the leaves from the herb sprigs and rub them and the fennel seeds into the meat too. Sprinkle the chops with salt and pepper, and drizzle over a little olive oil.

Place the finely sliced garlic in a shallow, heatproof baking dish with the remaining herbs. Nestle the chops amongst them, placing some below and some on top. Set aside in a cool place for several hours or overnight.

When ready to cook, preheat the oven to 110°C/225°F/Gas ¼. Heat a non-stick frying pan over a high heat, then sear the chops until browned. Return them to the baking dish and cook slowly and gently in the oven for about 45 minutes, or until done.

Recipe notes The sweet mild flavour of pork responds particularly well to a dry rub such as this, so I often leave the chops overnight, fully prepared in the baking tray, ready for slipping into the oven when I need them.

Brown the chops under a fierce grill [broiler] if you prefer, placing them close to the heat. For best results, they must be cut straight and thick, ideally from the rib.

Glazed gammon
Serves 10

½ ham-shaped gammon [raw smoked
country ham, bone in], weighing
about 2kg/4½lb
10 cloves
10 allspice berries
150ml/5floz/⅔ cup white wine or cider
1 onion, unpeeled
12 peppercorns

For the glaze
75g/3oz/½ packed cup brown sugar
2 tsp Dijon mustard
150ml/5floz/⅔ cup creamy milk
about 3 tbsp cloves

You will also need
1-2m/1-2 yds muslin [cheesecloth]
kitchen string

Soak the gammon overnight in cold water to draw out the salt. Weigh the joint to calculate the cooking time, allowing 40 minutes per 1kg/2lb 4oz.

Cut a small square from the muslin, tie the cloves and allspice berries in it and set aside. Use the rest of the fabric to wrap the gammon and tie neatly with string to secure, taking care the strings are not too tight and won't mark the skin. Place in a large pot, cover with water, and bring to a boil. The instant the water boils, remove the gammon, pour the water away and clean the pot. This soaking and blanching makes the gammon exceptionally juicy.

Return the gammon to the pot, cover with fresh water, then add the wine or cider, spice bag and onion. Bring the meat to the boil again and immediately reduce the heat to a simmer. Keep the water at 90°C/195°F, with the occasional bubble rising to the surface and cook according to

the time calculated, adding the peppercorns only for the last hour.

When the gammon is done, the skin will strip off easily, and the bone move easily, but it should not be so loose that the flesh breaks into pieces. Remove it from the pot, unwrap and place on an oven rack on the worktop with a large tray underneath to catch the drips. While the gammon is still warm, carefully peel off the rind.

Heat the oven to 170°C/325°F/Gas 3. Make the glaze by blending the sugar, mustard and milk together in a small bowl until smooth. Use a sharp, thin knife to score the fat diagonally in parallel lines across the meat in one direction, and then in the opposite direction, to form diamond shapes. Stud with the cloves, then brush the gammon with a coat of glaze.

Place the gammon on its rack near the top of the oven and cook for 40-50 minutes, painting with a little glaze every 15 minutes, and turning the joint to give an even, golden crust.

Recipe notes Poaching times for gammon are prone to change due to the many changes in meat brining and processing. If the gammon is tender when pierced with a skewer, and the skewer is piping hot when pressed against the inside of your wrist, and the bone is loose, it may be done before the recommended time is up. The internal temperature of the meat should be 80°C/175°F.

If desired, you can poach the gammon and remove the rind the day before serving. The following day, score the fat into diamonds and roast.

Use the sweet gammon stock the poaching creates for old-fashioned thick, hearty soups such as dried pea or lentil soup, or for cooking pulses.

Alsatian-style sausages
Serves 6

900g (2lb) canned or bottled *sauerkraut*
3 tbsp goose or pork fat, or butter
225g/8oz piece of streaky [slab] bacon,
thickly sliced, rind removed and
reserved
110g/4oz/1 cup onions, thinly sliced
55g/2oz/½ cup carrots, thinly sliced
8 sprigs parsley
2 bay leaves
6 peppercorns
10 juniper berries
150ml/5floz/⅔ cup white wine or
vermouth
580ml/1 pint/2½ cups chicken stock
1.35kg/3lb poaching sausages, such as
Strasbourg, merguez, garlic sausage,
chorizo, boudin blanc, black pudding,
or kosher beef frankfurters, or a
mixture
butter
salt and freshly milled white pepper

Drain the sauerkraut and place in a large basin of cold water to soak for 15-20 minutes or more, changing the water three times during soaking. Taste the cabbage and, when much of the briny flavour has been removed, drain it thoroughly.

Pick up small handfuls of the sauerkraut one or two at a time and squeeze out as much of the excess water as you can, then pick it apart gently to separate the strands.

Heat the oven to 170°C/325°F/Gas 3. In a large, heavy enamelled stewpot [Dutch oven], melt the fat or butter over a gentle heat and add the bacon, onions and carrots. Cover and cook slowly for 20 minutes without browning. Stir in the sauerkraut and, when it is well-coated and shining, cover again and cook slowly for another 10 minutes.

Tie all the herbs and spices together in a muslin bag and bury it with the reserved bacon rind in the sauerkraut. Season lightly with salt. Pour over the wine and stock and bring to simmering point on top of the stove.

Cover with a disc of buttered paper and the pot lid and place in the oven. Adjust the heat so that the casserole bubbles slowly for 3-5 hours, until all the liquid has been absorbed. This can be done overnight, on an automatic timer, or in a slow cooker if more convenient.

Within an hour of serving, bring a large saucepan of water to a simmer. Add the sausages, return to the boil, then immediately turn off the heat, cover and leave for 10 minutes.

Remove the sausages from the pan and set aside in a warm place. Reserve some of the poaching water to moisten the sauerkraut if it looks dry.

Forty minutes before serving, reheat the sauerkraut on top of the stove. Ten minutes later, nestle the sausages in the sauerkraut, cover again with the disc of paper and lid and simmer for 20 minutes or until the mixture is piping hot.

Slice the sausages and arrange them on top of the sauerkraut on serving plates. As everyone settles down to this wonderful meal, tip the leftovers back into the stewpot and keep it simmering so that all is hot for second helpings.

Recipe notes One of the most wonderful aspects of a trip to Paris is visiting the brasseries that were originally opened by the Alsatians. These gloriously old Art Deco places, filled with brass, are temples to Alsatian gastronomy and this sausage dish is a somewhat slimmed-down version of the traditional choucroute garnie I have often enjoyed in these places. Choucroute is the French word for sauerkraut or pickled cabbage. When sausages are cooked in it, they become exceedingly succulent and juicy, while the cabbage is flavoured with the delicious taste of the meats. Traditional choucroute garnie often includes smoked pork and thick slabs of charcuterie, but it can also be made from game birds.

Sauerkraut makes the rich meats easy to digest, so that you are able to treat yourself to a feast, without the inconvenience of suffering indigestion afterwards. A good digestion makes a happy person!

Serving sausages this way really is a complete meal in itself – there is no need for a starter – but do expect your guests and family to come back for seconds and thirds. One of the many charms of this dish is that it can be kept simmering almost indefinitely without spoiling. It is virtually impossible to over- or undercook it if you follow this method.

Serve the dish with small boiled potatoes, a pot of strong mustard such as Dijon, perhaps some little pickles such as gherkins and either a chilled Alsatian Riesling, lager or beer.

Venison with cranberry sauce
Serves 4

2 tbsp olive oil
8 medallions of red deer loin
about 1 tbsp red wine vinegar or
*   raspberry vinegar*
150g/5oz/⅔ cup crème fraîche
3 tsp Dijon mustard
about 8 tbsp cranberry sauce
salt and freshly milled black pepper

Heat a wide frying pan until very hot and add the oil. Season the venison and add it to the pan, pressing down on the meat to brown it on both sides. Cook for 3 minutes, then remove the medallions to an ovenproof plate and place in a low oven, or leave to rest in a warm place for 10 minutes.

Pour off any remaining fat in the pan and blot the pan lightly with paper towel to remove any excess.

When ready to serve, return the pan to the heat and add the vinegar, stirring well to scrape up all the meat juices encrusted on the bottom. Add the crème fraîche, mustard and cranberry sauce. Bring to a boil and simmer for about 5 minutes or until the sauce has thickened.

Adjust the seasoning to taste, correcting the sweet-sour balance with more vinegar or cranberry sauce as required. Divide the sauce between serving plates, place the medallions on top and serve immediately.

Recipe notes This is delicious served with plenty of mashed potato and crunchy, button-sized Brussels sprouts, or broccoli. Venison medallions are thick slices cut from the tenderloin. They weigh about 80g/2¾oz each, and have a mild, gamey flavour. Do allow three per person if you think two won't be enough.

Haunch of roe deer in huff crust
Serves 6

1.35kg/3lb haunch of roe deer or other
*   small, tender red deer*
1-2 tbsp groundnut or vegetable oil
1 quantity Huff Paste (page 178)
1 egg, plus 1 egg yolk
salt and freshly milled black pepper

To serve

1 quantity Clear Brown Gravy
*   (page 172)*
a little redcurrant jelly, rowan jelly or
*   crabapple jelly*

Ask the butcher to bone and tie the haunch, taking out the femur completely, and leaving just 7cm/2¾in of the shin bone. Weigh the meat and calculate the cooking time, allowing 15 minutes per 450g/1lb so the joint will be juicy and pink.

Pat the joint dry. Heat the oil in a large frying pan over a high heat and brown the venison all over. When completely browned, remove from the heat and set aside until cold.

Roll out the huff paste on a cool, flour-dusted surface, using plenty of pressure on your rolling pin to obtain a thin sheet of pastry. Whisk the egg and extra egg yolk together in a small jug with a pinch of salt, and set aside ready to glaze the pastry.

Wrap the cold meat in the pastry, painting the egg glaze along all the edges and pinching them firmly so that they stick together. Use a small sharp knife to trim away the excess pastry. Slide the haunch onto a non-stick baking tray or a tray lined with a sheet of Teflon, ensuring the seams of the pastry are on the underside. If desired, use the pastry trimmings to make braids, bunches of grapes and

tendrils, or other decorations, and press them onto the surface of the pastry. Brush the pastry all over with the remaining glaze and set aside to rest for 30 minutes.

Heat the oven to 200°C/400°F/Gas 6. Place the venison in the oven and bake for the required cooking time, or until done. The haunch should feel tender when pierced with a sharp skewer. Remove the joint from the oven and set aside to rest for 20 minutes, while you heat the gravy.

Crack open the pastry and discard it. Remove the strings from around the meat and carve into slices. Serve with the hot gravy and fruit jelly.

Recipe notes The huff crust is not meant to be eaten, it simply stops the lean flesh of the venison from drying out while in the oven.

Roe deer is sometimes known as 'the woodcock of the hill', and is extraordinarily difficult to shoot. It is best cooked to rare, and when overcooked turns grey and tough.

For reliability of supply, I always order venison from a Scottish company such as Donald Russell Direct. This also gives me peace of mind that the deer herds have been responsibly managed and shot by skilled professional stalkers on the wild heather moors. Indeed, the company's owner, Hans Baumann, is one of the best shots in Scotland.

Poultry

Poultry is easy to cook, and amiably receptive to a spectrum of flavours: Indian and Asian spices, as well as herbs from your window box. The pleasing texture of chicken appeals to all ages, and is reassuringly safe to many people. Grouse, pheasant and other game birds are amongst the jewels of British cuisine and worth exploring for their purity and health benefits. True, game can be very pungent, but those who love it enjoy the deep flavours that are enhanced by the wild foods on which game lives. In grouse there are hints of moorland, and in wild duck you can almost taste the reeds of the lakeside .

Fast ways with poultry

Stir-fry strips cut from chicken thigh or breast, or turkey escalopes, with cabbage or peppers, carrots, bacon, and small firm mushrooms.

Steam chicken and duck breasts with whole baby leeks and sprinkle with sesame dressing.

Char-grill chicken or duck breasts that you have marinated in a mixture of yogurt and sweet or spicy pimenton.

Dice the breast of poultry or game birds and add to a tomato or cream sauce. Simmer briskly for 5 minutes then serve with rice or noodles.

Pan-roast chicken, duck or game breast, then slice and add to rice pilafs or pasta, or serve warm on salads.

Bake a sliced chicken breast in a papillote with blanched strips of cavolo nero, a slice of parma or serrano ham, rehydrated dried porcini and a drizzle of olive oil.

It is essential that you always buy the best poultry you can afford. Try farmers' markets, independent butchers and mail order suppliers. They may at first seem expensive, but you will discover flavours quite different from the blandness of intensively farmed birds.

Ask your retailer if he or she knows how and where the poultry is farmed, and buy from someone you trust. Should you find tiny blood spots in the breast meat or broken bones and bloody spots around the damaged area, change your supplier.

What to look for and what to avoid

• The skin of chicken should be perfectly dry, creamy, with no signs of blood.
• Chickens and poussins should have plump rounded breasts.
• Avoid cheap, economy-labelled poultry. This has been produced by intensive, battery farming. Apart from the cruelty of the system, the birds cannot move sufficiently for them to build up muscle tissue, which is necessary for us to cook them successfully.
• Avoid ready-frozen poultry.
• Look for labels that give you confidence about the provenance of the bird.

• When shopping in supermarkets, try to buy organic and free range poultry. Treat with caution birds that may have been treated with hormones, antibiotics and chemicals. If in doubt, price is usually an indication of quality.

Storing and freezing

• Keep poultry cold and dry. If the temperature is below 4°C/ 39°F, large birds such as goose and turkey may be stored safely out of the refrigerator.
• Fresh whole poultry needs to be eaten within 5 days of purchase. Pieces such as breasts and thighs must be eaten within 2 days.
• Remove all the wrapping from the poultry when you get home, especially if it is polystyrene and plastic. Wrap in oiled parchment paper to prevent it drying out and place in the coldest part of the fridge immediately.
• Store birds on their breasts, wings up, to help them dry out.
• Most everyday poultry is wet-plucked and can harbour moisture under the wing bones, so an off-smell may develop after a few days in the fridge. If so, rinse it in a sink of cold water with about 150ml/5floz/⅔ cup of vinegar, and rub the back and

wings with more vinegar. Store the bird in a clean tea towel.
• Poussin freeze well, but you should avoid freezing chicken.
• As a townie, I would never freeze game, but in the country, when the game shooting season is short, and there is a glut of birds, it is often frozen and then used for stewing.
• Defrost frozen poultry or game in a fridge overnight, in its wrapping, then dry thoroughly, ideally in a cool draught, before cooking. Eat as soon as possible.

The principles of cooking poultry
The first thing is to understand that poultry breasts and legs cook differently, and whatever method of cooking we choose, we must respect this basic truth.

The breast needs minimum cooking at a very hot temperature, and the legs, which are used more than the wings during the bird's life, and hence have more muscle tissue, need longer slower, cooking at a low temperature.

Ideally we aim for a crisp skin and well-cooked but juicy flesh. All the recipes in this book take this into account. If you are cooking organic poultry, you may need to add a few extra minutes to the cooking time, and would do well to favour moist methods such as pot-roasting, cooking en papillote, and stewing.

Every bird is different, so make allowances for it. Game birds are a good example of how individual birds differ, and you will find those who truly enjoy eating game are the least critical of your cooking, as they understand this basic fact.

All poultry benefits from resting between the oven or stovetop and the table, giving the residual heat time to finish the cooking. This period, about 10 minutes, is not as long as that required for red meat. Indeed, it is usually the amount of time you need to get the plates out of the oven, to serve vegetables and pour wine, so it should fit naturally into the scheme of things. Just don't let your bird get cold, or try to keep it warm in an oven hotter than 25°C/80°F, where it would continue to cook and dry out.

How to tell when poultry is cooked
Cook poultry including chicken, domestic duck, poussin, guinea fowl, quail, goose and turkey to well-done, until there is no trace of blood in the flesh. I like to cook farmed poultry to an internal temperature of 82°C/ 180°F but there are other good indicators:
• If it is a whole bird, use a chef's fork to hold it neck up over a white plate, so the juices run from the cavity through the vent. Although they may look a bit cloudy, these juices should contain no trace of pinkness.
• The leg should wobble in the joint of a whole bird.
• Pierce the deepest part of the thigh with a skewer, then press with your finger near the hole. The juices will run clear when the poultry is cooked.

Rule of thumb
• A skewer inserted for 2 seconds into the thickest part of the bird, or piece of poultry, should feel piping hot when held against the inside of your wrist.

• The flesh should feel spongy when pressed with your finger.
• When cooking grouse, realize most people only eat the breast, which you should cook to rare, and if they really adore grouse, they will have no compunction sucking the leg bones.
• When cooking pheasant and partridge for formal occasions, only roast or pot-roast the crown, and use the legs for sauce making. The aim is to cook the breast until it is pearly pink.

The best advice I can give Always buy the best you can afford, and you'll be rewarded with fantastic results. Cheap chicken is produced by intensive farming, and is morally unacceptable. It has very little flavour, the flesh is immature, and no matter how much effort you put into cooking battery-farmed birds, they will always result in poor flavour and texture.

The best cooking methods My favourite methods for cooking poultry and game birds are:
Roasting. Whole chicken, duck, turkey and goose have a good layer of fat beneath the skin that melts in the oven and keeps the flesh of the birds juicy.
Pan-roasting. For chicken and duck breasts. Using a high heat for a very short period prevents evaporation and drying out.
Stewing. Ideal for tenderising the legs and thighs.
Pot-roasting. Tenderises the legs and thighs of whole birds yet the tight, heavy lid with a disc of buttered paper below prevents the steam and flavours escaping, and keeps the breast moist.

Roast chicken with its own jus
Serves 3-6

1 oven ready chicken
30g/1oz carrot, chopped
30g/1oz celery, chopped
30g/1oz mushrooms, chopped
30g/1oz onion, chopped
½ lemon
15g/½oz/⅓ cup thyme sprigs, plus an
*   extra 5 sprigs of thyme or rosemary*
2 tbsp softened butter
300ml/10floz/1¼ cups chicken stock
*   or water*
sea salt and freshly milled black pepper

Make sure the chicken is dry and not still cold from the fridge. Preheat the oven to 220°C/425°F/Gas 7.

Strew the vegetables across the base of a roasting pan. Stuff the cavity of the bird with the lemon half and 15g/½oz/⅓ cup thyme sprigs. Rub the outside all over with the butter, and sprinkle liberally with salt and a little pepper. Put a trivet or rack in the roasting pan and set the chicken on top, on its side. Place in the oven and roast for 10 minutes.

Reduce the temperature of the oven to 170°C/325°F/Gas 3 and keep cooking. When the vegetables turn a deep brown, add the stock or water and extra herbs to the pan and roast for 30 more minutes.

Turn the chicken over to its other side, using a chef's fork, and roast for another 30 minutes. Then turn the chicken breast upwards, to brown the skin for another 10 minutes or so. To test whether the chicken is done, use a chef's fork to help you hold it up over a white plate – the juices from the cavity should run clear. Also, the drumstick should be wobbly in the joint, and the internal temperature of the meat in the

thickest part of the thigh should be 82°C/180°F when tested with a probe thermometer. Remove the cooked bird from the oven, transfer it to a board, cover with foil and set aside in a warm place for 30 minutes.

Strain the cooking juices from the base of the roasting pan through a fine-meshed sieve and into a saucepan. Remove the excess fat on the surface of the jus with strips of paper towel. Bring the jus to a boil and boil it hard to concentrate the flavour – it should be strong and clear.

Meanwhile, carve the rested chicken. Pour the piping hot jus into a heated sauceboat, and serve.

Recipe notes Most chickens for everyday cooking come in three sizes: small, medium and large. A small chicken, less than 1.5kg/3lb 4oz, should take just over an hour to roast in total, and serves three people. A medium chicken, around 1.5kg/3lb 4oz, will serve four and take 70-80 minutes to cook. A large chicken, 2.25kg/5lb will take 95-100 minutes and serve six people.

Chicken is best cooked on its side, so that the juices run down into the breast to moisten it, and the legs (where the meat is most dense), are exposed to the heat of the oven. In the case of small and medium chickens, adjust the total timing by taking 10 minutes or so off the time the bird spends on each side.

Jus is a thin sauce with an intense flavour, made with stock and the juices from the roasting pan.

Roast chicken with honey, salt and cracked pepper crust
Serves 2-3

1.25kg/2lb 12oz chicken
2 tbsp softened unsalted butter
2 tbsp runny honey
1 tbsp coarsely crushed peppercorns
1 tbsp coarse salt [kosher salt]
2 cloves garlic, finely sliced
15g/½oz/⅓ cup tarragon or thyme

Heat the oven to 180°C/350°F/Gas 4. Cut off the tips of the chicken's wings, which tend to get tangled in the rack. Smear the bird with the softened butter, then thoroughly paint the skin with honey. Sprinkle all over with the pepper and salt, and sit the garlic and herbs in the cavity.

Place the chicken on a rack in a roasting pan and roast 45 minutes. Turn off the oven and leave the chicken inside, undisturbed, for a further 45 minutes so that it continues to cook in the residual heat.

Serve the chicken warm at this point, or wait until it is at room temperature. The juices will then have set to a light jelly, which is dressing enough for a side salad.

Recipe notes Nico Ladenis was a generous but strict mentor, friend and inspiration in my early years as a teacher. This recipe is based on one of his, and he suggests serving it with a green salad and warm Basmati pilaf.

I love cooking in a gentle, residual, falling heat as in this recipe – it is so much kinder to ingredients, especially high-protein foods.

Choose a plump, free-range corn-fed chicken for this dish. The butter must be very soft, at a 'dropping' consistency, meaning that it is so soft it drops off the spoon.

Pot-roast poussin with olive oil and herbes de Provence
Serves 1-2

1-2 poussins, at room temperature
1-2 tbsp herbes de Provence
2 tbsp olive oil
1 large lemon
salt and freshly milled black pepper

Heat the oven to 200°C/400°F/Gas 6. Season the birds with salt and pepper, then rub with the herbs.

On the stovetop, heat the oil in an ovenproof cocotte [Dutch oven] that will hold the poussins snugly. Add the birds and brown the breasts. When coloured, turn them over, cover with the lid and place in the oven. Reduce the temperature to 180°C/350°F/Gas 4, and cook for at least 45 minutes, or until a skewer inserted in one thigh comes out piping hot, the flesh is tender, and there are no traces of pink in the thigh joint.

Remove the birds from the pot and keep warm. Add a splash of water to the pan, scrape up the crusty bits from the base with a wooden spoon, and boil the pan juices hard for 2-3 minutes, or until they are thick enough to coat the back of a spoon.

Pour the light gravy through a fine-meshed sieve onto the birds and serve with lemon wedges and finger bowls, so that all the tender morsels can be chewed from the tiny bones.

Recipe notes This is one of my favourite mid-week suppers. Make sure the poussins are dry and at room temperature before cooking. If you have a scrap of lemon and onion leftover from anything else, place them in the cavities of the birds to give flavour and moisture.

Guinea fowl with lemon, juniper and bay rub
Serves 6-8

2 guinea fowl, about 1kg/2lb 4oz each
75g/3oz/¾ unsalted butter, plus extra for greasing
6 rashers unsmoked streaky bacon, rind removed
500ml/17floz/2 cups chicken or game stock
300ml/10floz/1¼ Bual or Malmsey Madeira
about 2 tbsp plain [all-purpose] flour
6 tbsp gin or genever
salt and freshly milled black pepper

For the marinade

5 juniper berries, cracked, plus 2 tsp juniper berries, left whole
4 tsp black peppercorns, cracked
20 white peppercorns, cracked
6 slices lemon
10 bay leaves
15g/½oz/⅓ cup thyme sprigs, tied with string

Place the guinea fowl in a cast-iron enamelled cocotte [Dutch oven]. Scatter the cracked juniper berries and black and white peppercorns over the birds, then add the lemon, bay leaves, thyme and the whole juniper berries. Cover with a heavy lid and leave in a cool place overnight.

When ready to cook, heat the oven to 190°C/375°F/Gas 5. Smear the birds liberally with 50g/2oz/½ stick of the butter. Cover the breasts with the bacon and sprinkle with salt. Turn the guinea fowl on their sides, cover closely with a disc of buttered paper, cover with the lid and place in the oven for 40 minutes.

Using a chef's fork to help you, turn the birds onto their other sides and continue cooking for 20 minutes.

Finally, remove the lid and turn the birds breast-up. Lift the bacon from the breasts but leave it in the cocotte. Cook for a final 15 minutes, or until the birds are done.

Remove the birds and bacon from the cocotte and keep warm. Lift out and discard the marinade ingredients with a teaspoon.

Place the cocotte on top of the stove. Add the stock and Madeira and boil hard, using a wooden spoon to scrape off the caramelized juices from the base of the cocotte. Boil briskly until the sauce is reduced to just over 570ml/1 pint/2¼ cups. Meanwhile, on a small dish, work the remaining 25g/1oz/¼ stick butter and flour together with a round-bladed knife to make a paste.

When the sauce has reduced, keep it boiling, and gradually whisk in small pieces of the butter-flour paste (beurre manie) until the sauce thickens enough to coat the back of a spoon.

Keep the thickened sauce hot on the stovetop while you carve the guinea fowl. Add the gin or genever to the piping hot sauce. Try not to let the sauce boil again, or the flavour of the gin will simply disappear, which is a terrible shame.

Strain the sauce through a fine-meshed sieve into a warmed sauce boat and serve immediately with the guinea fowl.

Recipe notes A dry rub or marinade is an easy way to make farmed poultry more flavoursome.

This is a recipe that pleases on all levels – the smooth, dark, rich sauce, the sweetness of the guinea fowl and its buttery tenderness, the flavours of the herbs and spices all trapped inside the heavy lid of the casserole. Serve it with a dish of stir-fried savoy cabbage and pancetta, little roast potatoes and a parsnip mash.

It is important that crusty dark deposits form on the base of the cocotte during roasting: these give body, colour and flavour to the sauce, but you must not use them if they have become bitter and burned.

There are four basic styles of Madeira and for this particular recipe it is best to use one of the sweet 'dessert' Madeiras Bual (or Boal) or Malmsey. If you have none, use ruby port or amontillado sherry to boil away the caramelized cooking juices (or to deglaze a roasting pan), in preference to red wine. Madeira is, however, very useful to keep in the kitchen for cooking as it keeps almost indefinitely once re-corked.

You can marinate the guinea fowl a day or so in advance, and leave it in the fridge in the casserole, ready to go in the oven. This will only improve the flavour. Pheasant, grouse and small chickens can be substituted for the guinea fowl if desired.

Grouse with wine, orange and brandy
Serves 4

4 young grouse
4 oranges
16 rashers streaky bacon, rind removed
15g/½oz/⅓ cup rosemary (optional)
90g/3oz/¾ stick butter
12 spring onions [scallions]
1 clove garlic, chopped
240ml/8floz/1 cup white wine
8 tbsp brandy
6 tbsp orange marmalade (optional)
salt and freshly milled black pepper

Preheat the oven to 250°C/490°F/ Gas 10, or the highest setting.

Rub the cavities of each bird with paper towel to ensure they are clean, then sprinkle with salt and pepper. Pare the zest from the oranges in long, large strips and juice the flesh. In the cavities of each bird, place a strip of orange zest, two rashers of bacon, and a sprig of rosemary, if using. Cover the breasts of each bird with two rashers of bacon.

Melt the butter in a cast-iron cocotte [Dutch oven] large enough to fit the birds snugly. Add the spring onions, garlic and a little salt and cook gently, without colouring.

Remove the onions from the pan and keep to one side. Increase the heat to moderate and pour in half the orange juice. Turn the birds one by one in the bubbling orange butter, but do not try to brown them. When the last one is done, pour in 8 tbsp of the white wine and boil until it has almost evaporated.

Return all the birds and the onions to the cocotte. Cover with a disc of buttered paper, tucking it deep down the sides of the birds. Cover with the lid of the cocotte and place in the oven. Reduce the oven temperature to 200°C/400°F/Gas 6 and cook for 15 minutes.

Meanwhile. cut the remaining orange zest into long thin strips. When the birds are done, remove them from the cocotte and place on an oven tray. Cover loosely with foil and set aside in a warm place to rest for 15-20 minutes.

Towards the end of the resting time, place the cocotte over a brisk heat, pour in the brandy and the rest of the white wine, and allow it to come to a rolling boil. Scrape down the sides of the pan with a wooden spoon, then add the remaining orange juice and thin strips of rind and continue boiling.

Start to carve the birds. The sauce should be very dark, and, as it bubbles away under your watchful eye, should eventually cover the back of a spoon. If you find the sauce a touch bitter, add the marmalade.

Strain the sauce through a fine-meshed sieve before serving, pressing down well to extract all the juices, and serve piping hot with the grouse.

Recipe notes When cooking game, always allow a bit of time and patience to take out any remaining feathers and quills, using a pair of tweezers, before you begin cooking.

To make the bacon thinner so that the rashers provide greater covering for the birds' breasts, take each rasher of chilled bacon and use the side of a knife to spread it firmly across the kitchen worktop.

If the sauce looks too buttery, be ready to thicken it with some cornflour [cornstarch] slaked in water.

Serve with fine French beans [haricot verts], game chips, parsnip crisps (page 121) or mashed potato.

Persian-style chicken pilaf with pistachios and barberries
Serves 6

For the chicken
675kg/1½lb chicken thighs, skinned,
  boned and trimmed
1 tsp saffron strands
1 tsp freshly ground white pepper
1 tsp ground ginger
1 large cinnamon stick
45g/1½oz/3 tbsp butter
2 onions, finely sliced
1.14 litres/2 pints/5 cups chicken stock
30g/1oz/¼ cup dried barberries, soaked
  in water
45g/1½oz/¼ cup nibbed pistachios
juice of 2 lemons
a few sprigs of flat-leaf parsley (optional)
salt and freshly milled pepper

For the rice
250g/8oz/1 heaping cup basmati rice
2 tbsp sunflower oil
½ onion, chopped
1-2 large garlic cloves, crushed
seeds of 4 cardamom pods, crushed
2 tsp cumin seeds
1 tsp ground turmeric
about 15g/½oz/1 tbsp butter
2 bay leaves

Rub the chicken with a little salt and freshly ground pepper. Place it in a cocotte [Dutch oven] with half the saffron, plus the white pepper, ginger, cinnamon and butter. Cook over a medium heat for 2–3 minutes.

Finely chop five slices of the onion and add to the pan with the stock. Bring to a boil, then reduce the heat, cover and simmer for 30 minutes. Add the remaining onions and cook until the chicken is very tender.

Meanwhile, preheat the oven to 180°C/350°F/Gas 4. Place the nibbed pistachios on a baking tray and toast in the oven for 5 minutes until crisp but not browned. Remove from the oven and set aside to cool.

Strain off 450ml/16floz/2 cups of the stock for cooking the rice, and strain the rest into a small, wide saucepan. Bring it to a boil and boil hard until the liquid has reduced in volume and become thick and shiny. Add the remaining saffron towards the end of cooking.

To prepare the rice, rinse it well and drain thoroughly. In a saucepan, heat the oil and gently fry the onion, garlic, cardamom, cumin and turmeric for about 5 minutes or until the onions are soft. Add the drained rice and butter and fry for about 2-3 minutes or until the rice is opaque.

Pour in the reserved 450ml/16floz/2 cups of stock, add the bay leaves, season well and bring to a boil. Cover, lower the heat to the gentlest simmer and cook for 8 minutes.

Remove the rice from the heat and set aside to rest, still covered, for about 5 minutes. Use a metal fork to stir it carefully, mixing in the drained barberries and pistachios.

Drape the chicken attractively over the rice on a large platter, and then pour over the hot sauce, or offer it separately. Sprinkle the chicken and rice with the lemon juice and garnish with parsley, if using, before serving.

Recipe notes The wonder of a chicken stew is that you get all the advantages of stewing, including fork-tender meat and a gorgeously aromatic sauce, in a comparatively short time.

Like all stews, this one can be made in advance and reheated, although I find the texture of the rice is best when freshly cooked. Serve it with a salad, or char-grilled aubergine with a yogurt and mint dressing.

Chicken tagine with apricots and prunes
Serves 4

1.57kg/3½lb chicken thighs
2 tsp ground cumin, or more to taste
350g/12oz/2 cups mixed pitted prunes
  and dried apricots
2–3 tsp ground cinnamon
2 large mild onions, sliced lengthwise
1 tsp ground turmeric
1 tsp ground ginger
groundnut or sunflower oil, for frying
100g/3½oz/¾ cup blanched almonds
1 large cinnamon stick, splintered
  lengthways
2 tbsp cornflour
15g/½oz/⅓ cup coriander [cilantro],
  chopped (optional)
salt and freshly ground pepper

Rub all the chicken pieces with the cumin and some salt and pepper and set aside for 1 hour.

Place the prunes and apricots in a saucepan with the ground cinnamon and cover with plenty of cold water. Bring to a boil, then reduce the heat and simmer for 30 minutes. Be sure not to overcook them, as they will be simmered again later.

In a flameproof casserole or cocotte [Dutch oven], cook the onions with the turmeric, ginger, salt, pepper and 125ml/4floz/½ cup of water for 15 minutes. Meanwhile, in a wide frying pan containing enough oil to give a depth of 5mm/¼in, brown the blanched almonds. Remove the nuts with a perforated spoon and set aside to drain on paper towel.

Using the same oil, brown the chicken evenly on all sides, then transfer to the pot of cooked onions. Add the splintered cinnamon stick and 250ml/9floz/1 cup of the poaching water from the fruit. >

Cover with a disc of buttered paper, put the lid on the pot and simmer for 30 minutes over a moderate heat.

Add the cooked fruit and some more of the fruit poaching water to the casserole and continue cooking until the chicken and fruit are done.

Place a colander over a large saucepan and gently tip the contents of the casserole into the colander, so that the juices drip into the saucepan.

In a small bowl, combine the cornflour with 2 tbsp cold water, stirring until smooth, then add the mixture to the saucepan. Boil hard until the sauce is really thick and smooth. Add the chicken and fruit to the pan, lower the heat and simmer until very tender. Stir in the fresh coriander, if using.

To serve, arrange the chicken on a serving platter and cover with the fruit and sauce. Sprinkle with the browned almonds and serve at once.

Recipe notes I love this tagine for its simplicity, the bold, dark and glowing colours, and the texture of soft, spicy fruit contrasted with whole crunchy almonds. It is based on a recipe by American food writer Paula Wolfert.

Plain dried fruit is becoming harder and harder to find these days. If you can only find semi-dried fruit, take extra care when poaching to prevent it falling apart. If, on the other hand, the fruit is very dry, you need to soak it for at least 1 hour beforehand and cook it a bit longer.

While the sauce is boiling, you may wish to remove the skin from the chicken, and trim off any bones (which will have become quite soft) with a cleaver or heavy knife.

Duck khoresh with bitter orange and pistachios
Serves 4–6

For the duck khoresh
3 tbsp sunflower oil or ghee
1 large onion, finely sliced
450g/1lb boned duck legs, cut into thin strips
2 large carrots, about 225g/8oz, peeled and cut into thin strips
2 tbsp dried or candied bitter orange peel, cut into thin strips
1 tbsp cornflour [cornstarch]
½ tsp advieh spice mix (see below)
1 tsp salt
freshly ground black pepper
300ml/10floz/1¼ cups fresh orange juice
2 tbsp lime juice, plus extra for seasoning
1 tbsp red wine vinegar
8 tbsp sugar, plus extra for seasoning
a pinch of saffron threads
2 large oranges, segmented, with white membrane removed

For the advieh spice mix
(makes 8 tbsp)
2 tbsp dried rose petals
2 tbsp ground cinnamon
2 tbsp ground cardamom
1 tbsp ground cumin

To serve
1 tsp slivered almonds
1 tsp slivered or chopped raw pistachios
a little mustard and cress

To make the advieh, place all the ingredients in a spice mill and grind until fine. Store in an airtight jar. Prepare the slivered almonds for the garnish by toasting them until golden in a hot dry frying pan, stirring often to prevent burning.

To make the khoresh, heat the oil in a medium-sized pot over a medium heat. Add the onions and stir-fry for 5 minutes until translucent. Add the duck and fry for 10–15 minutes, stirring occasionally, until golden brown. Add the carrots and orange peel, and stir-fry 1 minute longer.

Sprinkle in the flour and stir-fry for a few seconds longer, then add the advieh, salt and some pepper. Pour in the orange juice and bring to a boil. Reduce the heat to low, cover, and simmer for about 20 minutes, or until the duck is tender.

Adjust the seasoning to taste. Strain the mixture into a saucepan, setting the solids aside in a warm place. Bring the sauce to a boil and boil until the volume of liquid has reduced by at least half. Adjust the flavour, adding a little sugar or lime juice so that the dish is neither too sour or too sweet. Return the duck to the sauce and set aside.

Meanwhile, dissolve the saffron threads in 1 tbsp of hot water and set aside to infuse for 10–15 minutes.

In a small saucepan, combine the vinegar, lime juice, sugar, and the strained saffron water. Mix well and bring to the boil over a medium heat. Remove from the heat, gently add the orange segments and set aside to macerate for a few moments.

Transfer the duck stew to a serving dish. Carefully arrange the orange segments and some of their syrup on top. Cover and place in a warm oven for a short time until ready to serve.

Just before serving, sprinkle the khoresh with the toasted almonds, slivered pistachios and some mustard and cress. Serve hot, with steamed rice to accompany.

Recipe notes Khoresh is a Persian stew-cum-sauce made to serve with rice, which in that cuisine is a highly regarded part of the meal, not just a side dish. I lived in Tehran in the 1970s, working as a chef for a court official at the Shah's palace, and in that time came to understand and admire Persian food, which is one of the world's most ancient cuisines.

Advieh is a Persian spice mix, and there are almost as many recipes as there are cooks. Those made with dried rose petals are typical of the north-west of Iran. The recipe here, based on one from *A Taste of Persia* by Najmieh K Batmanglij, gives more than you need for one khoresh; try to use the remainder within three months otherwise the flavour will dissipate.

You will find all the ingredients you need for this dish in a Middle Eastern shop. The dried bitter orange peel in particular is a great find. It adds a striking new dimension to the classic combination of duck with orange sauce. While at the store, remember to stock up on dried barberries, saffron and dried mint, used elsewhere in this book.

This dish can be made entirely in advance and reheats very easily. Just keep the duck in its dark onion sauce, do not add the mixture of saffron, lime juice and orange segments, until just before serving.

Basmati pilaf with fresh green herbs (page 144) is a fine accompaniment to this dish.

If you do not care for duck or there is none available, lamb neck fillet and boned chicken are suitable substitutes in this recipe. You can also use chicken drumsticks, but will need to increase the cooking time of the khoresh to 55 minutes.

Chicken breasts stuffed with shiitake and chives
Serves 6

6 *chicken breasts, with skin and fillets*
300g/10oz *fresh shiitake or chestnut mushrooms, stalks removed, finely sliced*
30g/1oz/½ *cup chives, finely chopped*
a little truffle oil (optional)
groundnut or sunflower oil, for frying
salt and freshly milled black pepper

Remove the small fillets from the chicken breasts by peeling them off, and set to one side. Using the tip of a small, sharp, pointed knife, slit open the breasts, lengthways and horizontally, to make a pocket. Reach with the point of the knife deep into the thickest end of the fillet, but do not cut right through the breast. Season inside the pocket with salt and pepper.

In a frying pan, pour in enough oil to give a depth of about 5mm/¼in and heat. Lightly fry the mushrooms so that they are still meaty and juicy, then season and set aside in a sieve to drain and cool.

Reserve some of the mushrooms to use as a garnish. Fill the chicken with the remaining mushrooms, pushing them deep into the breasts, then sprinkle in the chives and trickle with truffle oil, if using. Set aside.

Place each of the reserved small chicken fillets between two layers of plastic wrap. Flatten them until almost paper-thin by bashing them evenly in two blows with the base of a saucepan. Peel away the plastic wrap, and lay the fillets over the stuffing of each chicken breast, to cover the pockets. Aim to get the flesh touching all the way around to help seal the pockets.

Heat the oven to 190°C/375°F/Gas 5. Meahwhile, heat a little more oil in a roasting pan, so that there is a thin film over the base. Season the chicken breasts and place them in the pan skin-side down to brown for a minute or so over a moderate heat.

Cover the breasts with pieces of buttered paper and place in the oven for 12 minutes. If desired you can flip the breasts over and sear the second side to make it a little crisper. Set the chicken breasts aside in a warm place to rest. Gently reheat the reserved mushrooms.

To serve, slice each breast at an angle into 3 or 4 thick slices. To do this, use a long, thin and very sharp knife and begin at the pointed end, using your elbow in a slicing movement but with a minimum of pressure. Arrange each breast, in a curve, on very hot serving plates and garnish with the mushrooms.

Recipe notes This tasty little stuffing turns a plain chicken breast into something quite special. You can cook this dish just as easily for two, six or 36 people but, depending on your oven, two chicken breasts will generally cook more quickly than six or more. If you want to prepare the breasts in advance, make sure the filling is cold before stuffing. They can wait overnight in the fridge, but must be brought to room temperature before roasting.

If you like, buy some additional chestnut mushrooms and fry them with the shiitake, using more oil and being sure to season them well. Serve these sautéed mushrooms around the cooked sliced chicken breasts, together with crisp green vegetables, buttered noodles (page 135), and clear brown gravy (page 172).

Chicken in cumin and yogurt marinade with roast vegetables
Serves 6

3 tsp ground cumin
200g/7oz/¾ cup Greek yogurt
6 large chicken drumsticks
6 tbsp extra virgin olive oil
1 red pepper, cut into chunks
1 yellow pepper, cut into chunks
2 small red onions, quartered
200g/7oz butternut squash, peeled and chopped
4 cloves garlic, squashed
12 sprigs flat-leaf parsley, chopped
salt and freshly milled pepper

Mix together the cumin, yogurt, salt and pepper to make a thick cream and slather it all over the chicken. Leave to marinate for at least 1 hour.

When ready to cook, preheat the oven to 200°C/400°F/Gas 6. Heat a roasting pan on the stovetop, then add the oil, vegetables, garlic and seasoning and toss to coat. Place the chicken, in its marinade, on top of the vegetables, and roast in the oven for 35-40 minutes, stirring the vegetables once during cooking.

When the chicken is done, a skewer inserted into the thickest part of the drumstick will come out piping hot. Divide the chicken amongst serving plates and scatter with the parsley. Stir the excess marinade into the vegetables, and serve with the chicken.

Recipe notes If you prefer, use four cubed chicken breasts instead of drumsticks and roast for 20 mintues. Stir them into the vegetables just before serving. Replace the peppers with bottled peppers if necessary, allowing them to heat through in the vegetable mixture for 5-10 minutes towards the end of cooking.

Jambonettes of duck
Serves 4

4 large duck legs or quarters, about 300g/10oz each, tunnel boned
2 tbsp sunflower, groundnut, or olive oil
salt and freshly milled black pepper
8 sprigs mizuna

For the stuffing
100g/3½oz chicken breast or pork fillet, chopped
160ml/5½floz/⅔ cup double [heavy] cream
15g/½oz/1 tbsp butter
1 heaped tbsp chopped shallots
70g/2½oz/½ cup cooked ham, very finely diced
30g/1oz/½ cup fresh spinach, finely sliced

You will also need
a needle and black thread

Make the stuffing. Place the chicken or pork fillet, the cream, a mixing bowl and the bowl and blade of the food processor in the freezer until icy cold. Meanwhile, melt the butter in a frying pan and cook the shallots gently until translucent, but not coloured. Add the ham and stir briefly, then scrape all the mixture from the pan and set aside to cool.

Purée the ice-cold chicken or pork in the food processor with a good dash of salt. Add a little of the cream, blending to give a thick smooth paste. Transfer this mixture to the chilled mixing bowl and gradually beat in the remaining cream with a rubber spatula.

Season the mixture generously: stuffing should have a bold flavour. Stir in the spinach, then the cooled shallot and ham, to give a fairly stiff mixture. Loosely fill the cavity of the duck legs with the stuffing, allowing room for it to expand, then sew the skin closed, trying to give the legs a triangular shape, so they look like little hams (jambonettes).

Preheat the oven to 220°C/425°F/Gas 7. Bring a kettle of water to the boil. Place the duck legs on a rack in the sink, then pour the boiling water over them. Let the water drain away quickly and pat the duck legs dry.

Heat the oil in a small roasting pan, season the jambonettes, and brown them carefully in the hot oil, pressing down gently and taking care you don't break the skin. Pour off the excess fat that has accumulated in the pan. Transfer to the oven and roast for 30 minutes. Turn once during cooking, and pour off the excess fat again.

Remove the black thread from the duck legs before serving. Slice with a fine, sharp carving knife to show the stuffing, and garnish with the mizuna sprigs. Chill, if serving cold, for an elegant picnic dish.

Recipe notes This impressive dish is not as complicated as it looks when you ask the butcher to tunnel bone the duck legs for you.

The jambonettes can be prepared up to two days in advance, and kept chilled, but bring them to room temperature before cooking. If necessary, the stuffing can be made the day before it is put into the duck legs and stored in the fridge in a covered container.

If you don't have space in your freezer for the food processor bowl or mixing bowl, you will need some ice. This will prevent the stuffing curdling, especially on a hot day.

There is no need to make any knots when sewing up the duck legs as a natural seal will form during roasting.

Eggs and cheese

'Something eggy on a tray,' was Noel Coward's first choice when the going got tough, and after a frantic day at the office, or a long, frustrating journey home, eggs are soothing, comforting and filling. I challenge any ingredient to be so versatile. Eggs take centre stage in dishes from simple poached eggs on toast to extravagant soufflé roulades, as well as providing a vital supporting role in other recipes such as sauces. Cheese on the other hand is fascinatingly diverse even before cooking. Most commonly made from cows', goats', or ewes' milk, it ripens, reaches its peak in aroma, taste and texture, then deteriorates. Man's ingenuity has given rise to hundreds of different varieties, each of which relies on the milk, the pasture, the microclimate, and the cheese maker for its distinction.

Fast ways with eggs and cheese

Toast some buttered slices of bread and top with sliced ham and grated cheese. Grill [broil] until hot and bubbling.

Stir-fry blanched spinach until hot and glossy then season well and top with smoked salmon and softly poached eggs.

Sprinkle two chopped hard-boiled eggs over a cooked bunch of asparagus and dress with vinaigrette.

Poach an egg for each person and serve on a bed of frisée, fried bacon lardons, and drizzle with vinaigrette.

Grate cantal cheese from central France and beat into mashed potatoes.

Crumble caerphilly from Wales over wholemeal toast and melt it gently.

Serve buffalo mozzarella or a soft or semi-soft goats' cheese with char-grilled aubergine [eggplant].

Freshness is key to purchasing both eggs and cheese, so choose a retailer with a high turnover of good stock. You will love specialist cheese shops and farmers' markets, as long as you are not in a hurry. Good cheese comes with a provenance and it is a part of its charm to be able discuss it fully with whoever is selling it. To buy from an affineur, who specially ripens cheeses at the shop, is a treasured experience; so is buying direct from a farm.

Go to shops where you can taste the cheese before you buy. Say when you wish to eat the cheese, and you will be advised where to keep it, and how to serve it at its best. On very warm days take a cool-bag with you when you go shopping, to ensure the cheese does not sweat and deteriorate before you get home.

Always check the use-by dates on eggs and buy the best you can afford, either organic or free range, ideally from a small independent producer, at a high-turnover delicatessen, farmers' market or farm shop.

What to look for and what to avoid

• Avoid battery-produced eggs, which will contain the antibiotics given to the hens. Doubt labels such as Fresh from the Flock, Deep Litter, and Barn Eggs. Instead look for the Organic and Free Range labels, or a named reliable producer.

• Always check eggs before purchasing them. Turn the box upside down and look for breakages or leaks. Open the box if possible, to check for cracks.

• Good recipes will help you select the best cheeses for cooking. Easy-melting cheeses include gruyère, fontina and emmental. They are just as good when served on a cheese board.

• Avoid huge, bland blocks of plastic-wrapped cheeses. Go for those in wax wrappings, or cheeses with rinds and crusts. Surface molds show quality and individuality.

• Avoid processed cheeses with a rubbery texture and pallid flavours. Instead choose soft or hard cheeses, and use them when fully ripe, at their best.

• When selecting cheese for

serving as part of a cheese board, look for artisanal farmhouse cheeses and classics such as Stilton and Reblochon produced by skilled cheese makers, not by large factories.

Storage and freezing

• Egg shells are porous, so must be stored hygienically, away from strong flavours, and in the fridge. Ironically, the worst place for them is the door, where the frequent movement causes the yolks and whites to swing.

• Egg whites can be frozen in clean, sealed jars, and used for baking meringues, soufflés and macaroons, however I don't recommend freezing the yolks.

• Cheeses store best in a cool, humid place such as a cellar or larder. Wrap them in waxed paper or damp muslin [cheesecloth], not in plastic wrap, in which they will sweat.

• If keeping cheese in the fridge, store it in a comparatively warm place such as the salad drawer. Loosely wrap it in waxed paper or damp muslin [cheesecloth], and place in a large sealed container, so it can 'breathe'.

• Allow cheeses to warm up a little before serving. They should be cool to the touch, and should never run out of their rind, or smell of ammonia. These are signs that they are past their best.

• Cheese can be frozen, if absolutely necessary. Hard rich cheeses such as gruyère, cheddar and parmesan freeze best. However, on defrosting, you may find that the texture of some cheeses has become crumblier and is best used for cooking.

The principles of cooking eggs

• Egg, like all proteins, sets when exposed to heat. Too much heat and the eggs will become rubbery. In the case of egg mixtures such as custards, too much heat will cause the mixture to separate.

• Eggs continue cooking in the residual heat of the pan. Scrambled eggs and omelettes must be removed from the pan before they have set firm.

• When heated and stirred gently in milk or cream, whole eggs or yolks will thicken the liquid. However, beaten eggs should never be whisked directly into a hot mixture, or they will scramble.

• Whisking the whites of eggs incorporates air bubbles, creating foam and an increase in volume. When cooked, these bubbles expand further in the heat, causing dishes such as soufflés to rise.

The principles of cooking cheese

• The overriding rule when cooking cheese is to use gentle heat and sensitive care. Remember: it is a melting process, not a cooking process.

• Disappointing results are not due to the quality of cheese you have bought, so much as the type of cheese you have chosen for the job required. A good recipe will specify the right cheese to use.

• When melting cheese for fondue mixtures, cut it into small cubes. Stir well over a gentle heat so that the fat does not seep from the cheese and the protein solidify.

• For gratins and other toppings, cheese should be grated. Varieties such as cheddar, fontina, gruyére, and emmental give the best results. Parmesan does not spread as well

as its cousins and works best when very finely grated and used on top of a very liquid sauce, or when mixed with cheeses that melt more smoothly.

• If you have to grill [broil] cheese, take care. An oven is the best place to melt cheese, not under a harsh, fast grill, unless you are inclined to watch very carefully.

• When making cheese sauces, choose strong varieties. Add the diced cheese to the creamy base just before serving. Never leave it to stew in a sauce waiting on the stovetop. A little starch, such as plain [all-purpose] flour or cornflour [cornstarch] cooked into the sauce helps keep the cheese from separating.

Serving a cheese board

• Choose a maximum of four cheeses, all in perfect condition and ideally produced by an artisan. You will need a blue cheese, hard cheese, a soft one, and a goats' cheese. You should be able to smell traces of the pastureland, mixed with the milk, in a really good cheese.

• For a winter and Christmas cheese board include a ripe Vacherin, which you eat with a spoon, and a Stilton. Surround with homemade oatcakes, freshly cracked walnuts, Muscatel raisins, unblanched almonds, small red apples, and a little dish of cumin, to nibble as an aid to digestion.

• For a summer cheeseboard choose softer, milkier, less pungent cheeses. Serve with grapes and celery, and a green salad. For a different effect, serve cubes of feta with watermelon, or vine tomatoes and black olives.

Hot broccoli mousses
Serves 4

softened butter, for greasing
1 tbsp sunflower oil
300g/11oz broccoli florets, trimmed
200ml/7floz/³⁄₄ cup vegetable stock
2 large eggs
4 tbsp double [heavy] cream
a little freshly grated nutmeg
salt and freshly milled white pepper

To serve
1 quantity Lemon Hollandaise (page 168)

You will also need
4 molds of 150ml/5floz/²⁄₃ cup capacity
a roasting tray bain-marie

Heat the oven to 180°C/350°F/Gas 4. Butter each mold twice, then place a disc of silicone paper in the bases.

Heat the oil in a saucepan, add the broccoli and cook gently for 2-3 minutes. Add the stock, season and bring to a boil. Cover and boil for 5 minutes, then remove the lid and cook another 5 minutes or until the broccoli is soft but the colour is still bright. Set aside to cool a little.

Transfer the broccoli and cooking liquid to a blender or food processor and purée until fine. Add the eggs, cream, nutmeg, salt and pepper and blend until smooth. Pour the mixture into the molds and cook in a bain-marie of steaming water in the oven for 35-40 minutes.

To serve, turn the mousses out of the molds and cloak them with plenty of sauce. Serve immediately.

Recipe notes These mousses are ideal served as a substantial starter on a winters' night, or as a vegetarian main course. If you prefer, serve them with a warm vinaigrette (page 163).

Parmesan custards
Serves 4

For the custards
softened butter, for greasing
150ml/5floz/²⁄₃ cup whipping [heavy]
  cream
150ml/5floz/²⁄₃ cup milk
80g/2³⁄₄oz/11 tbsp Parmigiano Reggiano
  cheese, finely grated
2 large eggs, plus 1 large egg yolk
salt and freshly milled white pepper

To serve
a few long strips of romaine lettuce,
  cut from the heart
a little Anchovy Dressing (page 162)
4 Parmesan Crisps (page 182)
4 strips shaved Parmigiano Reggiano
  cheese, plus 2 tbsp, grated
a few snipped chives

You will also need
4 molds of 150ml/5floz/²⁄₃ cup capacity
a roasting tray bain-marie

Heat the oven to 130°C/250°F/Gas ½. Brush the molds with softened butter, ideally twice, chilling them between each buttering.

To make the custards, combine the the cream, milk and cheese in a small saucepan and bring to a simmer. Turn off the heat, move the pan to a cooler spot, cover and leave to infuse for at least 45 minutes.

In a medium bowl, whisk the eggs and extra yolk together until thick and smooth. Reheat the cream mixture until it is hot, but nowhere near boiling. While whisking the eggs very gently, gradually strain the hot cream mixture through a sieve onto the eggs. Stir well to combine and season with salt and white pepper.

Ladle equal quantities of the mixture into each mold and cover with buttered paper. Place in a bain-marie of steaming hot water and make sure the water comes at least halfway up the sides of the molds.

Place the bain-marie in the middle of the oven and cook for about 40 minutes, or until the custards are just set, wobbly in the centre and lightly set around the edges. Remove from the water bath and chill for at least 2 hours before serving.

To serve, toss the strips of lettuce in the anchovy dressing in a bowl, using only enough dressing to coat the greens lightly. Season to taste with salt and pepper. Run a paring knife around the edge of each custard, dip the base of the mold into very hot water and turn out onto a serving plate. Drizzle each plate with a little anchovy dressing.

Top each custard with a parmesan crisp. Scatter the grated cheese over the lettuce and arrange a little on top of the parmesan crisp. Sit a cheese shaving on top, sprinkle with the chives and serve immediately.

Recipe notes This recipe is based on one by Thomas Keller of The French Laundry restaurant in the Napa Valley.

All the elements of the dish can be prepared days in advance and assembled just prior to serving. The custards will keep for up to 3 days in the refrigerator.

Make the cheese shavings by rasping a wedge of Parmigiano Reggiano with a vegetable peeler and keep the shavings in a small, lidded container until required for garnishing.

Goats' cheese mousselines
Serves 4

For the mousselines

softened butter, for greasing
2 cloves garlic
about 125ml/4floz/½ cup milk
300g/10oz/1¼ cups soft fresh rindless
  goats' cheese
200ml/7floz/scant 1 cup whipping
  [heavy] cream
100g/3½oz chicken breast fillet,
  skinned and sliced
salt and freshly milled white pepper

To serve

4 sprigs of chervil or mizuna
a few snipped chives
a few rocket leaves, or similar leaves
6 black olives, stoned and chopped
a little Warm Tomato Vinaigrette
  (page 163)

You will also need

a chilled metal mixing bowl
4 molds of 150ml/5floz/⅔ cup capacity
a roasting tray bain-marie

Heat the oven to 170°C/325°F/Gas 3. Lightly brush the molds with softened butter, ideally twice, chilling them between each buttering.

Meanwhile, place the garlic and milk in a small saucepan. Bring it to the boil and cook until the garlic is tender. Drain, discarding the milk, then peel and crush the garlic.

In a food processor, purée the goats' cheese and cream briefly – not too much or the mixture will curdle. Remove from the bowl and set aside. Don't wash out the processor.

Place the chicken, garlic and a large pinch of salt in the processor bowl and purée until fine. Add a little of the cream mixture, process thoroughly, and season generously.

Transfer the chicken mixture to the chilled metal bowl and, using a rubber spatula, beat in the rest of the cream-cheese mixture by hand, a little at a time, until it is absorbed. The mixture should look shiny, thick and floppy.

Using a table knife, spread the mixture around the sides of the molds, then fill the centres, tapping on the worktop to remove air bubbles. Cover each with a square of buttered paper.

Sit the molds in a bain-marie of steaming hot water and place in the oven, turning the heat down to 160°C/310°F/Gas 2½. Cook for 20 minutes, or until set, being careful not to overcook. Remove from the oven and leave to stand in the bain-marie until ready to serve.

Turn out and serve hot, garnished with a sprig of chervil or mizuna, the rocket, chives, olives, and some warm tomato vinaigrette.

Recipe notes It is important to keep the equipment and the mixture very cold to prevent separation.

Pre-cooking the garlic in the milk mellows its flavour.

These make a good starter or lunch dish. If there is a delay in taking them to the table it's not a problem – the mousses will stay warm in the bain-marie for about 30 minutes.

Peppery, crisp salad leaves are the perfect contrast to the richness of the mousse. You could use a pesto-flavoured vinaigrette instead of the tomato one, if you prefer.

Soufflé roulade with crème fraîche and caviar
Serves 12-15

For the filling

200ml/7floz/scant 1 cup crème fraîche
30g/1oz/2 tbsp butter
150g/5oz caviar such as Sevruga, or
  golden herring roe
20g/⅔oz/⅓ cup chives, finely cut

For the roulade

425ml/14floz/1¾ cups milk
75g/2½oz/¾ stick butter
60g/2oz/6 tbsp plain [all-purpose] flour
4 tsp lemon juice
3 eggs, separated, plus 1 egg white
sunflower oil, for greasing

For the garnish

335g/12oz rocket or frisée
240g/8oz cooked white lobster meat, cut
  into thick round slices
15 sprigs chervil
salt and freshly milled white pepper

You will also need

a shallow baking tray measuring
  33 x 23cm/13 x 9in

Line a sieve with paper towel and set over a mixing bowl. Place the crème fraîche in the sieve and leave to drain for at least 1 hour in the fridge.

To make the roulade, preheat the oven to 170°C/325°F/Gas 3. Brush the shallow baking tray with sunflower oil, then line it with plastic wrap, allowing a small border of plastic around the edges of the tin (these will disappear in the heat of the oven, but don't worry about it).

'Paint' the plastic wrap into position with a dry brush – a few creases here and there will not matter.

To make the sauce base for the soufflé mixture, heat the milk in a small saucepan until it is barely simmering. Meanwhile, in a separate saucepan, melt the butter, add the flour and, using a wooden spoon, stir continuously for a few minutes.

Working over a moderate heat, pour the hot milk over the butter and flour mixture, whisking very vigorously so that no lumps form. Bring to a boil, stirring constantly, until the sauce is thick and shiny. Whisk in the lemon juice, then remove the pan from the heat and set aside to cool.

When the sauce is tepid, add the egg yolks and stir until completely blended. In a large clean bowl, whisk the egg whites to a shiny dense foam. When the whisk is lifted from the foam, the tips of the peaks formed should flop over. Gently and lightly fold the sauce mixture into the egg whites until evenly distributed.

Spread the mixture evenly into the prepared tin, tapping it against the worktop to burst any large air bubbles. Bake for 35-40 minutes until golden-brown and firmish to the touch. Remove the tin from the oven and place on a rack to cool.

Turn the cooled roulade out onto a clean tea towel and peel off the plastic wrap. Lay another tea towel over the surface and use the ends of both to help you turn the roulade over so that the shiny side is on the new tea towel. Use a knife to neatly trim the edges of the short sides.

To finish making the filling, melt the butter and allow it to cool. Place the drained crème fraîche in a mixing bowl and add the cooled butter, whisking well. Season generously with salt and pepper, then chill well.

Spread the cream mixture over the roulade. Cover this with the caviar, followed by the chives. Use the tea towel underneath the roulade to help

you roll it up carefully. Place the roulade on the upturned oven tray in the fridge until ready to serve.

Trim the edges of the roulade, then cut it into slices using a hot, sharp, thin-bladed knife and wiping the blade between each slice.

Divide the rocket or frisée leaves amongst the serving dishes, and place a portion of roulade on each. Top with a slice of lobster and a sprig of chervil and serve.

Recipe notes Reliably retro, this recipe is one for special occasions. The finished roulade improves if kept in the fridge for 1-2 days.

If the roulade is very soft and inclined to flop, you can achieve a perfect log shape by wrapping it in plastic wrap then positioning the roulade between two rolling pins and leaving it in the fridge until well-chilled and set. Keep the rolling pins in place by standing weighted objects, such as food cans, next to them.

If you have to leave the sauce for any length of time before continuing to make the roulade, place a buttered paper on the surface of it.

Avoid using lumpfish or any caviar that is dyed in this recipe as the colour will run and ruin the presentation.

Aubergine sandwich stack with dolcelatte and mozzarella
Serves 6

6 large, straight sprigs of rosemary
6 large tomatoes
2 long, thin aubergines [eggplant]
1 large courgette [zucchini]
juice of 3 lemons
extra virgin olive oil, for greasing and frying
1 tbsp dried oregano
85g/3oz dolcelatte or gorgonzola cheese, crumbled
85g/3oz mozzarella, cut into 6 slices
a little aged balsamic vinegar
butter, for greasing
sea salt and freshly milled black pepper

Heat the oven to 180°C/350°F/Gas 4. Pick the leaves from the lower end of the rosemary sprigs, leaving a small tuft of leaves at the top. The trimmed sprigs will be used as skewers when it comes time to serve. Set the sprigs and picked leaves aside separately.

Cut two 'cheeks' about 1cm/½in thick from each tomato, reserving the remainder for use on another occasion. Discard the seeds from the cheeks. Season with salt and pepper and drizzle with a little olive oil. Place the cheeks on a baking tray and roast for about 20 minutes or until they are just tender and lightly coloured. Remove from the oven and set aside.

Slice the aubergine and courgette into 12 rounds about 1cm/½in thick. Place in a mixing bowl. Add the lemon juice and a little olive oil, the picked rosemary leaves and some salt and pepper. Set aside to marinate for at least 1 hour.

Heat some olive oil in a large frying pan and fry the sliced aubergine and courgette in batches. Remove and drain on paper towel. >

To assemble the sandwiches, arrange the cooked tomato, aubergine and courgette in layers, sprinkling them with oregano, salt and pepper as you go. Top each stack with the cheeses and set aside until ready to finish.

When almost ready to serve, heat the oven to 180°C/350°F/Gas 4. Secure each stack with a cocktail stick and place in a buttered gratin dish or on a baking sheet. Roast for about 15 minutes or until the stacks are heated through.

Remove from the oven and replace the cocktail sticks with the rosemary skewers. Serve with the smallest drizzle of well-aged balsamic vinegar.

Recipe notes The combination of melted cheese and aubergine in this attractive starter is rich and satisfying. It also makes a good vegetarian main course or side dish for roast lamb.

When making the stacks, don't be too ambitious. Keep them low and fat rather than tall and thin or they may slide apart in the oven. Once you have built the stacks, the dish can wait for several hours before roasting.

If you find the mozzarella on top of the stacks becomes dry and tight in the oven, top with a little more crumbled blue cheese and return to the oven until the cheese melts.

Tomato cheeks are rounds of flesh produced by cutting vertically down both sides of a tomato, leaving a strip in the centre.

If you prefer, serve the stacks with a warm vegetable vinaigrette instead of balsamic vinegar. You could also char-grill the aubergine and courgette instead of frying them, and include a smear or two of pesto in the layers.

Char-grilled figs with taleggio fondue
Serves 4

4 firm black figs, halved lengthways
8 thin slices prosciutto
24 sprigs of thyme, trimmed
a little olive oil, for brushing

For the salad garnish

2 tomatoes, seeded and diced
2 tbsp diced red onion
10 basil leaves, cut in strips, or torn
a trickle of extra virgin olive oil
a few drops of balsamic vinegar
a large pinch of caster [superfine granulated] sugar, or more to taste
a pinch of salt

For the fondue

80g/3oz taleggio or fontina cheese
20g/⅔oz/4 tsp unsalted butter
125ml/4floz/½ cup whipping [heavy] cream

Make the salad garnish by combining all the ingredients in a mixing bowl. Cover with a square of damp kitchen paper and chill until required.

To make the fondue, remove the rind from the cheese and cut the paste into cubes. In a small saucepan, melt the butter, then add the cream and cubed cheese. Heat until the cheese melts then bring a very gentle boil and cook until the mixture is thick enough to coat the back of a spoon. Keep the sauce warm, over a very low heat.

Use the ham slices to wrap the figs, enclosing three sprigs of thyme in each half. Use scissors to trim the ham so that there is a single layer of ham around the fruit and the joins are on the cut side of each half. Set aside or chill until ready to cook.

To cook the figs, heat the oven to 220°C/425°F/Gas 7. Meanwhile, heat a char-grill pan or a hot non-stick frying pan. Brush the ham-wrapped figs with a little olive oil, then place the flat-side down on the hot pan, pressing gently to sear them. Cook over a medium heat for approximately 3 minutes on each side, until deeply coloured. Then, transfer the figs to the oven for a few minutes, until they are piping hot all the way through.

Arrange the figs on serving plates, garnish with the lightly chilled tomato and onion salad, and serve with the hot fondue.

Recipe notes In my work arranging cookery programmes with chefs and food writers, Antony Worrall-Thompson has been one of the most lavish with his time, recipes and ideas. This is one of my favourites, which he demonstrated at the Divertimenti cookshop in London.

You can use any air-dried ham such as Parma, speck or Serrano in this recipe. It must be soft and pliable or you will have difficulty wrapping the tender figs. Unwrap the ham only at the moment it is required.

The figs, salad and melted cheese fondue may be prepared hours in advance, and are easily assembled just before serving. Just spritz the thyme sprigs with water from a spray bottle to freshen them up. Gently reheat the fondue in a small saucepan on the stovetop. Finishing the figs in the oven is optional. I do it in the winter, but not in summer.

Beans and pulses

Fast ways with pulses and tofu

Whizz up a houmous by blending rinsed canned chickpeas [garbanzos] in a food processor with extra virgin olive oil, a little tahini, lemon juice, and some salt and pepper.

Toss rinsed, canned flageolet beans with cubes of smoked chicken, toasted flaked almonds and a creamy vinaigrette flavoured with herbs.

Combine rinsed, canned cannellini beans with drained canned tuna and mild red onion. Dress with vinaigrette.

Wrap plain or marinated tofu in a papillote and bake until hot. Serve with Japanese, Chinese or Southeast Asian condiments.

Dice a litte plain tofu and add to hot miso soup, allowing it to heat through before serving.

Purée tofu in a blender with soft herbs such as parsley and chives and a little water to make a spread or a dip.

Although associated with a worthy style of vegetarian cooking, dried beans are the main ingredient of many much-loved regional rustic recipes, such as French cassoulet and Tuscan ribollita, a pasta and bean soup. Soya bean curd or tofu similarly has a reputation as a health food, yet it originates in the vibrant cuisines of China, Japan and Southeast Asia. Beans, pulses and tofu all carry other flavours readily, but with a cook's skill and ingenuity, they can also form the centrepiece of some quite distinguished gourmet recipes.

Dried beans and pulses are the edible seeds of leguminous plants such as chickpeas [garbanzos], lentils, cannellini beans and soya beans. They are a healthy source of protein and fibre and most, though not all, are low in fat. Health food stores have traditionally been the easiest places to find a wide range of dried beans and lentils, however as the gourmet qualities of specific varieties becomes more appreciated, it is increasingly easy to find excellent brands in fine food shops and supermarkets.

Fresh soya bean curd or tofu is like a dairy product, a thick, pale, smooth, custardy cheese made from a milky liquid produced from soya beans. Also rich in protein, it can be silky or crumbly, snow white or slightly yellow. Fresh tofu is found in chiller cabinets, packaged in the whey left over from the pressing process. Long-life tofu is available from the ambient grocery shelves.

What to look for what to avoid

• Always check the sell-by date on packs of dried beans and pulses. The earlier in the season you buy them, the better.
• Buy often and in small quantities from a shop that smells fresh and has a high turnover of stock.
• Dried beans and pulses should be clean and plump, with shining unbroken skin.
• Beware of little stones, tiny insects and other foreign objects, especially if buying from open sacks. Modern processing techniques mean that many packs of lentils are fairly clean, however it is wise to check before cooking, especially for little stones of the same dimensions as the lentils.
• Beans and pulses should be of even size, so that they cook to tenderness in an equal period.
• The older your dried beans and pulses, the longer they take to cook. They are also more inclined to fall apart on cooking, therefore are best for purées.
• Always check to sell-by date on packs of fresh tofu as it has a very short shelf life, and the fresher the tofu the better it will taste.
• Blocks of firm-pressed tofu are easier to cut and cook in stir-fries, than silken tofu, which is better for puréeing. Organic tofu tends to be crumbly.
• Tetrapacks of tofu, even when firm-pressed, have a very smooth, slithery texture similar to junket. Some people who have never eaten tofu before prefer this to the crumblier varieties, however the flavour is not as good as that of freshly made tofu.

Storing and freezing

- Dried beans and pulses are designed for long storage. Kept from the harvest, they were the reliable staples that provided nutrients during the long winter months when it was impossible to grow food to eat.
- Store dried beans and pulses in a cool dark place in an airtight box or jar.
- Pulses are less expensive bought dried rather than canned, but dried beans take much longer to prepare. It is a good idea to cook more than you need for one sitting and freeze the remainder. Place the cooked drained beans in polythene bags and seal. Defrost them slowly in fridge before use.
- Cooked pulses do not store well in the fridge and tend to quickly become smelly.
- Fresh chilled tofu needs to be cooked and eaten within a few days of purchase, and the sooner the better as the soya flavour becomes stronger over time.
- If you have opened a pack of tofu but have not used all of it, store the remainder in a lidded plastic box, covered with fresh water, and place in the fridge. Replace the water with fresh each day until ready to cook it.
- Tetrapacks of tofu have a long shelf life and can be stored in the grocery cupboard. So can snow-dried tofu, a Japanese speciality.

The principles of cooking pulses Our aim in cooking pulses is to:
- Soften them to a soft, mealy, floury consistency, using water or stock to simmer until tender.
- Fill them with flavour, using a stock, herbs and spices including chillies and garlic, or vegetables such as onions and tomatoes.

Dried beans need to be soaked in water for 4-12 hours before cooking. This helps shorten the cooking time. Sit them in a cool place, and change the water several times during soaking.

When ready to cook, place in a large deep pot and cover with plenty of water. Add your chosen flavourings, but do not add salt. Bring to a boil, and boil hard for 10 minutes, then reduce the heat to a gentle simmer and cook, topping up with boiling water from the kettle as necessary. Start to test for doneness after an hour. Drain and season before serving.

If using a slow-cooker, bring the pulses to a boil in a saucepan for 10 minutes, then drain and rinse before simmering as above in the slow-cooker.

Dried beans need at least an hour's cooking when cooked as part of a stew. If you are stewing chicken or lean lamb neck fillet, which are done in an hour, part-cook the pulses before adding them to the stew. They will help to thicken the stew too.

To maintain their vivid colour, dark lentils may be blanched before simmering, however they do not need to be soaked.

If using canned beans and pulses, always rinse thoroughly before cooking or serving.

The principles of cooking tofu Our aim in preparing tofu is give it flavour, and sometimes a particular texture. There is actually no need to cook it.

The Chinese and Japanese have used strong flavours such as soy sauce and sesame with tofu for thousands of years, but you could also use it like paneer, the firm fresh Indian cheese, and combine it with spinach and other vegetables in spicy dishes.

To prepare tofu, read the side of the packet on how to 'refresh' it. Some varieties require rinsing in cold water, some are steeped in hot water, others need to be pressed briefly under a plate.

How to tell when pulses are cooked

- Dried beans are cooked when they are tender, and squash to a purée when pressed against the side of the pot. The skins of several will break at this stage.
- Pulses are never served al dente, so if you have to serve them, and have run out of time, finish them in the microwave, in short bursts of high heat.
- Brown and green lentils are done when the inside is soft but the skin still has a distinct texture. Cook them any longer, and they will collapse into a slime.

The best advice I can give If you have never cooked dried pulses before, begin with lentils, as they do not need soaking and are ready to eat in about 20 minutes. Also try using canned pulses. Nestle a ham bone from your local deli, or a few cubes of chorizo or garlic sausage amongst the lentils. Add several sprigs of thyme, then water or stock to cover, and simmer for 30-40 minutes to give a robust dish. Whatever you do, always use plenty of liquid.

When first starting to cook with tofu, use authentic Oriental and Southeast Asian recipes.

Marinated tofu
Serves 4-6

250g/8oz tofu
2 tbsp dark soy sauce
2 tsp sugar
1 tbsp grated fresh ginger
3 tbsp sunflower or groundnut oil
2 tbsp sesame oil

Cut the tofu into cubes or strips and place in a porcelain or heatproof dish. Cover with the soy sauce, sugar, ginger, neutral oil and sesame oil. Marinate for 30 minutes.

Steam, or bake en papillote in a foil parcel until hot, and serve with a selection of vegetables.

Recipe notes Full of protein, tofu is a handy alternative to fish or meat, should you have a vegetarian friend at your table. This is a marvellously simple way of preparing it so that it can be easily incorporated into a dinner designed for meat-eaters.

Spicy Chinese tofu salad with dried shrimp and ginger
Serves 4-6

250g/8oz tofu
2 tbsp dried shrimp, rinsed
2 tbsp dark soy sauce
2 tsp sugar
1 tbsp grated fresh ginger
3 tbsp sunflower or groundnut oil
2 tbsp sesame oil
a few drops hot chilli oil or Tabasco sauce (optional)
2 medium red chillies, deseeded and cut into small rounds
4 large spring onions [scallions], slashed finely

Cut the tofu into rectangles or cubes as desired. Place on paper towel to absorb any excess moisture. In a small bowl, soak the shrimps in just enough water to cover for 30 minutes, then drain and reserve the liquid.

Chop the shrimp finely and place in a large serving bowl with their soaking liquor. Add the soy sauce, sugar, ginger, the two oils, plus the chilli oil or Tabasco sauce if using, and stir to combine. Add the tofu and spring onions and mix again. If the tofu is large or delicate, pour the dressing over it instead.

Leave to stand for at least 30 minutes, turning the tofu once or twice as it marinates. Just before serving, add the chillies and serve at room temperature.

Recipe notes This simple recipe, prepared by my Chinese culinary mentor, exquisite cook and friend, the late Yankit So, packs a substantial amount of flavour. Serve it as a starter or as part of a Chinese or Southeast Asian meal. It is also wonderful taken on picnics.

White bean and basil mash
Serves 4

300g/10oz leeks, trimmed of most of the green, finely sliced
2 cloves garlic, finely sliced
1 tbsp olive oil, plus extra to serve
400g/14oz can of cannellini beans, drained and rinsed
about 400ml/14floz/1¼ cups light chicken stock or vegetable stock
½ tsp salt
½ tsp freshly milled black pepper
8 large basil leaves, shredded
a little extra virgin olive oil

In a shallow pan, stir-fry the leek and garlic in the olive oil until the leek is bright green. Add the beans, and enough stock to barely cover them. Bring to the boil, cover and cook for 5 minutes at a rapid simmer.

Add the salt and pepper, then cook uncovered until all the liquid has evaporated. Remove the pan from the heat and set aside to cool.

Stir in the shredded basil, then mash everything together using the back of a fork, or a stick blender, to produce a chunky paste. Trickle over a little extra virgin olive oil just before serving.

Recipe notes A great recipe from a great book, *Cook at Home with Peter Gordon*, this is unbelievably quick to make, but tastes as though it has taken a lot of time and trouble.

You can prepare it in advance and reheat in a microwave, or on top of a double boiler, adding some fresh basil just before serving.

Peter spreads this mixture on crostini. I find it works very well as a side dish and serve it with hot and spicy foods, such as roasts, or with marinated lamb or beef steaks.

Falafel

Serves 4

*400g/14oz can of chickpeas [garbanzos],
 drained and rinsed*
1 very small onion, chopped
1 clove garlic, crushed
*10g/⅓oz/¼ cup coriander [cilantro]
 leaves*
1 tsp ground cumin
1 tsp ground coriander
a little cayenne, to taste
2 tbsp plain [all-purpose] flour
a pinch of bicarbonate [baking] soda
salt and freshly milled black pepper
*sunflower or groundnut oil,
 for deep-frying*

Purée the drained chickpeas in a food processor. Add the onion, garlic, coriander leaves, spices, flour and bicarbonate of soda and blend to a paste, using plenty of seasoning. The paste must be very smooth if it is to hold together. Set aside to rest for at least 30 minutes.

Using wet hands, shape the mixture into little patties or rissoles about 4cm/1½in diameter. Let them rest for another 15 minutes, or longer.

To cook, pour enough oil into a deep-frying pan to give a depth of 14cm/5½in and heat through.

Slowly deep-fry the felafel until they are a dark, rich golden brown, turning once during cooking. Drain well and serve immediately.

Recipe notes In some countries felafel are made with uncooked dried white beans, soaked until tender, or a mixture of chickpeas and white beans, but I have found that using canned chickpeas makes the felafel more digestible. Serve these with green coriander and coconut chutney (page 164) – the flavour is fantastic.

My succotash

Serves 4

*4 fresh ears of corn, or 450g/1lb canned
 corn kernels*
300ml/10floz/1¼ cups vegetable stock
60g/2½oz/heaping ¼ cup couscous
50g/2oz/½ stick butter
*100g/3½oz spring onions [scallions],
 sliced*
150g/5oz red and yellow peppers, sliced
*120g (4oz) cooked or canned butter or
 lima beans*
*120g/4oz/scant 1 cup cooked or
 defrosted peas*
salt and freshly milled black pepper

If using fresh corn, preheat the oven to 240°C/475°F/Gas 9. Peel back the husks and try to remove as many of the silks as you can. Re-wrap the corn in the husks, then wrap each with a sheet of foil. Bake for 15-20 minutes, or until the kernels are tender. Remove from the oven and set aside to cool. Once cool, cut the kernels from the cobs and discard the husks and cobs.

Bring 150ml/5floz/⅔ cup of the stock to a boil in a small saucepan. Place the couscous in a bowl, then pour most of the stock over it. Leave to stand for 15 minutes to rehydrate.

Heat the butter in a large shallow pan, and add the spring onions and peppers. Stir briefly, then add the beans, peas, corn and the remaining stock. Bring to the boil and cook for 10 minutes, until the vegetables are tender and the stock is absorbed.

Stir the couscous into the pan and season to taste. Allow the succotash to heat through before serving.

Recipe notes The Native Americans, using their stored ingredients, originally cooked succotash for the pilgrims. You will probably find most of the contents of this recipe 'stored' in your home too.

Hominy grits (a type of rough white cornmeal) is used in the Southern States of America for this dish but can be difficult to come by in Europe, so I use couscous as a readily available substitute. Leave out the couscous if you prefer, but I love the way it soaks up the juices to give a comforting, satisfying dish.

Similarly the authentic lima beans can be difficult to find, but butter beans are in all supermarkets and their large size provides a nice contrast to the small corn kernels and green peas. I love the creamy consistency of butter beans.

This succotash is heaven under a Thanksgiving turkey but is good with all roasts and especially game. Even children love succotash, and it reheats perfectly in the microwave. You could serve it as a vegetarian main course, perhaps packed into a little loaf tin and unmoulded onto a plate, then garnished with chives. A good variation is to add a little finely sliced, deseeded mild chilli.

Chickpea and spinach curry
Serves 4

250g/9oz spinach
2 tbsp olive oil
1 large onion, chopped
2 cloves garlic, crushed
20g/¼oz/3 tbsp fresh ginger, peeled
and chopped or grated
1 large red chilli, finely chopped
2 tsp turmeric powder
2 tsp medium Madras curry powder
3 cardamom pods, cracked
1 tsp mild garam masala
400g/14oz can of chickpeas, drained
and rinsed
400ml/14floz/1¾ cups can coconut milk
(optional)
salt

Put a kettle of water on to boil. Place the spinach in a colander and pour the hot water from the kettle over it. Set aside to drain thoroughly.

In a wide, shallowish pan, heat the olive oil and fry the onion, garlic, ginger and chilli for 5 minutes, stirring occasionally.

Add the turmeric, Madras curry powder, cardamom and mild garam masala to the pan and cook for 4 minutes, stirring over a gentle heat. Tip in the blanched spinach, together with a little water to moisten the ingredients if necessary, and stir well.

Add the chickpeas, season with salt, and cook for 3-4 minutes or until piping hot. The curry is ready to serve now but, if desired, you can add the can of coconut milk and a dash more salt and allow to heat through before serving.

Recipe notes This is a favourite mid-week meal, consisting mainly of store-cupboard ingredients combined with a bag of fresh spinach. Eat this curry Indonesian style with spoons and forks or serve with plain boiled rice, jasmine rice or a pilaf.

Haricot beans can be used in place of chickpeas if desired. In summer, add a large handful of freshly-shelled peas, and simmer for 8 minutes or until tender before adding the chickpeas. If you suddenly expect guests, include the coconut milk and add a large handful of cooked rice sticks to the pan at the same time.

When preparing large spinach leaves, fold them in half lengthways, hold tight, and rip off the stalk with the ribs, then discard.

Another ideal vegetable for this dish would be Swiss chard, which these days is making its presence felt more often in supermarkets and farmers' markets. Most of my friends with gardens grow it, for its appearance as much as its flavour, which is a bit like asparagus and so delicate that in some parts of Europe it is used to make sweet tarts. Swiss chard has large, thick, fleshy white stems and a dark green leaf with white ribs. After washing, cut off the leaves and shred them finely, then cut the stems into diagonal strips. When you come to cook the curry, add the stems first and allow them to soften for a few minutes before adding the greens.

Puy lentils with cumin, chilli and coriander
Serves 4

115g/4oz/scant ½ cup Puy lentils
1 shallot, finely chopped
about 580ml/1 pint/2½ cups) double-
strength vegetable bouillon, made
from a powder
1 large red chilli, deseeded and finely
chopped
1 tsp ground cumin
15g/½oz/½ cup fresh coriander leaves
[cilantro], chopped
salt and freshly milled pepper

Place the lentils in a large pan of cold water and place over a high heat. When the water boils, strain and rinse the lentils well. Clean the pan.

Return the lentils to the pan with the chopped shallot and vegetable bouillon and bring to the boil again. Simmer gently for 15-20 minutes, or until the lentils are almost cooked. Add extra hot water or stock if necessary, as the lentils will swell during cooking. Take care, also, that they do not become too salty.

Remove the pan from the heat and allow the lentils to cool in the stock, before draining off the excess liquid. Stir in the chilli, cumin, fresh coriander and extra seasoning, if required, then reheat before serving.

Recipe notes Lentils and other pulses were highly prized by the ancient Greeks and Romans, who understood their excellent nutritional value. Out of respect, they named many of their statesmen after pulses – Cicero from the chickpea and Fabian from the fava bean or dried broad bean. The lentil took its name from the lens of the eye, thanks to its identical shape. Puy lentils in particular, with their >

dainty, pebbly, stippled appearance, take their name from an area of France, and their flavour from that region's volcanic soil. Like all pulses, they need all the help they can get with added flavourings, to bring out their mealy, satisfying quality.

I like to serve this dish in baked potatoes with a dollop of strained yogurt on top, or alongside lamb and poultry. It is particularly good served with pork chops baked in spices, herbs and garlic (page 72), bobotie (page 64), slow-cooked lamb with Baharat spices (page 69) and North African fish bake with fennel and pickled lemons (page 54). If you have any lentils leftover, stir them into the basmati pilaf with fresh green herbs (page 144) for an easy yet wholesome mid-week supper.

You can cook the lentils up to a day in advance of serving, then reheat the dish in a microwave oven if desired. Alternatively, it can be gently reheated in a saucepan on the stovetop, adding 2 tbsp water to loosen the mixture and prevent drying and scorching.

French regional-style lentils
Serves 8

225g/8oz/1 heaping cup Puy lentils
1 bouquet garni
1 shallot, halved, studded with 1 clove
1 large carrot, finely chopped
2 cloves garlic, crushed
4 tbsp duck fat or olive oil
about 1 tbsp butter
180g/6oz/1 cup pancetta, lardons of bacon, or streaky bacon, finely chopped
1 large onion, finely chopped
15g/¹⁄₂oz/¹⁄₂ cup flat-leaf parsley, finely chopped
salt and freshly milled black pepper

Place the lentils in a saucepan of cold water and bring to a boil. Immediately remove from the heat, drain and refresh under cold running water. Set the lentils aside to drain thoroughly while you rinse out the saucepan.

Return the lentils to the pan and cover with 1 litre/1¾ pints/4¼ cups of water. Add 1 tsp salt, plus the bouquet garni, clove-studded shallot, carrot and half the crushed garlic. Bring to a boil then simmer over a low heat, uncovered, skimming from time to time. If too much water evaporates, add hot water from the kettle. Cook for 15-20 minutes, until the lentils are only just tender. Take care as they easily overcook. Remove from the heat and drain. Discard the bouquet garni and shallot.

Combine 2 tsp of the duck fat or olive oil in a frying pan with the butter and heat gently. Fry half the bacon until the inside base of the pan becomes deep golden brown.

Stir in the finely chopped onion, which will help to deglaze the tasty brown bits on the base of the pan, and cook gently with a dash of salt.

Add the remaining bacon and cook slowly until done.

Add the lentils, then toss in the remaining garlic and the parsley, plus a few tablespoons of duck fat, if desired. Adjust the seasoning to taste and serve warm or hot.

Recipe notes I confess to being a huge fan of Joël Robuchon, although I have only eaten at his restaurant once. He has the gift of being able to make just a few humble ingredients into a mouth-watering dish, the raison d'etre behind the best of French and Italian country cooking. This is my version, evolved over time, of one of his recipes.

Serve these lentils with confit or roast duck, pork, game, salmon and anything richly fatty, including foie gras, in which case you should omit the final flourish of duck fat.

This recipe can be made two days in advance of serving. The lentils reheat well in a conventional oven or microwave, especially if well moistened with duck fat. Use a perforated spoon to serve them, so that it's easy to drain off any excess fat.

Slightly undercooking lentils is preferable to overcooking them as it makes the pretty, little, bright beads collapse into a slimy mash.

If you are using a non-stick frying pan to fry the bacon, the juices will not caramelize on the base of the pan and create a deep golden colour, but you should proceed with the recipe anyway when the bacon is cooked.

Soups and stocks

Chilled in summer and warming in winter, soups can be a cook's best friend. They discreetly use up fruit and vegetables, slightly past their best, and are always entirely prepared in advance of serving. In winter we can send them out on a winter's walk in a thermos, drink them in front of the fire in mugs, or serve them for lunch with bread and cheese. At finger food parties, soup can makes an elegant appearance in little espresso cups. In hot weather, we can use our imagination to present soup glamorously as a frappé, or in a glass bowl buried in ice. Perhaps best of all, soups are wonderfully comforting and nutritious, and form an important source of fluid in our diets.

Fast ways with soups and stocks

Fry a punnet of mushrooms and stir into store-bought chilled mushroom soup with a few drops of truffle oil.

Heat a carton of stock in the microwave. Flavour with honey and tamari, then pour over a bowl of lightly cooked noodles and broccoli florets.

Simmer yesterday's cooked vegetables in water, then whizz in a blender with chopped parsley or chives.

The foundation of many good soups is lightly flavoured stock, a clear broth sometimes called a bouillon, which can be drunk on its own from a bowl, or from a mug as a nutritious hot beverage.

Stock is simply made by simmering meat, poultry or fish bones and sweet vegetables in water until and flavour tastes clear and fresh. Vegetable stock is made only of vegetables.

A strong, concentrated, reduced or boiled-down stock, is the essential backbone of all hearty gravy sauces. A good independent butcher will keep you well supplied with bones for stock-making. Chicken, beef, lamb and game are all suitable, though it is best to match the flavour of the stock to the meat with which the resulting sauce will be served. Beef, lamb and venison bones require cutting into small pieces with a bandsaw to generate the flavour you require for a superlative stock – do ask your butcher in advance for this service.

On the other hand, thick vegetable soups need not be made with stock at all. They can be produced very simply by whizzing up cooked vegetables in a blender with water until thick, creamy and velvety. Such is the smooth, silky texture that they are sometimes called a cream soup, even though they often contain no cream at all.

Soups can be complete meal in a bowl when they contain pulses, or pieces of fish, meat, poultry or noodles. These hearty dishes were called 'mouthful soups' in old English cookery books.

What to look for and what to avoid

• Chilled ready-made soups and stocks can be three or four times the price of home-made, but are undeniably handy.

• When buying chilled soups from a store, look at the sell-by date. For the freshest soup, go for the longest shelf-life.

• Choose ready-made soups and stocks with as few ingredients as possible on the label, with no gums, stabilizers or additives.

• If buying a can of soup, it should have no dents or bulges. Choose only reliable brands.

• Some families like to have a cans of Cream of Mushroom and Cream of Chicken soup to hand. I make no comment, except that they can be useful when added to a hasty casserole, and helpful in making a quick sauce.

• I like to have a few cans of clear clam broth or consommé in the cupboard in case I need a fish or meat stock at very short notice.

• Avoid the dried packets of soups, packed full of chemicals. When heated, the smell and taste will stay with you far longer than you will find welcome.

• Some exceptionally good stocks are available in glass jars from fine food stores, including speciality varieties such as veal and game stocks.

• Buying ready-made chilled fish stock is a good alternative for those who don't like the smell of fish stock being made at home.

• Japanese dashi powder, from specialist Oriental stores and some supermarkets, is a handy alternative to fresh fish stock. Simply add water for an excellent stock to use with seafood dishes or in shellfish risottos.

• Good quality vegetable bouillon powders are readily available in supermarkets and food halls and are an excellent alternative to home-made stocks.

Storage and freezing

• Stocks rich in bones set to a jelly, and these store well in the fridge for up to five days.

• All stocks store exceptionally well and safely in the freezer.

• Meat, fish and poultry stocks attract bacteria. They need to be heated quickly before serving and chilled quickly before storing. Never leave stock, or soups containing stock, in warm place for any length of time.

• On a hot day, you may need to place freshly made stock in a large jug and plunge into a bucket of ice to rapidly dissipate the heat before chilling.

• Most plain, cooked vegetable soups store well in the freezer. If you have a glut of vegetables, they will in the main store better as a soup than as raw vegetables.

• Fresh soup can be stored in the fridge for no more than four days, especially if it contains cream.

The principles of cooking soups and stocks
Our aim in cooking stocks, bouillons and clear soups is to gently simmer, not boil, during the initial stages of cooking, and to slowly draw out all the flavour of the ingredients into the water, so the resulting broth tastes rich and good.

Later, when all the flavourings are spent, strained and discarded, the surface fat and froth must be skimmed off, and the resulting clear, glowing liquid can be boiled to concentrate its flavour for whatever use you intend it for.

Our aim in cooking soup is to cook it lightly and with integrity, so the soup tastes as fresh, clean and lively as the fresh ingredients from which it was made. It should not taste pungent or stewed.

It is important to allow soups to cool slightly before puréeing them in a blender, otherwise the steam will blow off the lid, potentially scalding the cook as well as creating mess.

Putting the soup though a vegetable mill (mouli-legumes) will give an ultra-soft, luxurious consistency be removing the skins of peas, corn kernels or pulses. For a faster result, stick blenders are useful for puréeing soups in the saucepan.

How to tell when soups and stocks are cooked

• When a stock or clear broth is done, the flavour and aroma should be strong. It should taste of what you made it from, either fish, meat, chicken or game, sweetened by a small amount of vegetables. The vegetables should never overpower or dilute the main flavour. The stock or broth should also be sparkling clear from repeated skimming and a little boiling.

• After cooking the vegetables until very soft, and whizzing in a blender, a puréed soup should be creamy, shining and fluid.

• When making a chunky soup, the broth should taste deliciously robust, and all the solid ingredients must be tender and small enough to sip from a spoon.

The best advice I can give All soups, broths and stocks should taste good, with a judicious amount of salt and pepper to help bring out the flavours. Follow basic recipes to begin with, then when you are pleased with your results, start being more experimental.

Add chopped fresh herbs to bowls of soup, or to the pot in the very last stages of cooking, so they don't stew. Herbs loose their green colour in the heat.

Invest in a vegetable mill (mouli-legumes), a stick blender and an upright blender. They speed up the soup-making process, give a wonderful texture and are a delight to use.

Green pea soup
Serves 4

30g/1oz/¼ stick butter
1 heart cos [romaine] or little gem
lettuce, cut into fine strips (optional)
500g/17oz green peas, fresh or frozen
1 tsp salt
a pinch of sugar

Melt the butter in a deep saucepan, then add the lettuce, peas, salt and sugar. Cover and cook gently for 10 minutes, until the peas are thoroughly soaked in butter.

Pour in 500ml/17½floz/2¼ cups of cold water and bring to a boil. Simmer briskly for about 8 minutes or until the peas are quite tender.

Remove the saucepan from the heat and cool briefly. Whizz the soup in a food processor or a blender until it is a thick, smooth purée. Pass it through a sieve or a mouli-legumes [vegetable mill] and return to the saucepan. When ready to serve, reheat the soup gently and divide amongst serving bowls.

Recipe notes This soup can be made in advance and reheated the following day. If you like, some chopped ham, bacon or smoked pancetta, cooked or softened in a little hot butter, may be sprinkled over each serving just before taking it to the table. The soup also doubles as a sauce that is particularly good served with fish.

Chlodnik with dill, cucumber, beetroot and prawns
Serves 6

2 tbsp red wine vinegar
2 tsp salt
½ tsp sugar, or to taste
225g/8oz cooked beetroot [beets],
peeled and coarsely grated
1 tbsp arrowroot
150ml/5floz/⅔ cup soured cream
110g/4oz cooked peeled prawns or
shrimp, roughly chopped
½ medium cucumber, peeled, deseeded
and sliced
2 spring onions [scallions], sliced
2 large red radishes, chopped
3 tbsp fresh dill
2 tbsp lemon juice
freshly milled white pepper

To serve
12 cooked prawns or shrimp, peeled
½ spring onion [scallion], slashed into
splinters
2 tbsp chopped beetroot [beet]
2 tbsp chopped cucumber
6 sprigs dill

Place 4 tsp of vinegar in a small bowl with 1 tsp salt and the sugar. In a large stainless steel or enamelled saucepan, bring the beetroot and 850ml/1½ pints/3¾ cups cold water to a boil over a high heat. Add the vinegar mixture, reduce the heat to moderate and simmer slowly for about 20 minutes.

In a small bowl, combine the arrowroot and 1 tbsp cold water and stir until smooth. Bring the soup to a boil and, using a hand whisk, stir in the arrowroot mixture. Boil and whisk for 3 minutes until the soup has thickened lightly.

Strain the soup through a sieve, reserving the liquid and cooked beetroot separately. Allow to cool. Whisk the soured cream into the beetroot liquid, then stir in the cooked beetroot, prawns, cucumber, spring onions, radishes, dill, lemon juice and the remaining vinegar. Add salt, pepper and sugar to taste.

Cover with plastic wrap and refrigerate for at least 2 hours, or overnight, until thoroughly chilled.

When ready to serve, divide the soup amongst chilled cups or glasses. Add two prawns per serving and sprinkle with the remaining garnishes.

Recipe notes A wonderfully chunky soup, the recipe is based on one in the *Time Life Cooking of World* series. Try serving it New York-style in Chinese take-away containers, or large chilled glass goblets.

You could use bottled beetroot, but some brands are very sour and some are very sweet, so adjust the flavourings accordingly. Avoid any jars containing large amounts of chemicals as these will interfere with the natural sweet flavour.

If you prefer to cook your own beetroot, be careful not to puncture the skins before boiling. Boil them slowly and steadily for about 1 hour or until they're tender, and peel the beetroot while they're still warm.

For best results, make sure the intestines are removed from the prawns. To do this, run the point of a sharp thin knife around the larger C-curve of the prawns, and lift out the little brown thread.

To slash spring onions, cut them lengthways from top to bottom in quarters. Then, slice them diagonally into short pieces. The splintered effect looks very pretty as a garnish.

Courgette and parmesan soup
Serves 4

2 tbsp olive oil
700g/1½lb courgettes [zucchini], chopped
1 garlic clove, sliced
1 litre/1¾ pints/4¼ cups chicken or vegetable stock
1 tbsp chopped parsley
125g/4½oz/1 heaping cup Parmigiano Reggiano cheese, grated
salt and freshly milled white pepper

Heat the oil in a saucepan. Add the chopped courgettes, cover and cook gently for 20 minutes, adding the garlic after about 10 minutes.

Pour in the stock and add some salt and pepper. Bring to a boil then lower the heat and simmer gently for about 5 minutes.

Remove the pan from the heat and cool briefly before liquidizing the soup to a smooth and velvety cream.

Return the soup to the saucepan, and add the parsley and cheese, if using. Reheat gently, adjust the seasoning to taste and serve with char-grilled ciabatta bread.

Recipe notes One of the best parts of my work as a presenter is that I often get the chance to help new cookery authors in their careers. This recipe is adapted from the debut of vivacious young American, Amy Willock.

Don't boil or microwave the soup once you have added the cheese, as it will become gummy.

To make it in advance, cook up until the mixture is puréed, then cool and store. Just before serving, bring it to the boil, then lower to a simmer, add the cheese and serve immediately. Alternatively, you can leave the parmesan cheese out altogether.

Curried pear and parsnip soup
Serves 4

40g/1½oz/3 tbsp butter
1 small onion, chopped
½-1 tsp medium Madras curry powder
350g/12oz parsnips, peeled and coarsely chopped
350g/12oz pears, peeled and cored
700ml/1 pint 4floz/3 cups light chicken stock
4 tbsp crème fraîche, whisked (optional)
salt and freshly milled white pepper

Melt the butter in a saucepan, add the onion and curry powder and cook gently, uncovered, for 5 minutes, until the onion is tender but not coloured.

Add the parsnips and chicken stock to the saucepan. Bring to a boil then lower the heat and simmer briskly for 20 minutes. Add the pears and simmer for another 10 minutes, or until the vegetables crush easily against the side of the pan when pressed with the back of a spoon.

Remove from the heat and cool briefly. Purée the soup in a blender until smooth and shining, then season with salt and pepper. Reheat as necessary and serve with a swirl of crème fraîche, if desired.

Recipe notes: This wintry recipe can be made using stock made from a cube or powder if desired.

As with all spice cooking, take care to cook the curry powder gently. Do not let it burn or it will become bitter.

Purée the soup in a food processor by all means, but only a blender will give you a glorious velvety texture.

At the end of winter, parsnips will have a hard woody core that will simply bounce about in the machine. Just remove them, and continue to purée the remainder.

Mushroom cappuccino
Serves 4

70g/2½oz/5 tbsp butter
2 tbsp olive oil
2 cloves garlic, crushed
450g/1lb chestnut mushrooms, sliced or chopped
250ml/9floz/1 cup whipping [heavy] cream
200ml/7floz/¼ cup milk
300ml/10floz/1¼ cups vegetable stock

For the topping
about 300ml/10floz/1¼ cups skimmed milk
a little freshly grated nutmeg (optional)
3-4 tbsp finely cut chives (optional)
salt and freshly milled black pepper

You will also need
a stick blender, capuccino frother or espresso machine with steam arm

In a large heated saucepan, combine the butter, oil and garlic and stir-fry over a medium heat. When the mixture is sizzling, add the sliced mushrooms and continue stir-frying for 3-4 minutes.

Cover and simmer for 10 minutes, until all the mushroom liquid has evaporated. If this is not the case, remove the lid and simmer briskly.

Pour in half the cream and simmer until the mixture reduces to a chunky, thick consistency. Add the milk and half the stock, and bring to the boil for a minute or so.

Remove from the heat and cool briefly. Transfer the mixture to a blender. Add the remaining cream and stock and blend until frothy. Reheat the soup gently.

To serve, warm the skimmed milk in a pan then froth up with a stick blender or cappuccino-style milk frother. Alternatively, use the steam arm of an espresso machine to heat and froth the milk.

Pour the hot soup into the warmed serving bowls and top with the foam. Finish, if you like, with a light dusting of nutmeg, and/or snipped chives.

Recipe notes You may like to add more stock or water for a lighter consistency, but I prefer the intense flavour produced using the quantities of liquid given here in the recipe. Stock made from vegetable bouillon powder is fine for this soup.

For speed, slice the mushrooms on the slicing blade of a food processor.

The yield here is for soup-bowl-sized portions. This recipe serves six when presented in cappuccino cups, and 20 if served in espresso cups at a crowded party. Soup makes a pleasant change from finger and fork food at parties, especially if many of your canapés are based on pastry cases, bruschettas and croûtes.

Chicken soup – and stock
Serves 4-6

3kg/6lb 8oz whole chicken
a little sunflower or groundnut oil
1 large onion, unpeeled but halved
200g/7oz carrots, sliced
150g/5oz celery, sliced
200g/7oz tomato, deseeded and sliced
200g/7oz dark mushrooms, sliced
1 large bouquet garni comprising 5 sprigs of thyme, 5 sprigs of parsley, 5 sprigs of rosemary, 2 bay leaves, 2 cloves garlic and 6 peppercorns, tied in a leek leaf or with string
enough filtered water or bottled still mineral water to cover the ingredients by 20cm/8in

Heat the oven to 200°C/400°F/Gas 6. Paint the chicken lightly with oil, place in a roasting pan and roast near the top of the oven for 45 minutes. Turn once or twice during cooking to brown evenly, and drain off the fat and liquid from time to time, keeping them separate if you can.

Meanwhile, brown the onion, carrots and celery in the oven or in a non-stick frying pan.

When the chicken is a good deep brown colour, transfer it to a large, deep stockpot, draining off all the fat. Deglaze the roasting pan, if the caramelized cooking juices do not taste burnt, with 120ml/4floz/½ cup water and reserve the liquid.

Add the browned vegetables, tomato, mushrooms and bouquet garni to the stockpot. Pour in the deglazing and roasting liquids and enough filtered water to cover the ingredients by 20cm/8in. Bring to the boil slowly, then simmer slowly for at least 1½ hours, skimming from time to time, to remove all the fat and foam from the surface.

Remove the chicken and vegetables with tongs, without disturbing the liquid too much, and set aside on a tray. Ladle into a jug enough of the golden, clear stock to serve the soup, and remove the fat from the surface using strips of kitchen paper. Season to taste with salt. Keep the remaining stock simmering in the pot.

Using two forks to help you, pick out and shred the chicken from the bones. Divide this and the vegetables amongst soup bowls. Toss all bits of gristle, bones and tomato skins back into the stock pot, to continue cooking. Pour the reserved stock into the soup bowls and serve.

Recipe notes To cure everything from heartache to headache, as a pick up after financial foolishness or a fever, a steaming chicken soup is a legendary restorative broth.

Continuing to simmer the chicken remnants in the pot after you have made the soup will produce a dark brown chicken stock of rich flavour that can be stored and used for other dishes long after your delicious soup has been enjoyed.

Chicken stock
Makes 3 litres/5 pints/about 3 quarts

3kg/6lb 8oz chicken bones and
* trimmings, fatty bits removed*
a little sunflower or groundnut oil
* (optional)*
200g/7oz carrots, cut in 10cm/4in pieces
150g/5oz celery, cut in 10cm/4in pieces
200g/7oz tomato, quartered and deseeded
200g/7oz dark mushrooms, cut in
* 10cm/4in pieces*
1 large onion, unpeeled, halved
1 large bouquet garni comprising 5 sprigs
* of thyme, 5 sprigs of parsley, 5 sprigs*
* of rosemary, 2 bay leaves, 2 cloves*
* garlic and 6 peppercorns, tied in a*
* muslin bag*
enough filtered water or bottled still
* mineral water to cover the ingredients*
* by 20cm/8in*

You will also need
a large piece of muslin [cheesecloth] or
* 2 smaller pieces*

Heat the oven to 200°C/400°F/Gas 6. Paint the bones and flesh lightly with oil, if using. Place in a roasting pan, set it high in the oven, and cook for at least 45 minutes, turning once or twice to brown evenly. Drain off the fat and liquid that accumulates in the bottom of the pan from time to time, keeping them separate if you can.

When the bones and meat are deep brown, transfer to a large stockpot, draining off all fat. If it's not burnt, deglaze the pan with 120ml/4floz/ ½ cup water and reserve the liquid.

Heat a heavy frying pan on the stovetop. When hot, place the onion cut face down in the pan, cook until it is black, then transfer to the pot.

Brown all the remaining vegetables in the oven or in a non-stick frying pan. Transfer the vegetables to the stockpot. Add the bouquet garni and reserved deglazing and roasting liquids, then pour in enough filtered water or bottled still mineral water to cover the ingredients by 20cm/8in.

Bring the pot slowly to the boil, then simmer slowly for 4-5 hours so that small bubbles occasionally rise and break through the liquid. Skim from time to time to remove the fat and foam that accumulate on the surface. Top up with extra water as necessary during the first 2 hours of cooking.

When the cooking time is over, use tongs to remove and discard the chicken and vegetables, trying not to disturb the stock too much. Use strips of kitchen paper to help you remove all fat from the surface.

Place a double thickness of damp muslin in a sieve high above a deep bowl. Ladle the stock through, then set aside to cool. Remove all further traces of fat before further use.

Recipe notes This light stock is ideal for use in rice and pulse dishes and vegetable soups. The amount produced may seem small for such a large quantity of bones, but these days chicken has a very mild flavour.

One of the easiest ways to collect a good quantity of chicken bones and trimmings is to save those from roast chickens and other dishes. Store them in a bag in the freezer and make stock when you have at least 1.5kg/3lb 5oz. Alternatively, buy chicken wings from a supermarket or chicken carcasses from an independent butcher.

For sauces where a stronger stock is required, and for jus, simpy boil the finished stock in a clean saucepan. Making chicken stock with stock in place of water is a good, quick way of producing a darker, meatier stock of powerful flavour.

Fish stock
Makes 1 litre/1 ¾ pints/8 ¼ cups

30g/1oz/¼ stick butter
500g/1lb 4oz white fish bones, chopped
* into pieces*
1 medium carrot, finely sliced
1 leek, white part only, finely sliced
½ celery stalk, finely sliced
4 shallots, finely sliced
4 button mushrooms, finely sliced
a scrap of fennel (optional)
4 tbsp dry white wine
2 tbsp white wine vinegar
1 clove garlic, unpeeled
1 bouquet garni comprising a few
* parsley stalks, a few thyme sprigs and*
* 2 bay leaves*
1 litre/1¼ pints/8¼ cups filtered water
* or bottled still mineral water*
½ tsp peppercorns, cracked
salt

You will also need
a piece of muslin [cheesecloth]

Remove any gills from the fish carcasses with scissors. Soak the fish bones in plenty of clean, cold water for about 1 hour, changing the water periodically until it runs clear.

Heat the butter in a deep saucepan, add the carrot, leek, celery, shallots, mushrooms and fennel, if using, and cook very gently for 10 minutes.

Pour in the white wine and vinegar, then add the garlic, bouquet garni and fish bones. Bring to a simmer for 1 minute or so, until the volume of liquid has reduced by half.

Top up the saucepan with filtered water, bring to the boil and simmer for 20 minutes. Add the peppercorns simmer for another 5 minutes.

Line a sieve with damp muslin and ladle the stock carefully through it. Do not try to press down on the ingredients, just allow the stock to drip peacefully through. Add salt to taste and cool before using.

Recipe notes Do be fussy about your fish bones. Say no to fins, too many fish heads, and all bones other than those of plaice, sole, brill, turbot and halibut (although the latter two usually go to the expensive restaurants).

I cut the bones into pieces using secateurs. It saves my kitchen scissors, and is easier than chopping the bones up with a knife.

By a 'scrap' of fennel, I mean the feathery fronds at the top of a bulb of fennel, sometimes called Florence fennel. It is traditionally associated with fish cookery, including stocks and sauces, throughout Europe and has a mild anise flavour.

The flavouring vegetables used in this stock may be cut into pretty shapes and used to decorate a fish dish afterwards – they will still be slightly crunchy and full of flavour. You could, for example, cut the leek into long strips or spaghetti, and the carrot into stars.

Brown beef stock
Makes 3 litres/5 pints/about 3 quarts

3kg/6lb 8oz beef bones and trimmings, fatty bits removed
a little sunflower or groundnut oil (optional)
200g/7oz carrots, cut in 10cm/4in pieces
150g/5oz celery, cut in 10cm/4in pieces
200g/7oz tomato, quartered and deseeded
200g/7oz dark mushrooms, cut in 10cm/4in pieces
1 large onion, unpeeled, halved
1 large bouquet garni comprising 5 sprigs of thyme, 5 sprigs of parsley, 5 sprigs of rosemary, 2 bay leaves, 2 cloves garlic, 6 peppercorns, and 2 cloves, tied in muslin bag
enough beef stock to cover the ingredients by 20cm/8in

You will also need
a large piece of muslin [cheesecloth] or 2 smaller pieces

Heat the oven to 200°C/400°F/Gas 6. Paint the bones and meat lightly with oil, if using. Place in a roasting pan, set it high in the oven, and cook for at least 45 minutes, turning once or twice to brown evenly. Drain off the fat and liquid that accumulates in the bottom of the pan from time to time, keeping them separate if you can.

When the bones and meat are deep brown, transfer to a large stockpot, draining off all fat. If it's not burnt, deglaze the pan with 120ml/4floz/ ½ cup water and reserve the liquid.

Heat a heavy frying pan on the stovetop. When hot, place the onion cut face down in the pan, cook until it is black, then transfer to the pot.

Brown all the remaining vegetables in the oven or in a non-stick frying pan. Transfer the vegetables to the stockpot. Add the bouquet garni and

reserved deglazing and roasting liquids, then pour in enough beef stock to cover the ingredients by 20cm/8in.

Bring the pot slowly to the boil, then simmer slowly for 4-5 hours so that small bubbles occasionally rise and break through the liquid. Skim from time to time to remove the fat and foam that accumulate on the surface. Top up with extra water as necessary during the first 2 hours of cooking.

When the cooking time is over, use tongs to remove and discard the meat and vegetables, trying not to disturb the stock too much. Use strips of kitchen paper to help you remove all fat from the surface.

Place a double thickness of damp muslin in a sieve high above a deep bowl. Ladle the stock through, then set aside to cool. Remove all traces of fat before further use.

Recipe notes You can also make a brown game stock by following this recipe and substituting game bones and game stock for the beef bones and stock. I have mixed pheasant, partridge and other birds with venison bones and meaty on occasions and have found it works well.

Vegetables

Blanch young spinach
with a kettle, then stir-
fry gently in olive oil
and serve with salmon
baked en papillote and
drizzled with balsamic
vinegar and extra
virgin olive oil.
Grill [broil] large, flat
mushrooms and halved
tomatoes, sprinkled
with salt, pepper and
herbes de Provence.
Serve topped with a
poached egg.
Boil asparagus then
serve with melted
butter, parmesan
shavings, salt crystals
and freshly milled
black pepper.
Stir-fry a selection of
vegetables that taste
good together in a little
olive or groundnut oil.
Cook until crunchy
and glistening.

I cannot think of a meal that does not benefit from the addition of vegetables, whether it is grilled [broiled] field mushrooms for breakfast, char-grilled aubergine with fish fillets for lunch, or a steak with roast vegetables in the evening. Fresh vegetables introduce an enormous variety of colour, texture, flavour and nutrition to our diets and, apart from their vital role as accompaniments, can be made into myriad outstanding dishes in their own right.

Although supermarkets have come a long way in offering a wide variety of vegetables, I still prefer buying from farmers' markets, farm shops and greengrocers. Here you will find seasonal produce, carefully displayed in cool, dim surroundings that smell of earth, leeks and onions. You can often find unusual vegetables which are fun to buy and experiment with by dipping into recipe books when you get home.

If buying vegetables in supermarkets, the best value for money can be found in loose vegetables, which are often fresher too. Supermarkets are also helpful in supplying recipe cards for exotic vegetables, helping you to enjoy the bounty of many different countries and gradually increase your repertoire of vegetable dishes.

A trip to a specialist ethnic shop will result in authentic fresh produce for exotic recipes. For example, the tiny white pea aubergines [eggplant] found in the curries and stews of Southeast Asia are quite different from the many different types of purple, oval aubergines sold in Turkish shops, and are cooked in completely different ways.

It must be mentioned that there is nothing like home-grown vegetables. The incomparable flavours of freshly picked peas, beans and asparagus have to be tasted to be believed. To avoid huge gluts, which can put you off the whole process, stagger your planting by six weeks to three months. That way, you will always be eating new and fresh vegetables, and will never feel guilty about moldering stocks in the garage.

What to look for and what to avoid
• Try to buy seasonal produce wherever possible. I have a nagging doubt about vegetables that have been carried half-way across the world, and look 'fresh'. There are all sorts of chemical processes that can fool us in our search for healthy produce. On the other hand, London Heathrow deals with tonnes of fresh produce and has an ultra-fast clearing system. A friend assures me the asparagus he imports, which was growing in a Zimbabwean summer on Monday, can be on our plates for Wednesday night's supper.
• Buy as fresh as possible. Colour is a good indication. Green vegetables should be a vibrant, intense green, with no traces of yellow. Brown, bruised edges tell you fennel and globe artichokes are past their best.
• Buy from countries that make

sense to you. Tomatoes are a sunshine crop, so why would one buy Dutch or Belgian tomatoes? Tomatoes should be a deep red when you buy them.

• Firmness and plump skins are other indicators of freshness. Avoid wizened courgettes [zucchini] and aubergines [eggplant], just as you should avoid any vegetables that are too large or overblown for their type – they could have been over-watered and over-fertilised.

• Look at the stalks. Avoid aubergines [eggplants] that are black or withered, or asparagus if the butts are dry and woody.

• Asparagus is at its best with narrow, tapered points, not sprouting little buds. Likewise broccoli should have a head as compact as moss, dark green to blue in colour, rather than yellowy green and ragged.

• Small green vegetables such as mangetout, French beans [haricot verts] and peas should shine, crack when your bend them, and smell sweet and grassy.

• Cabbages should squeak when you cut them, and give up a few drops of moisture.

• If you are buying in a large supermarket, avoid the 'reduced to clear' labels on vegetables. There will probably be a slime underneath in the polystyrene tray, and they are persuading you to take it away for them.

Storing and freezing

• In general, it is best to buy fresh vegetables in small quantities on a frequent basis and use them quickly for maximum nutritive value and quality of flavour and texture.

• Most vegetables are best kept in the drawer in the fridge, but only for a short while. Normal plastic bags keep vegetables plump but also make them sweat. Keep an eye out for special vegetable storage bags that aim to prolong freshness.

• Winter vegetables such as onions, swede [rutabaga], turnips and marrows store well in a cool dark place such as a cellar. Onions keep for months, so it is worth stocking up. They store well in a salad drawer too, as long as they are dry and unwrapped.

• Tomatoes should never be stored in the fridge, but on a sunny window sill.

• Celery will continue to grow if kept in a jug of water.

• Fresh garden vegetables can be home-frozen. Many growers find they can wash and dry their crop and simply place it in the freezer in strong bags, especially for short periods. However food safety advice recommends blanching vegetables prior to freezing. In many respects, they store better as soup (see page 105).

The principles of cooking vegetables

Our aim is twofold:

• When cooked and served simply, we want to preserve the flavour and characteristics that nature gave them, without interfering with the colour and integrity of each vegetable.

• When making composite vegetable dishes we want to complement their natural flavours with other vegetables, seasonings and condiments. Many countries with sunny climates have fantastic recipes for vegetable dishes that improve in flavour if kept for a day.

How to tell when vegetables are cooked

• A key requirement is to soften the fibre and cellulose, to make them more digestible. Cook the onion family until soft and caramelized whenever possible as these are notoriously indigestible.

• Vegetables should otherwise be cooked how you like them. Crisp, squeaky carrots are loved by some; others prefer them soft and mealy.

Rule of thumb You can't really tell whether a vegetable is cooked just by looking. If you bite the vegetable and it is appetisingly crunchy, it is done. If you taste it and like it, it is done.

The best advice I can give Be curious and bold. Learn to experiment with vegetables, collect tips and recipes from good cookery writers.

The best cooking methods for vegetables

• **Blanching.** Ideal for fresh green vegetables, and baby varieties.

• **Boiling.** Use when making purées of swede [rutabaga], parsnip, celeriac [celery root], Jerusalem artichokes and beetroot [beets].

• **Steaming.** Especially good for organic vegetables, so you can really appreciate the flavour.

• **Roasting.** With a little fat, it is ideal for parsnips, carrots, peppers, red onions, shallots, garlic, butternut squash.

• **Deep-frying.** This brings a crisp dimension to meals and is lovely for strips of root vegetables.

Glazed broccoli and sugar snaps
Serves 10

220-340g/8-12oz sugar snap peas
220-340g/8-12oz broccoli florets
15g/½oz/1 tbsp butter, or a trickle of
*   extra virgin olive oil*
salt and freshly milled black pepper

Bring a large quantity of salted water to a rolling boil in a deep pot with a pasta insert or blanching basket.

Meanwhile, destring the sugar snap peas and slice them diagonally lengthways once or twice. Cut the broccoli into bite-sized pieces.

Add the vegetables to the boiling water and, when they are brightly coloured and still crisp (sometimes the cooking water will not have returned to the boil), remove the blanching basket and drain.

Turn the hot vegetables in butter or olive oil, season and serve immediately.

Alternatively, if you want to serve them later, remove the blanching basket from the pot and plunge the vegetables into a large basin full of ice and water, to halt the cooking. Don't throw out the cooking water! As soon as the vegetables are cold, remove and drain. They can now wait for several hours, stored in a plastic bag in the fridge.

To reheat them, heat the butter with a little of the cooking water in a wide shallow pan. When it is boiling, toss the vegetables in the pan until they're steaming hot but still colourful. Season well with salt and pepper and serve immediately.

Recipe notes This basic recipe can be used for a variety of vegetables including topped and tailed french beans, mangetout [snow peas], asparagus tips, baby carrots, baby corn, baby turnips cut in quarters, thick batons of swede, runner beans sliced diagonally into diamond shapes, courgettes [zucchini] halved lengthways then sliced, and trimmed cauliflower florets.

Choose whatever mixture is fresh, vibrant and catches your eye. Allow about 55-85g (2-3oz) fully trimmed vegetables per person as part of a three course menu. Add the vegetables to the pot according to the length of time they take to cook. Root vegetables take longest, green vegetables take almost no time at all, so throw in any carrots and turnips first, allow them time to cook, then add the green vegetables.

There is no need to refresh the vegetables each time. Refreshing is only useful when cooking for a crowd, or if you wish to cook the vegetables in advance of serving. When cooking just for yourself, follow the basic instructions, but don't refresh them – simply keep them hot for a few minutes, in a sieve set over the hot cooking water, whilst you get the rest of the meal ready.

If you would prefer to reheat the vegetables in a microwave oven, take the cold, drained vegetables and layer them in a microwave-safe buttered dish, seasoning as you go. Cover with a few very small dabs of butter or a trickle of olive oil, then with plastic wrap. Reheat at the highest setting for 6-8 minutes. Plunge your finger into various parts of the bowl to check all is piping out. Then, wait for 1 minute and reheat again for 1 minute, so that the vegetables do not transfer a lot of their heat to the dish.

Jade cucumber with dill
Serves 4

2 cucumbers
15g/1oz/⅓ cup small bunch dill, finely
*   chopped*
a little sunflower or groundnut oil
salt and freshly milled white pepper

In a pot with a blanching basket, bring a large quantity of salted water to the boil. Meanwhile, peel the cucumbers and halve them lengthways. Use a teaspoon to scoop out and discard the seeds, then cut the flesh into half-moons. Prepare a bath of iced water to refresh the cucumber.

Place the cucumber in the blanching basket and plunge it into the boiling water for about 8 seconds. Then remove the basket and plunge the cucumber into the icy water. When it is cold, lift the basket and drain the cucumber, then transfer to paper towels and leave to absorb all the excess moisture.

Heat a large frying pan or wok. Add the oil and, when it is almost smoking, stir-fry the cucumber and dill together for 30 seconds, or until piping hot. Season to taste and serve the cucumber immediately.

Recipe notes To remain crisp, it is important that you blanch the cucumber very briefly, as the vegetable is almost entirely water.

Make jade noodles to accompany salmon and fennel ravioli (page 132) by cutting the cucumber flesh into fine noodles after deseeding, then proceeding with the recipe above.

Char-grilled Mediterranean vegetables
Serves 6

1 fennel bulb
1 red pepper
1 yellow pepper
1 courgette [zucchini]
1 aubergine [eggplant]
about 6 tbsp extra virgin olive oil
juice of 1 lemon
3 cloves garlic, thinly sliced
3 sprigs rosemary, lightly crushed
2 tsp herbes de Provence, or 3-4 sprigs
*   of thyme*
1 tsp fennel seeds
salt and freshly milled black pepper

Slice the fennel bulb into 1cm/½in slices lengthways and steam until soft, about 3-4 minutes. Set aside.

Cut the cheeks from the red and yellow peppers, and slice away the ribs, so that the cheeks sit flat. Trim and slice the courgette as thinly as you can, and cut the aubergine evenly into thick rounds.

Lay all the vegetables in a shallow dish with the olive oil, lemon juice, garlic, herbs and fennel seeds, and a few grinds of black pepper. Turn them to coat evenly with the marinade, and add more olive oil and lemon juice if the mixture seems too dry.

Heat a ridged grill-pan or barbecue then cook the vegetables on each side, pressing them down well to brown the surface. Serve within the day, either at room temperature or hot, seasoning with salt before taking the vegetables to the table.

Recipe notes Serve this dish as a starter, or as an accompaniment to roast or grilled meat or fish that has been well-moistened with a flavoured oil or big wedges of lemon.

If you wish to reheat the vegetables, place them in a single layer on an oven tray and warm them through for 20-30 minutes in an oven set to 180°C/350°F/Gas 4.

One of the things I like best about this recipe is that each of the vegetable components can be served as a dish in their own right. The char-grilled aubergine is terrific served as a starter with yogurt flavoured with dried mint.

Steamed then marinated and char-grilled fennel also makes a wonderful starter served with a garlicky mayonnaise and country bread, and works well as a vegetable accompaniment to jambonettes of roast duck (page 86).

The grilled courgette is lovely rolled around cubes of hard goats' cheese then secured with a cocktail stick and dusted with finely chopped lemon zest, basil and black pepper.

Chargrilled peppers make a nice crunchy bed for firm grilled [broiled] or barbecued fish such as swordfish.

There are not many dried herbs that earn shelf-space in my kitchen but every year I replace my herbes de Provence with a fresh little terracotta pot. When you drive up into the hills of Provence, behind the azure coast, the dry hard perfume of thyme, fennel, oregano and bay sits on the breathless midday heat, reminding you that it is time for a chilled glass of rosé and a grill at the *feu de bois*, local restaurants in which food is cooked over a wood fire.

Sweet yellow peppers with capers and crumbs
Serves 4-5

5 yellow peppers, about 1.6kg/3lb 8oz
olive oil, for greasing, plus extra virgin
*   olive oil, for drizzling*
40g/1½oz/¼ cup fresh coarse breadcrumbs
2 tbsp small capers, rinsed
6-8 cloves garlic, crushed
2 large handfuls flat-leaf parsley leaves,
*   chopped*
6 tbsp grated Parmesan cheese
100ml/3½floz/½ cup white wine
salt

Heat the oven to 200°C/400°F/Gas 6. Quarter the peppers, removing the stems, ribs and seeds.

Spread a film of oil over the base and sides of two shallow ovenproof dishes. Lay the peppers skin-side down, closely packed in a single layer. Strew with the breadcrumbs, capers, garlic, parsley, some salt, then the cheese. Spoon the wine evenly over the top and drizzle with olive oil.

Cover with foil and bake for 30 minutes, swapping the dishes around halfway through cooking. Remove the foil, return the dishes to the top shelf of the oven, or put them under a preheated grill [broiler], and cook until deliciously charred.

Set aside to cool for 15 minutes, then drizzle over a little cold pressed extra virgin olive oil and serve.

Recipe notes When offered as a starter with a rustic loaf of sourdough, this recipe serves four to five people. It serves eight to ten as a vegetable side dish and is good with baked or grilled meat or fish, a crunchy green salad, and noodles trickled with a little roast garlic oil (page 166).

Florentine fennel gratin
Serves 6-8

3 fennel bulbs
285ml/10floz/1¼ cups double [heavy]
    cream
75g/3oz/¾ cup grated Parmesan cheese
a little softened butter
salt and freshly milled white pepper

Using a serrated knife, cut the fennel
lengthways into 1cm/½in thick slices.
In a pan of boiling salted water, cook
them until the central core is tender
but the fennel slice still holds its shape.
Drain and set aside. Alternatively,
steam the fennel instead of boiling it.

Meanwhile, in a small saucepan,
boil the cream vigorously until it has
reduced and thickened enough to
resemble mayonnaise.

Place the fennel slices in a single
layer in a buttered gratin dish.
Reassemble any untidy slices if
necessary, then season with salt and
pepper. If desired, you can cover the
dish with plastic wrap and set aside
for several hours until ready to cook.

When ready to cook, slather the
reduced cream over the fennel to
coat, sprinkle with the Parmesan and
dot with a little butter.

Preheat an overhead grill [broiler]
to its highest setting. Place the dish
on a tray high under the grill and cook
until hot and bubbling. Serve at once.

Recipe notes This must be the easiest
version of this dish, and it can be
prepared completely in advance.
I find it particularly useful to serve
with plain roasts and grills as the
creamy consistency of the gratin gives
a saucy texture to the meal.

You can make and serve this in a
large gratin dish, or individual ones,
each containing a slice of fennel.

Violet artichokes in olive oil and white wine with sweet vegetables
Serves 4

2 lemons
16 small violet artichokes
200ml/7floz/¼ cup extra virgin olive oil
150g/5oz carrots, finely diced
250g/9oz small onions, finely diced
200ml/7floz dry white wine
3 cloves garlic, peeled
8 sprigs thyme
4 bay leaves
10-12 parsley stalks
6 black peppercorns, cracked
salt and freshly milled pepper

Squeeze one of the lemons and place
the juice in a large bowl of water.
Halve the other lemon and set aside.

Remove plenty of the outer layers
of leaves from the artichokes. It may
seem a lot, but it is a normal process.
With a sharp, serrated knife, cut off
all but 2cm/¾in of the stalks and
slice about 2cm/¾in off the tips of
the leaves, then halve the artichokes
lengthways. As you go, rub them all
over with the cut lemon, and as you
finish, toss into the bowl of water and
lemon juice. If you are interrupted,
rub the cut part of the artichoke on
which you are working.

Wash the prepared artichokes under
cold water, drain and pat dry. Pour
the oil into a shallow saucepan and
heat gently. Add the carrot, onion
and artichokes and cook for about
5 minutes, stirring occasionally with
a wooden spoon, until the vegetables
are a pale golden colour.

Add the wine and enough water
to cover the vegetables, then add the
garlic, 4 sprigs of thyme, the bay
leaves, parsley stalks, crushed
peppercorns and a little salt. Simmer

gently for about 20 minutes. Test the
artichokes with a point of a knife,
they should be tender but still firm
when they are done. Cook for a little
longer if necessary.

To serve, arrange the artichokes in
a shallow dish, with the garlic and
only a sprinkling of the carrot and
onion. Set aside in a warm place.

Remove the parsley stalks from the
pan. Discard the thyme and replace it
with the remaining 4 fresh sprigs.
Bring the cooking liquid to a boil and
boil hard until the volume of liquid
has reduced by one-third. Strain it
over the warm artichokes and serve.

Recipe notes Best in the spring and
summer, these little artichokes are
lovely with baked fish, or as a starter,
or as part of a fork supper or party
table. The real success of the dish
depends on the quality of the
artichokes, which must be very small,
ripe and tender, otherwise the outside
leaves will be hard and inedible and
the results will be bitter. You need to
trust a good supplier, as the
artichokes will all look the same.

Wear gloves when preparing the
artichokes to avoid staining your
hands. The lemons prevent the
artichokes going black, so rub any
part of the cut artichoke, including
the leaves and stalks, as you go.

When preparing this dish for large
numbers of people, you can decrease
the amounts of carrot and onion
used in proportion to the artichokes.

Sesame asparagus
Serves 10 at a buffet

700g/1½lb asparagus spears
3 tbsp sunflower oil or soft butter
4 tbsp sesame oil
4 tbsp lemon juice
4 tsp toasted sesame seeds
salt and freshly milled black pepper

Put a kettle of water on to boil. Meanwhile, break off the stub ends of the asparagus. If they break cleanly and crisply, it will prove the asparagus is fresh. Lightly scrape away the green outer skins of the stalks with a potato peeler, leaving the tip intact.

Pour the boiling water from the kettle into a deep roasting tray and salt well. Keep at a boil on the stovetop. Place the asparagus in the water, cover with a cloth, and boil until tender. Drain immediately and refresh briefly under cold running water. Drain again and pat dry.

Slice the spears diagonally into pieces of 4cm/1½in and set aside.

In a large pan, heat the sunflower oil or butter. Add the sesame oil, lemon juice and some seasoning. When hot, add the asparagus and toss to coat well. Transfer to a warm serving dish, scatter with the sesame seeds, and serve immediately or the asparagus will discolour.

Recipe notes This recipe can be served hot or cold. If you want to serve it cold (or at room temperature) be sure to use sunflower oil instead of butter for the best consistency.

Combine the asparagus with the dressing (most importantly the lemon juice) only at the last minute. In my experience, horseshoe peelers are the best for peeling asparagus.

Slow-roast tomatoes with garlic, thyme and basil

1kg/2lb 4oz small ripe tomatoes
extra virgin olive oil
15g/½oz/¼ cup bunch fresh oregano or
*   thyme, leaves stripped from the stem*
a few leaves of basil
3 cloves garlic, finely sliced
3 tsp caster [superfine granulated] sugar
salt flakes
freshly milled black pepper

You will also need

a 500g/2lb capacity Kilner jar, or
*   similar, in which to store them*

Heat the oven to 120°C/230°F/Gas ½. Halve the tomatoes and, using the tip of a teaspoon, winkle out the seeds and discard them.

Line a large baking tray with foil. Drizzle with some oil, sprinkle with salt and pepper, and spread the tomatoes out on the tray. Pour a little more oil evenly over the tomatoes. Strew with most of the herbs and garlic, keeping the remainder for later. Then sprinkle with the sugar and some more salt and pepper. Cover the tray very loosely with foil.

Roast the tomatoes slowly for 3-4 hours, until they have given up some of their juices. Remove the foil for the last 30 minutes or so of cooking and, if you wish, raise the heat to the highest setting, to lightly char the tomatoes. Trickle over a little more oil if they are starting to look dry.

Season again to taste, then transfer the tomatoes to a preserving jar. Add the remaining herbs and garlic and cover with extra virgin olive oil.

Store in a cool place, or the fridge for up to a week. Just before using, place the preserved tomatoes in a warm spot for an hour or so.

Recipe notes Remarkably flavoured and brilliantly coloured, slow-roast tomatoes are essential to have on hand for bruschetta, salads, couscous dishes, and to accompany red meat and poultry. Try them chopped and mixed with a can of cannellini beans to spread on thick granary toast, or under pan-roasted fillets of fish. They are good tossed with pasta (add some of the oil in the jar) and are very useful for garnishing, as they bring a touch of exquisite colour to the plate. You could also label the jar and tie it with ribbon to give as a gift.

Although they are obviously a wonderful dish to prepare in advance, once cooked, the tomatoes must be kept in fridge and eaten within a week. Thyme is the best herb for roasting but for a different dimension the tomatoes can be sprinkled with extra basil just before serving.

For the optimum taste, never store fresh tomatoes in the fridge. Ideally buy them a week or so before you need them, to give them time to ripen. I try to find those grown in the sunshine of Italy or Spain. Those from Naples have the added advantage of a sweet and dynamic flavour imparted by the volcanic soil of the area.

Carrot and swede purée with mustard seeds and ginger
Serves 4

300g/10oz carrot, peeled and cut into
  large chunks
300g/10oz swede [rutabaga], peeled and
  cut into large chunks
2 tbsp olive oil
1 tsp black mustard seeds
2 pieces crystallized ginger in syrup,
  finely chopped, plus 3 tbsp of syrup
15g/½oz/1 tbsp butter
salt and freshly milled white pepper

In separate saucepans of boiling salted water, cook the carrot and swede until they are soft enough to squash against the sides of the pans. Drain, then return each vegetable to its pan to steam-dry over a low-to-moderate heat, shaking the pan frequently so that each piece of vegetable comes into contact with the hot base of the pan. Continue until the carrot and swede are dryish and floury, being careful not to let them burn.

Transfer the carrot and swede to a food processor and whizz until creamy. Check the mixture for any woody lumps of vegetable, and discard them as necessary.

Heat the oil in a large, lidded frying pan. Add the mustard seeds and cook over a medium heat, keeping the lid nearby in case the mustard seeds start to pop. Add the ginger syrup, then the vegetable purée and cook for a moment or so to make the purée fluffier.

Add salt and pepper to taste and stir in the butter. Mix in the finely chopped ginger and serve.

Recipe notes My friend Kate Sloane cooked this for me first, with her large country house packed full of guests and children. She cooks diligently and expertly for family and friends every weekend, in between bringing in yet more armfuls of fresh produce from the garden.

This recipe suits all roasts, and is particularly good in winter, when carrots and swedes are full of starch and the ginger is in the shops.

It can be made in advance, frozen and reheated in a microwave oven. For Christmas, when fridge space is tight, freeze and store this mixture in convenient portions in Ziploc bags.

Some people don't like swede and the French dislike it so much they tend to use it as cattle feed. But I love its vivid orange colour, its sweetness, and when mixed with a spice such as cinnamon, or in this case preserved ginger, it is transformed into something moist, colourful and delicious, yet inexpensive. Swedes can also be served alone as a fluffy purée, or cut into thick strips, boiled until just a little crunchy and mingled with crisp green vegetables for a colourful side dish.

As swedes are very large, heavy and dense, it is best to peel them with a horseshoe peeler and cut with a sharp, heavy knife.

Corn puddings
Serves 6

20g/⅔oz/1½ tbsp butter, plus extra for
  greasing.
15g/½oz/2 tbsp plain [all-purpose] flour
3 pinches salt
2 eggs plus 3 egg yolks
225g/8oz frozen corn kernels, defrosted
  and drained, or canned kernels, plus
  extra to garnish
250ml/9floz/1 cup whipping [heavy]
  cream
freshly milled white pepper

You will also need
a roasting tray bain-marie
6 aluminium molds of 150ml/5floz/
  ⅔ cup capacity

Heat the oven to 160°C/310°F/Gas 2½. Melt the butter and set aside to cool. Grease the molds. Sift the flour with the salt and pepper and set aside.

Place the whole eggs and extra yolks in a blender, and whizz until frothy. Add the corn and blend until the mixture is fairly smooth but still slightly textured by the kernels.

Transfer the mixture to a bowl, stir in the flour, then add the melted butter and cream. Mix well. Adjust the seasoning to taste.

Pour the mixture into the prepared molds and place in a roasting tin of steaming water, so the water comes at least halfway up the sides of the molds. Bake for about 1 hour, until the tops are brown, and a skewer inserted in the centre of a pudding comes out clean. A little longer will not harm them – cover with foil if they darken too quickly.

Remove the puddings from the water bath, leave them to set for 5 minutes, then run a knife round the edges, and unmould onto hot plates.

Garnish the puddings with the extra corn kernels, reheated in a little water or in the microwave.

Recipe notes I first cooked these bright yellow little puddings as part of a Thanksgiving dinner for Emma Soames, grand-daughter of Sir Winston Churchill, and people have been asking me for the recipe ever since. When cooking to try and celebrate a festival observed in another country, it is fun to use the festival's key ingredients in a way that suits your menus and your kitchen. It sometimes gives rise to your best and most original dishes.

Corn is a comparatively new vegetable to British shores and people love its sweetness and soft texture. Combine it with turkey, which has a fairly bland flavour, and you'll find the corn really helps the bird taste its best. These puddings are also good with glazed gammon (page 72).

Apart from being unusual, they are wonderfully reliable when feeding guests, and with this master recipe you can make a variety of vegetable puddings, providing you use a cooked purée and follow the method and quantities given here. My most successful variations have been with parsnips, swede [rutabaga], turnips, asparagus tips and pumpkin. Leeks give the puddings a beautiful pale green colour but really need to be cooked and sieved before adding to the mixture. However, the effort is sometimes worth it, because the flavour they then bring to your roast meat and poultry is gorgeous.

Deep-fried parsnip crisps
Serves 4-6

4 parsnips
at least 2 litres/3½ pints/8½ cups
  groundnut or corn oil

Peel the parsnips with a good strong horseshoe peeler. Then use the peeler to cut them lengthways into thin strips.

In a deep-fryer or large saucepan with blanching basket, heat the oil to 180°C/350°F. Working in small batches, place the parsnips in the basket and dip into the hot oil. Cook until golden, lifting the basket as soon as the crisps are cooked and the bubbles stop forming.

Gently shake off the excess oil. Place a layer of crumpled kitchen paper on a baking tray and spread the crisps out in a single layer. Keep them warm in a low oven while you cook the remainder of the parsnips.

Recipe notes Serve these crisps wherever you need something crunchy. I like them with all grills and roasts, especially fillet of beef, roast game and duck.

Heat the oil and check it. It should be palest gold, with no odour or taste. If there is one, it will transfer to your food. If you don't have the luxury of a custom-built deep fryer, fry using an ascending temperature. As you immerse the food, raise the heat. This will keep the temperature steady, and combat the cooling of the oil by the cold ingredients.

You can keep deep-fried food warm for 30 minutes or so in an oven set to 110°C/225°C/Gas ¼. However, once cold, they cannot be reheated in an oven, or they will go turn black and produce a lot of smoke.

Deep-fried onion rings
Serves 4

1 large onion
150ml/5floz/⅔ cup milk
a handful of flour
at least 2 litres/3½ pints/8½ cups
  groundnut or corn oil
sugar
salt

Cut the onion into thin rings, then place in a dish, cover with the milk and leave to soak for 30 minutes or so.

Lift the onion rings from the milk and place them in a wide sieve. Scatter with the flour and shake off the excess until only a fine coating remains on the onion rings.

In a deep-fryer or large saucepan with blanching basket, heat the oil to 180°C/350°F. Working in small batches, place the coated onion rings in the basket and dip into the hot oil.

Lift the basket as soon as the onion rings are golden and gently shake off the excess oil. Place a layer of crumpled kitchen paper on a baking tray and spread the rings out in a single layer. Keep warm in a low oven while you cook the remainder.

Just before serving, toss the onion rings in sugar and salt, and eat hot.

Recipe notes Try serving these on top of fried fillets of white fish sat on a glossy portion of stir-fried spinach, or with roast fillet of spiced beef (page 62). Deep-fried onion rings are also delicious as a snack in their own right, especially when served outdoors at a barbecue.

Salads

In Britain we have emerged from the nineteenth century criticism that 'the salad was the glory of every French dinner and the disgrace of most in England'. We have not yet come to feel the need for salad every day, like the Europeans and Americans, or developed the Lebanese passion for raw salad ingredients with lunch and dinner, or the Iranian habit of beginning meals with fresh herb leaves and cubes of white cheese to aid digestion. However we have come to realise that heat and our everyday cooking methods destroy the vital nutrients required for health found in vegetables. Helped by stores' promotion of new products, our salad making has come a long way.

Fast ways with salads

Trickle olive oil and a few drops of aged vinegar over prepared salad leaves from the supermarket, then sprinkle with salt crystals and finely milled pepper.

Quarter little gem lettuces and drape with strips of preserved roasted red pepper and anchovies. Add cherry tomatoes and drizzle with basic vinaigrette for an authentic Spanish salad.

Mix the juices and oils from store cupboard ingredients into your dressings, tasting first to make sure they are good. Try the oil from cans of anchovies and tuna, and the marinade from jars of olives, sun-dried tomatoes and roasted peppers.

Use chicory spears as little boats to hold dips, savoury pastes, or mini-salads and serve as canapés.

Salads cover a wide and fascinating range of dishes and recipes. Some are prepared from a mix of raw, young leaves, herbs and vegetables. Just as easily, we can make substantial salads to form a main course, by including cooked eggs, roast beef, cheese, smoked fish and seafood. Salads are now served warm or cold, so the possibilities are infinite.

Personally, I love salads that are as close as possible to nature, the garden plot or the forest. In Swiss mountain pastures you find mint, thyme, salad burnet, marjoram and chives growing within a yard of each other. I adore growing my own, or seeking wild food whilst out walking or wading, and I love that squeaky-clean feeling I get after eating wild, raw food.

The joy of a fresh salad is the combination of sweet, bitter and peppery leaves, the colours of russet, burgundy, beetroot-red baby chard, purple basil leaves, the icy green of the crunchy ribs of lettuce, and the bold British racing green of iron-rich spinach. I don't mind the inclusion of a few little good-looking leaves with shy flavour, such as mizuna and Japanese shiso. Just like a beautiful meadow, each and every leaf earns its place, and just like a meadow, a salad is, or should be, slightly different every day.

If you cannot grow your own salad leaves and herbs in a window box, allotment or garden – I promise you, it is easier than you think and a fraction of the price – the supermarkets maintain a fresh selection of salads in convenient portions year-round. Although I tend not to buy bags of prepared salad, it is good that these bags contain leaves that are not sold separately, like frisée, and they are an excellent way to be introduced to new leaves and ideas. I hope one day these retailers progress to the bins of dry, loose, perfect, crunchy salad leaves such as those sold in Zurich and Canada.

Seek out a greengrocer whose produce is dry, fresh and sprightly, with a brisk turnover. Dreary, mop-head frisées, or slimy lettuces are not worth considering, you will never revive them at home. Hunt out a farm shop or a stand at a farmers' market where salads and herbs are handled with respect. These fragile ingredients are short-lived and naturally susceptible to decay in bad weather.

What to look for and what to avoid

• Bagged salads and baby spinach leaves should have no trace of moisture in the bag, and should look perky, not flaccid.
• When buying loose salad vegetables, look for a sensitive arrangement of tender greens, not jammed or flung on top of each other. Leaves should be spry and crisp with vivid green edges.
• Look for radishes, celery and baby carrots filled to bursting with juice and sporting a good topping of springy leaves.
• Avoid slimy, floppy and dead salad leaves, limp cucumbers, floppy soft radishes and Belgian chicory that is not snow-white.
• Take your business to shops that smell cool and fresh.
• For salad dressings, choose fine quality oils and mellow vinegars. Good to have in the cupboard are first-rate cold pressed extra virgin olive oil and nut oils, dark vinegars such as balsamic and sherry vinegars, plus clear rice and champagne vinegars.

Storing and freezing

• In order to have fresh salad on hand the moment you need it, wash and dry all the leaves when you get home, by soaking them in water, especially if the salad is more limp than perky.
• Spin the more robust leaves dry, and air-dry the others, to avoid bruising.
• When your washed leaves are dry, place them in a plastic box, covered with a paper towel, then an airtight lid. They will keep for a few days this way but should be eaten as soon as possible.
• Large bunches of coriander [cilantro], parsley, mint, thyme, rosemary and dill need to be rinsed of all sand, and soaked if necessary. Stand the bunch in a jug, covered by a large, loose plastic bag and leave in the fridge for a few days.
• Small bunches of herbs (about a handful, or 15g/½oz/⅓ cup) should be rinsed and soaked if necessary, then sprayed with water from a spritzer bottle. Lay them in a long, loaf-shaped dish, with damp paper towel between each variety, and cover with plastic wrap. They will keep in the fridge for a few days. (Note that there is a fine line between damp and wet – when damp the herbs keep well, when wet you may find they rot.)
• Tomatoes and avocados should be kept on a sunny window sill and eaten as soon as they are ripe.
• Bunches of watercress can be kept upside down in a bowl of water overnight, but not longer.
• Oils for dressings should be stored in a cool, dry, dark place. However walnut and hazelnut oils deteriorate very quickly and are best kept in the fridge and used within five weeks.
• All home-made dressings, and particularly those containing eggs, can be kept in the fridge for no more than a week.

The best advice I can give Although you can put anything into a salad, don't. Start with the classic combinations, using good recipe books to help you. Keep leaf salads light, subtle and dainty. When you feel you are ready to experiment, start gradually, adding different ingredients, and tasting to see if they complement each other as you go.

Include as many soft herbs as you can, such as chervil, tarragon, summer savory, and flat-leaf parsley. Experiment with chive and borage flowers, but take care with nasturtiums, you might find them too peppery.

Learn to dress a salad with your fingertips, rather than the salad servers. Your fingertips are wonderfully gentle and thorough, allowing you to feel for the undressed parts of the salad.

Remember to wash salad very thoroughly, if it has not been grown for a supermarket.

The best preparation methods for salad vegetables The transformation of plain, raw vegetables into a salad relies on chopping and cutting skills. I know I should enjoy munching on raw carrots, but I am far more partial to forking my way through a finely grated carrot salad, with its inviting mouth-feel and sweet, honeyed dressing.

Invest in top-quality utensils. First is the heavy, sharp knife required to crack open a dense ball of cabbage, then the attachment on your food processor to grate it effortlessly into coleslaw. Use a serrated knife for slicing tomatoes, fennel, citrus fruit, and raw baby artichokes. A mandoline will help you produce flawless wafer-thin discs of cucumber and other vegetables.

Green salad
Serves 4

175-250g/6-9oz/1½-2¼ cups mixture of
salad and herb leaves
1 tbsp Basic Vinaigrette or Creamy
Vinaigrette (page 162)

To prepare the leaves, fill a sink or
large basin with cold water. Tear off
or cut away any bruised or slimy
parts from the leaves and place in the
water. Gently stir the leaves to
dislodge any sand, which will sink to
the bottom of the basin. If the leaves
were limp (they usually are, when
you buy them in a city), they will be
crisp when they start to rise above
the surface of the water. This can
take a couple of hours, but is really
worth the wait. Scoop the leaves out
of the water and drain them in a
colander. For very sandy, gritty
leaves, repeat the soaking process
twice in clean water.

Spin the leaves in a salad spinner,
or if they are particularly delicate, let
them air-dry in a cool draught. If
you have the time, pat them dry with
paper towel. Tear the prepared leaves
into bite-sized pieces, removing and
discarding any brown edges.

To serve, pour the dressing into a
salad bowl, whisk well, then sit the
salad servers in the bowl. Lay the
leaves on top, then, when the time
comes to serve the salad, toss the
leaves gently, coating them evenly
with the vinaigrette dressing, and
serve immediately. Alternatively,
serve the salad in individual salad
bowls, with the vinaigrette handed
separately in a jug.

Recipe notes Try to find a good
independent greengrocer for bright
and new salad leaves, rather than

flimsy ones that bruise and break
when you wash and toss them.
Bagged salads are better than no
salad, I suppose, but I consider it one
of life's little luxuries to have at least
one salad every day made from
home-grown fresh leaves and herbs.

You will need about 45g/1½oz of
mixed salad leaves and herbs per
person, but make sure you include as
many herbs as possible. Choose from
parsley, tarragon, chervil, lovage
leaves, nasturtium leaves, chives,
chive flowers, wild garlic and basil.
When it comes to salad leaves,
rocket, baby spinach leaves, lollo
rosso, lollo bianco, radicchio, cos or
romaine lettuce, curly lettuce, baby
red chard, pousse, baby frisée, corn
salad, little gem lettuce leaves and
mizuna are all suitable.

As long as they were fresh when
you bought them, salad leaves keep
perfectly, after washing and drying,
for about 5 days in a plastic box in
the fridge. Place a few sheets of paper
towel between the leaves and one
under the lid. They can also be
wrapped in a tea towel. You will find
the leaves become even crisper after a
day or so in the fridge.

Serve a green salad at the end of
the main course, on your big plates,
so the meat juices mingle deliciously
with the vinaigrette dressing.
Alternatively, serve it with the cheese
course, so fragments of cheese make
their way into the salad, or serve
separately after the main course to
freshen up the appetite for pudding.

Mixed salad
Serves 4

45g/1½oz french beans [haricot verts]
(optional)
60g/2oz/½ cup salad leaves, such as
curly lettuce, rocket [arugula] or baby
spinach, washed and dried
12 sprigs flat-leaf parsley or chervil
25g/1oz/⅓ cup red onion, finely sliced
12 black olives, stoned
½ red pepper, deseeded and cut into
chunks
90g/3oz feta or mozzarella cheese, cut
into 1cm/½in cubes
1 avocado
4 tsp Basic Vinaigrette (page 162)
sea salt and freshly milled black pepper

If using the green beans, bring a pot
of salted water with a blanching
basket to a boil. Add the trimmed
beans and cook for 30 seconds or
until bright green, then lift out the
basket and plunge the beans into icy
cold water. Drain and dry.

Tear the salad leaves into bite-sized
pieces. Pour the vinaigrette into the
bottom of a deep salad bowl. Add
the salad leaves, herbs, red onion,
olives, red pepper and cheese.

Peel the avocado, cut it into cubes,
and add to the salad with some salt
and pepper. Turn the salad gently, to
coat each leaf to glistening perfection
and serve immediately.

Recipe notes If preferred, you can
dress this salad with a trickle of extra
virgin olive oil and a few drops of
balsamic and/or sherry vinegar, in
which case add them to the bowl just
after the avocado.

If appropriate, taste the marinating
oil from your container of olives – it
may be worth including a little of it in
the salad dressing too.

First course salad
Serves 4

160g/5½oz Parma ham, bresaola,
  smoked halibut or salami, finely sliced
60g/2oz/½ cup salad leaves, such as
  baby spinach, mizuna, baby chard,
  corn salad or maché, washed and
  dried
½ tsp dressing, made with a clear
  vinegar
sea salt flakes and freshly milled black
  pepper

Lay the meat or fish in straight lines
across four medium-sized serving
plates. In a large bowl, toss the salad
leaves in the dressing.

Bundle up one portion of dressed
leaves lightly in the palms of your
hand, to make a little ball, then place
it in the centre of one plate. Repeat
with the rest of the salad.

Sprinkle over the salt crystals, grind
over the pepper, and serve immediately.

Recipe notes For meat lovers,
particularly, this makes an easy
starter, and takes advantage of the
increasingly imaginative range of
charcuterie and smoked meats and
fish sold ready-sliced in small packs.

Rocket and cherry tomato salad
Serves 4

½ tsp Basic Vinaigrette Dressing (page
  162)
180g/6oz/1½ cups rocket [arugula]
  leaves, washed and dried
8 cherry tomatoes
sea salt flakes and freshly milled black
  pepper

Place the rocket in a salad bowl. Add
the tomatoes, then the dressing. Toss
and sprinkle lightly with the salt and
pepper before serving.

Recipe notes It is important not to use
too much dressing, or the salad will
be dark, oily and soggy.

When making this salad for a
different number of people, you
simply need to allow 45g/1½oz/
⅓ cup rocket leaves and two cherry
tomatoes per person.

Sweet-sour cucumber salad
Serves 4

½ cucumber
2 tbsp caster sugar
2 tbsp white wine vinegar
1 tbsp fresh dill, chopped
coarse [kosher] salt and freshly milled
  white pepper

Run a canelle knife or the tines of a
fork down the sides of the cucumber
to decorate. Then thinly slice the
cucumber, place it in a colander and
sprinkle with coarse salt. Cover with
a plate that fits inside the colander,
and weight it so that it presses down
on the cucumber. Leave to stand for
30 minutes to draw the juices.

Thoroughly rinse the cucumber of
salt, then press it dry on absorbent
paper. In a mixing bowl, combine the
sugar, wine vinegar and 4 tbsp water
and season with salt and pepper.

Add the cucumber slices and dill to
the dressing and leave to marinate
for several hours before serving.

Recipe notes Disarming, modest and
understated, this is a recipe I would
never be without. It's important on
the hottest day, with cold roast
chicken, poached or baked salmon or
salmon trout, as well as in winter,
when it provides a crisp contrast to a
creamy fish dish served hot.

Chinese rainbow salad with sesame and soy dressing
Serves 4-6

225g/8oz carrots, peeled
1½ tsp salt
350g/12oz cucumber
6 large dried Chinese mushrooms
1 medium red pepper, deseeded
7 spring onions [scallions], trimmed
5 tbsp groundnut or corn oil
200g/7oz/2 cups beansprouts

For the dressing

2 tbsp sesame oil
4 tsp rice vinegar
2 tsp soy sauce
salt and freshly milled black pepper

Run a canelle knife along the sides of the carrots. Slice very thinly on the diagonal. Place in a bowl, sprinkle with 1 tsp of salt and leave for 15-30 minutes. Canelle the cucumber, then halve lengthways and deseed. Slice very thinly on the diagonal. Place in a bowl, sprinkle with ½ tsp salt and leave for 20 minutes.

Place the mushrooms in a heatproof bowl, cover with warm water and leave to soak for 15 minutes.

Cut the red pepper into thin strips and set aside. Halve the spring onions lengthways, then cut into 5cm/2in sections on a sharp diagonal. Keep the white and green parts separate.

Make the dressing by combining all the ingredients in a jar with 2 tsp water and shaking them together.

Drain the cucumber and carrot thoroughly, keeping them separate. Squeeze out the excess water from the mushrooms, but leave them damp, then slice into the thinnest possible slivers, discarding the tough stems.

Heat a wok over a high heat until smoking. Add 4 tbsp of the oil and swirl it around. Add the white parts of the spring onion and stir a couple of times. Stir in the mushrooms, then the carrots and red pepper. Sliding the wok scoop to the bottom of the wok, flip and turn the ingredients vigorously over a high heat for about 2 minutes or until the vegetables are barely cooked and still very crunchy.

Add the green parts of the spring onion and the beansprouts. Stir a few times more, then remove to a large plate or baking tray to cool. If water starts to ooze from the vegetables, drain and discard it.

When the vegetables are cool, mix in the cucumber. Stir in the dressing and toss well. Cover and chill before serving, or serve at room temperature.

Recipe notes This recipe is from Yan-Kit So, who had indisputable taste in food and clothes. A poignant memory is of her large Yves St Laurent and Celine carrier bags, in which she carried her wok, cleaver and ingredients whenever she came to teach at my school.

The subtle dressing of sesame and vinegar makes this colourful plate of lightly stir-fried vegetables all the more delectable. Rainbow salad can be prepared well ahead of time, and if refrigerated, will keep overnight without losing its crunchiness. The salting of the vegetables draws out their moisture, intensifying their natural flavours.

If desired, you can add water chestnuts to the wok when the vegetables are nearly done, and stir in some cooked cellophane noodles after you add the cucumber.

Serve this salad as part of a Chinese or Southeast Asian menu, or with cold roast duck, cold beef, or the spiced beef fillet (page 62).

Caesar salad
Serves 4

2 small cos or romaine lettuce hearts
6 or more shavings of Parmigiano Reggiano cheese
salt and freshly milled black pepper

For the croûtons

80g/3oz/¼ stick salted butter
1 clove garlic, crushed
3 slices good white bread, crusts removed, diced

For the dressing

2-3 tbsp Anchovy Dressing (page 162)
45g/1½oz/⅓ cup Parmigiano Reggiano cheese, grated

To make the croûtons, heat the oven to 180°C/350°F/Gas 4. Melt the butter gently in a small saucepan, then add the garlic and leave to infuse, keeping the butter on a very gentle heat for at least 10 minutes.

Pour the flavoured butter onto a baking tray and add the cubes of bread. Roast in the oven for 10 minutes, then turn the croûtons over using a fish slice or spatula, and roast on the other side for another 5 minutes or so, watching carefully to ensure they do not burn.

Use a sieve to strain the croûtons, then drain them on crumpled paper towel. Taste and add a little more salt if necessary, then set aside while you finish the salad.

To make the dressing, put the anchovy dressing and the grated cheese in a small blender or food processor and whizz until the mixture is smooth, thick and creamy.

Slice the lettuce, or tear it into bite-sized pieces and place in a salad bowl with the dressing. Toss well, then divide amongst serving plates. >

Scatter with the croûtons, top each portion with the parmesan shavings and take to the table.

Recipe notes From the moment Caesar salad became fashionable in London some years back, my male students were seeking out the sweetest cos or romaine lettuce hearts with which to make it. It certainly became the salad of choice for ladies who like to lunch on a lettuce leaf.

I think part of its popularity is the bold flavour of the parmesan cheese, which grates to a fine powder and flavours the dressing. Together with the anchovies and garlic, it makes this salad a substantial, satisfying and delicious light meal or starter.

The croûtons will keep for a few days in an airtight box. To reheat them, stir-fry the croûtons quickly in a frying pan with a little olive oil.

To make a chicken Caesar, char-grill or pan-roast some chicken breast fillets, then cut them into strips. Turn them in plenty of the cheesy dressing before adding them to the salad. You could also try replacing the croûtons with capers, and the lettuce with baby shrimp, and serve the mixture on spears of chicory as a canapé.

Orange, red onion and coriander salad with cinnamon dressing
Serves 4

4 ripe sweet oranges
½ red onion, finely sliced
1 pomegranate, seeded (optional)
15g/½oz/¼ cup coriander [cilantro]
  leaves

For the dressing
2 tbsp sugar
½ tsp cinnamon
1 tbsp orange flower water
2 tbsp orange juice
a pinch of salt

Using a very sharp serrated knife, cut away the rind of the orange, leaving the flesh free of all pith and skin.

Working over a mixing bowl, with the knife blade lying flat against the membrane separating one segment from another, cut towards the centre of the orange until the cutting blade reaches the middle. Lift the knife blade so it stands vertical, resting on the next membrane to the right, then push the cutting edge to the right, and the segment will pop out free of pith and skin. Continue all the way around the orange. When you have finished, squeeze the pithy remains to extract the fresh orange juice. Repeat with the remaining oranges and set aside.

If using the pomegranate, drive a knive into the fruit, as if to cut it in half lengthways, but as soon as you can, put down your knife and break open the pomegranate with your fingers. Use a round-tipped teaspoon to winkle out the seeds so they remain looking like whole, shining jewels, then set aside in a bowl.

Place all the ingredients for the dressing in a blender. Blend well then adjust the seasoning to taste – the dressing should be sweet and warmly spiced with a note of salt.

Arrange the orange segments on serving plates. Top with the onion slivers and coriander, and pomegranate seeds if using. Pour the dressing over the salad and serve. In summer, chill the salad before serving.

Recipe notes Serve this salad as a starter, or after a tagine or Middle Eastern dish, or another highly spiced main course. Ideally it should be presented on brightly coloured plates. My favourite is blue, anything from turquoise to cerulean and azure.

Pomegranates are seasonal, so don't be disappointed if you cannot find them. Try the Persian shops first. A ripe pomegranate is the colour of deep ruby or garnet, and ever-so-slightly wizened.

There is another way to successfully segment oranges, so choose the one that suits you best. After peeling the fruit, cut towards the centre of the orange with your knife blade lying flat along one membrane. Repeat on the other side of that segment. The segment will slide out, again perfectly clean of pith and skin. I don't always use a sharp serrated knife – my small Japanese ceramic knife makes a good job of segmenting oranges too. Alternatively, for this salad you can slice the oranges instead of cutting them into segments.

Pasta, noodles and couscous

Fast ways with pasta

Toss boiled fresh noodles with cream, grated parmesan, sea salt and freshly milled black pepper.

Use freshly made aromatic garlic oil or warm tomato and herb vinaigrette to dress spaghetti.

Stir crème fraîche and caviar through steaming hot pasta.

Combine short shapes such as penne with chunks of chorizo, black olives and extra virgin olive oil.

Pour melted butter flavoured with fresh sage over filled pasta parcels brought from an Italian specialist.

Toss long fine ribbons such as tagliolini with grated parmesan, finely shaved white truffles or truffle oil, and a little melted butter.

Buy basil pesto from a good deli and toss with trenette or linguine.

Chop plenty of fresh parsley and stir through cooked spaghettini with canned vongoles (little clams) and olive oil.

There is something about pasta that almost everyone finds pleasurable, from tiny children to the most demanding gourmet. When combined with the simplest of cooking methods, pasta gives even the most timid cooks the courage to cook. Authentic Italian dried pasta offers supreme convenience as well as quality and value. From there it is an easy step to preparing dishes of couscous and Oriental noodles, incorporating exciting textures and flavour combinations from North Africa and the Far East.

Italians usually eat pasta once a day as a first course. We have adopted it as the ultimate comfort food for midweek suppers, dinner parties, buffets, snacks and just about everything else, but the results are often poor and unappetising.

So much is written today on how to make and cook fresh pasta that I sometimes feel it is all designed to veil its simplicity and make it appear more difficult than it really is. In fact, I reckon it is almost quicker to make fresh pasta than it is to write out the recipe for it.

What to look for and what to avoid

• For the most part, Italians eat golden yellow dried pasta. It is much easier to cook than fresh pasta, especially for large numbers of people.

• The best pasta is made from durum wheat semolina, which produces a strong, fast-drying pasta that is elastic when cooked, and softens on the outside while remaining firm within.

• Pasta can be made with a variety of gluten-free grains for those with wheat allergies, however quality varies between brands. Some disintegrate on boiling. Look in food halls and organic retailers for the superior Italian gluten-free varieties, or those made in Australia.

• When making pasta from scratch, try to use farina 00, a particularly fine Italian strong durum wheat flour. If you cannot get it, good quality bleached strong bread-making flour will work just as well.

• Eggs used in fresh pasta dough should be the best you can find. I sometimes use two yolks for a warm, buttery coloured pasta.

• Mass-manufactured ravioli has nothing of the tenderness of fresh ravioli. It is a bit like eating chewy, soggy footballs, and it takes a long time to cook.

• Fresh pasta should be cooked as soon as it is made, so commercially produced 'fresh' pasta is not true fresh pasta. I avoid it, because it is often slimy and tasteless.

The principles of cooking pasta

• Use a lightweight, deep pot with two handles for it will be easy to lift when full of liquid.

• The ratio of water to pasta should ideally be 10:1. Plenty of boiling water in the pot allows the water to retain its full heat when the pasta is added, and allows excess starch to boil free.

• As a general guide, use 1 tsp salt to 1 litre/1¾ pints/8¼ cups water, and 100g/3½oz pasta to 1 litre/1¾ pints/8¼ cups water.

• Only add olive oil to the water if boiling large sheets of pasta or ravioli, as it prevents sticking. For other pastas, oil is unnecessary.

• Blanching baskets and pasta pan inserts help you get the cooked pasta out of the hot water in the quickest possible time, and lets you return it to the boiling water easily should you discover it is under-cooked.

• Once the water has reached a rolling boil, introduce the pasta to the basket gradually, and stir it well to prevent sticking.

• Remember that the pasta continues to cook during the draining process, so build this factor into your timing.

• On draining, shake the pasta well to release the moisture. Keep some of the cooking liquid to thin down sauces if necessary.

• Try cooking pasta in chicken stock rather than water for a good flavour. After cooking, reserve it, cool and freeze for use in soup.

• Egg pasta will swell slightly when cooked due to the protein in the egg. It is richer and more filling than eggless pasta, therefore you need less per portion.

• Only cook small amounts of fresh pasta at one time. The weight of it, and the water, will cause it to tear. The maximum I will cook is 450g/1lb fresh pasta to serve 4-6 people.

• Different batches of flour absorb moisture at different rates. When making pasta from scratch, be prepared to add plenty of extra flour as necessary, and add it as early in the mixing process as possible to prevent streaky dough.

• Be prepared to use a hand-held hair-dryer to help dry sheets of freshly made pasta more quickly.

• If you are using a vegetable purée to flavour or colour the pasta, make sure it is as creamy and smooth as possible, or the noodles will be difficult to cut.

How to tell when pasta is cooked

• Cooking time varies depending on the shape and density of the pasta chosen. Note the instructions given on the pasta packet and expect it to take a minute or so less than it says.

• Check for doneness by tasting a few pieces from various parts of the pan. Aim for an al dente texture. This means 'to the tooth'. The pasta should be tender yet firm and just a little resilient. Long pasta should also be supple when you bend it.

• When cooked, fresh pasta must not taste of dough.

• Overcooked pasta will break easily and be soggy and tasteless.

How to toss pasta in sauce Place a little of the hot sauce in the base of a pasta bowl and add the shining, jiggling pasta to it. With two large wooden spoons, toss the noodles in the sauce. As with dressing a salad, lift and stir until only the lightest film of sauce remains on the pasta. Each angle, frill, edge and fluting must be visible. Then place a spoonful of the sauce on top of the mound of pasta and serve immediately.

If the sauce is not ready for the pasta, whatever you do, don't leave the pasta to stand or it will congeal, no matter how perfectly you have made and cooked it.

Quickly pour a little olive oil or melted butter over the cooked pasta and toss. Then it may wait a few moments. Return the bowl of pasta to the top of the pasta cooking saucepan to keep warm.

If the sauce has boiled away, or you do not have enough to coat the pasta, add a little of the starchy cooking water to thin or 'stretch' it and blend thoroughly.

Rule of thumb Northern Italy is the traditional home of egg pasta. Cream, eggs and other substantial ingredients are used in the sauces. Plain dried pasta originated in the hotter South of Italy, where the sauces are based mainly on olive oil and tomatoes. If they include meat, it will be in small proportion to the rest of the sauce.

Tips for using couscous

• Making traditional couscous is a long process. The modern quick-cooking varieties on sale in supermarkets need only to be covered with hot stock and left to stand for 15 minutes before stirring through with a fork.

• If you have the time, lightly rub the rehydrated couscous through your fingers to make it fluffy.

• Couscous can bring height and drama to a buffet display. Pack the couscous into a large, tall bowl, then gently tip it out onto your serving dish. It will keep its shape. Decorate with nicely cut pieces of roast red pepper, char-grilled courgettes [zucchini], currants and flat-leaf parsley.

• Couscous salads can be even more delicious the day after making, as the flavours will have had time to meld.

Salmon and fennel ravioli
Serves 4-6

For the dough
1 tsp sunflower or olive oil
a pinch of salt
3 egg yolks
125g/4oz/scant 1 cup plain strong white
*   [all-purpose] flour or Type 00 Italian*
*   flour, plus extra for dusting*

For the filling
10g/⅓oz/½ tbsp butter
60g/2oz/½ cup fresh fennel, finely
*   chopped*
60g/2oz/½ cup onions, finely chopped
2 tbsp double [heavy] cream
4 tsp fennel seeds, crushed and sieved
90g/3oz salmon or pink trout fillet,
*   deboned and thinly sliced*
1 yolk, beaten with a little salt
salt and freshly milled white pepper

To serve
285ml/10floz/1¼ cups whipping [heavy]
*   cream*
a pinch of saffron threads
½ quantity Jade Noodles (page 114)
12 sprigs of dill, to garnish

You will also need
several large trays lined with tea towels
*   and dusted with semolina*
a hand-cranked pasta machine
a wheel ravioli cutter (optional)
a ruler

To make the pasta dough, place the oil, salt, egg yolks and flour in a food processor with 2 tbsp water and blend. Squeeze the dough into a ball (it should be firm and tough) and leave to rest under an upturned bowl for 1 hour while you make the filling.

Place the butter in a small frying pan. Add the fresh fennel and onions and fry gently until softened. Add the cream, bring to a boil and simmer briskly until the mixture is a thick paste. Add the fennel seeds and season with a little salt and pepper.

Set the pasta machine to the widest setting. Take small amounts of dough about the size of an egg and roll them through the rollers. Then fold each piece of dough in half, and feed it through again, folded side first. Work in sequence so that each portion of dough has equal resting and kneading times.

When the dough feels ultra-smooth and firm, it is time to start stretching the pasta. Bring the rollers together by one notch. Feed each piece of dough through once, without folding. Repeat, in sequence, bringing the rollers together, notch by notch, each time you pass the dough through. Continue through to the last notch on the pasta machine. The sheets will become longer and longer, so cut them with a sharp knife or scissors to fit your trays. If the dough feels sticky at any time, dust lightly with flour.

It is important not to abandon the pasta at this stage, it is just the right consistency to tuck over and seal the filling. Using a ravioli cutter, cut the pasta sheets into squares of 7cm/3in diameter. Alternatively, use a large round cookie cutter or a knife.

Brush the edges of each piece of pasta with a little beaten egg yolk. Place a small spoon of fennel paste on one piece of dough, then cover with the fish, leaving a decent border all around. Season the fish with a light hand. Place a second piece of dough over the top, yolk-side down, and seal with your fingers, pressing gently but firmly onto the pasta below. Repeat with the remaining ingredients. Lay the finished ravioli on trays lined with tea towels and dusted with semolina and, if necessary, place in the fridge to chill until ready to cook.

To make the accompanying sauce, infuse the saffron threads in 2 tbsp boiling water for 15 minutes. Meanwhile, in a small saucepan, boil the cream until it reduces enough to coat the back of a spoon. Season to taste with salt and pepper, then strain the saffron liquid through a small sieve into the cream sauce. Stir to combine and set aside.

To cook the ravioli, bring a pot of salted water to the boil. Slip the ravioli into the boiling water, and cook for 2-3 minutes or until the salmon turns pink, stirring gently so they do not stick together. Lift out and drain briefly on a tea towel to mop up the excess water.

Meanwhile, reheat the saucepan of saffron cream sauce, whisking well, and reheat or finish the jade noodles in a large frying pan.

Serve the ravioli in shallow bowls with the saffron sauce poured over, the jade noodles to one side, and decorated with the dill sprigs.

Recipe notes The trick of making ravioli is keeping the pasta soft and supple until the ravioli are sealed and finished. If you can find it, Italian Type 00 soft wheat flour makes the silkiest, smoothest ravioli.

All the elements of this recipe can be made well in advance of serving.

When seasoning the ravioli filling, go easy on the salt. It could make the filling weep, and the ravioli will become sticky, which is a problem especially if making them in advance.

If you wish to avoid a creamy sauce, use the warm tomato and herb vinaigrette (page 163). There is also no need to incorporate the cucumber noodles unless desired.

Really fresh pasta
Serves 4-6

4 egg yolks
125g/4oz/scant 1 cup plain strong white [all-purpose] flour, or Type 00 Italian flour, plus extra for dusting

You will also need
several large trays lined with tea towels and dusted with semolina
a hand-cranked pasta machine with noodle cutters

Place the egg yolks, flour and 1 tbsp water in a food processor and blend to a dough. Squeeze the dough into a ball (it should be firm and tough) and leave it to rest under an upturned bowl for 1 hour.

Set the pasta machine to the widest setting. Take small amounts of dough about the size of an egg and crank them through the rollers. Then fold each piece of dough in half and feed it through again, folded side first. Work in sequence so that each portion has equal resting and kneading times.

When the pasta feels ultra-smooth and firm, it is time to start stretching the pasta. Bring the rollers together by one notch. Feed each piece of dough through once, without folding. Repeat, in sequence, bringing the rollers together, notch by notch, each time you pass the dough through. Stop either at the penultimate notch, or go right down to the last one if you want the pasta to be very fine. The sheets will become longer and longer, so cut the dough with a sharp knife or scissors to fit the size of your trays. If the dough feels sticky at any time, dust lightly with flour.

Now test the pasta – it should not stick together, when folded on itself and pressed. If it does, leave it to dry naturally for a bit longer, or dry it with a hair dryer if you are in a hurry. It should be the consistency of damp chamois leather. Too moist and the noodles will stick into clumps, too dry and the pasta will be too brittle to cut.

Slot the noodle attachment of your choice onto the pasta machine and run the fine sheets effortlessly through the noodle cutter. Reaching under the machine, catch the noodles, fold them into little nests and sit them on the towels dusted with semolina.

Ideally, they should be cooked immediately. Alternatively, the tray of pasta nests can be placed somewhere warm and airy to dry, or the noodles can be draped over a rod.

To cook, bring a large pot of water to the boil, adding enough salt to make it taste like sea water. Throw the pasta into the boiling water and cook for 2-3 minutes, or as little as 20 seconds, depending on how 'fresh' it is. Stir carefully once or twice during cooking to prevent the noodles sticking to the bottom of the pot. Drain, reserving a little of the cooking water to help toss the pasta, depending on how you wish to serve it.

Recipe notes As standard, a hand-cranked pasta machine comes with two sets of cutters, one for fettuccine or tagliatelle, and another for thin angels' hair noodles. You can make both with this dough recipe.

The trick is to dry the pasta sheets sufficiently after stretching, and before you cut them into noodles, so the noodles do not stick together during further drying or cooking.

Don't cook and serve more than one quantity of the recipe given here at a time, as the fresh noodles are very delicate and inclined to break up in the boiling water.

Scallion fettuccine with smoked salmon
Serves 4

about 115g/4oz spring onions [scallions]
225g/8oz/1⅔ cups plain strong white [all-purpose] flour, plus extra for dusting
1 large egg, beaten

For the sauce
320ml/11floz/1⅓ cups crème fraîche, whipping or double [heavy] cream
100g/3½oz smoked salmon, cut into strips
salt and freshly milled black pepper

You will also need
several large trays lined with tea towels and dusted with semolina
a hand-cranked pasta machine with noodle cutters

To make the scallion fettuccine, finely mince the spring onions until they are smooth. Place in a measuring jug and make sure you have exactly 100ml/3½floz/scant ½ cup.

Place the onion mince in the bowl of a food processor. Add the flour, then the beaten egg and process briefly until a dough is formed. Squeeze the dough into a ball, adding extra flour or semolina as necessary to stop it being too sticky, then set aside under an upturned bowl for 1 hour.

Set the pasta machine to the widest setting. Take small amounts of dough about the size of an egg and roll them through the rollers. Then fold each piece of dough in half, dust liberally with flour and feed it through again, folded side first. Work in sequence so that each portion of dough has equal resting and kneading times.

When the dough feels ultra-smooth and firm, it is time to start stretching the pasta. Bring the rollers together by one notch. Feed each piece of dough through once, without folding.

Repeat, in sequence, bringing the rollers together, notch by notch, each time you pass the dough through. Stop at the penultimate notch. The sheets will become longer and longer, so cut the dough with a sharp knife or scissors to the size of your trays. If the dough feels sticky at any time, dust lightly with flour.

Now test the pasta – it should not stick together, when folded on itself and pressed. If it does, leave it to dry naturally for a bit longer, or dry it with a hair dryer if you are in a hurry. It should be the consistency of damp chamois leather.

Slot the fettuccine attachment onto the pasta machine and run the sheets carefully through the cutter. Reach under the machine to catch the noodles and hang them over a rod of dowel or saucepan handles.

Make the sauce in a large, shallow pan. Boil the cream over a brisk heat until well-reduced. Add the smoked salmon and allow to infuse briefly. Season with pepper and a little salt, and keep warm.

To cook the pasta, bring a large pot of water to the boil, adding enough salt to make it taste like sea water. Slip in the pasta and cook for about 5 minutes or until the pasta is al dente. Drain thoroughly.

Combine the cream sauce and fettuccine in a warmed serving bowl and serve immediately.

Recipe notes I have adapted this from a traditional recipe of the Savoie, one of the most tranquil places in the world, where I have cooked and taught. The kitchen window looked out onto mountains and pastureland,

and two cows with bells around their necks made soothing, deep chimes as we chopped and cooked. The water from the tap was icy, pure and sweet. We gathered our own mushrooms and fresh herbs from alongside the mountain track, and in winter plunged the stockpot into the snow to cool.

There, the scallions were soup greens such as lovage and nettles, cooked with an onion, then made into a purée and incorporated into the dough. This is a simpler version, but I would not try it unless you have made pasta before. Why not warm up by making basic fresh pasta (see left) a few times, and then when you have mastered it, try this recipe?

Mince the spring onions very finely or the dough will be difficult to cut into noodles. Use a mincer, the chopping blade of a food processor, or a similar electric mixer attachment for a good result.

Due to the high moisture content of the onions, the dough will always be a bit sticky, and will take longer to firm up than regular pasta. Once the noodles are dry, they can easily wait a few of hours before cooking and serving, as can the sauce.

The sauce can be made with smoked trout too, if desired. You may need to experiment with your local choice of smoked salmon – some varieties are saltier than others and too much of this flavour can spoil the sauce. Alternatively, replace the fish with grated beaufort or fontina cheese, or crumble hard goats' cheese over the top.

Buttered noodles
Serves 6

350g/13oz good quality dried noodles,
or 450g/1lb fresh noodles
55g/2oz/½ stick unsalted butter, diced
salt and freshly milled pepper

Bring a large pot of salted water to the boil, using 1 tsp of salt per 1 litre/ 34floz/4¼ cups of water so that the water tastes as salty as seawater. Add the pasta and cook. Meanwhile, in a small saucepan, gently melt the butter.

When the noodles are cooked, drain them, reserving about 150ml/5floz/ ⅔ cup of the cooking water in a jug.

Combine the melted butter and cooking water, adding a little extra boiling water from a kettle if the mixture seems too salty. Grind some pepper into the sauce and pour it over the noodles. Toss gently until evenly coated and serve immediately.

Recipe notes For this side dish, choose fairly wide pasta ribbons such as pappardelle, and fine unsalted butter, preferably from the Charente or Normandy.

If you like dried noodles very tender, rather than al dente, do not boil them longer. Instead, take the pan off the heat and leave them to poach in the cooking water for a few minutes after boiling, to allow them to soften without breaking up.

Pasta shells with ricotta and spinach, in a tomato sauce with thyme and garlic
Serves 4

12 large conchiglie pasta shells
225g/8oz fresh leaf spinach
225g/8oz/1 cup ricotta
butter, for greasing
a little freshly grated nutmeg
salt and freshly milled black pepper

For the sauce
2 tbsp olive oil
2-3 cloves garlic, crushed
675g/1lb 8oz tomatoes, chopped
6 sprigs thyme
3-4 tbsp grated parmesan cheese

Cook the pasta in a blanching basket in a large pot of boiling, salted water, stirring carefully as you add the pasta to prevent the shells from sticking. Boil for about 10 minutes, then lift out the basket and drain the pasta shells on a tea towel, open side down so that all the excess water runs out.

Bring a kettle of water to the boil. Place the spinach in a sieve or colander and pour the hot water from the kettle slowly over the spinach to blanch it. Alternatively, use 'washed and ready to cook' spinach and cook it in a microwave oven according to the packet instructions.

Drain as much water from the spinach as you can. Place the leaves on a clean tea towel, roll it up and twist the ends like a toffee wrapper to extract all the moisture, then untwist and set aside to cool.

Place the cooled spinach and the ricotta in a food processor and whizz until smooth. Season to taste with nutmeg, salt and pepper. Carefully spoon the stuffing into the pasta shells and place in a buttered baking

dish with the open side of the pasta shell facing downwards.

To make the sauce, heat the oil in a shallow saucepan. Add the garlic and allow to infuse gently, so the oil takes on the flavour of the garlic. Add the tomatoes and the leaves from the thyme sprigs. Simmer the sauce for 20-30 minutes or until it is thick.

When almost ready to serve, heat the oven to 180°C/350°F/Gas 4. Spoon the sauce over the filled pasta. Sprinkle evenly with the grated cheese and bake for 15-20 minutes or until the sauce is bubbling. Serve piping hot.

Recipe notes This recipe is from one of my culinary heroines, Katie Stewart, when she was the original Times Cook. It is a great example of her skill as a writer. The dish is without ostentation, but beautifully balanced and exceptionally useful.

The spinach and ricotta filling is of just the right consistency to fill the shells – not too stiff and not too runny. Another advantage is that you do not have to blanch and peel the tomatoes in order to make the sauce.

Each part of this dish can be made well in advance, but I like pouring the sauce over the shells and topping with cheese just before baking, to give the most even coating.

Saffron couscous salad
Serves 4-6

85g/3oz mangetout [snow peas]
a large pinch of saffron threads
45g/1½oz/3 tbsp butter
350ml/12floz/1½ cups light chicken or
  vegetable stock
250g/9oz/heaped 1 cup couscous
85g/3oz cooked tiger prawns
75g/3oz/½ cup pitted olives
15g/½oz/¼ cup mint leaves
salt and freshly milled black pepper

For the dressing
100ml/3½floz/scant 1 cup extra virgin
  olive oil, warmed slightly
juice of 2 lemons

In a large saucepan of boiling water, blanch the mangetout for just under 1 minute, then drain and refresh in ice-cold water. Drain the mangetout again and set aside to dry thoroughly before slicing them finely lengthways. Meanwhile, combine the saffron threads and 2 tbsp boiling water in a small dish and leave to infuse for at least 10 minutes.

Melt the butter in a wide, shallow saucepan. Strain the saffron liquor into the pan, add the stock and bring to a boil. Stir in the couscous, then cover and remove from the heat. Leave to stand for 10-12 minutes.

Transfer the couscous to a large bowl, breaking up any lumps with a fork or your fingers. The grains should have absorbed all the liquid. Add the prawns, sliced mangetout, olives and mint leaves.

To make the dressing, gently warm the olive oil and lemon juice in a small saucepan, whisking to combine.

Pour the dressing over the couscous, then toss and season to taste with salt and pepper. Allow >

the salad to stand for 10 minutes or so before serving, to give the couscous time to absorb the dressing.

Recipe notes Couscous, flavoured with vegetables and herbs, is a staple in my cookery programmes. Apart from being a great accompaniment to the lamb shanks with mustard, rosemary, chickpeas and caramelized onion (page 66) or slow-cooked lamb with Barahrat spices (page 69), it can stand on its own as a starter, or as a main course supper or luncheon dish, and can be made a few days in advance of serving.

For a delicious variation, omit the prawns altogether. Replace the mangetout with 100g/4oz celery, trimmed and finely diced, substitute 75g/3oz/⅔ cup toasted pine nuts for the olives, use chopped parsley instead of mint leaves, include two small spring onions [scallions], finely sliced, and whisk a pinch of powderd cinnamon into the dressing.

Couscous with apricots and roasted coriander seeds
Serve 4-6

1 tbsp coriander seeds
3 tbsp extra virgin olive oil
½ tsp salt
170g/6oz/¾ cup couscous
120g/4oz/⅔ cup semi-dried or dried apricots, chopped
3 tbsp chopped flat-leaf parsley or coriander [cilantro]
salt and freshly milled black pepper

Heat a frying pan until very hot, then dry-fry the coriander seeds, rolling them often to toast evenly. When the seeds are deeply aromatic and almost starting to smoke, tip them into a mortar and, when cool, grind to a powder using the pestle.

Place 300ml/10floz/1½ cups water in a saucepan with 2 tbsp of the olive oil, and the salt, and bring to a boil. Stir in the toasted coriander seeds and the couscous, cover the pan and remove from the heat. Leave to stand for 5 minutes, covered.

Using a fork, gently mix the dried apricots and fresh herbs into the couscous and add salt and pepper to taste. Drizzle with the remaining 1 tbsp of olive oil just before serving.

Recipe notes A great midweek recipe, this is one to try a with roast or pot-roast chicken, or serve with vegetables for a non-meat supper. The roasted coriander seed gives a rounded, warm flavour to the couscous, and goes well with the dried apricots too.

If there is any left over, you can reheat it in the microwave for a minute for a second meal, or take it as part of a packed lunch to work, instead of the usual sandwich.

Soba in chicken and soy broth with wilted watercress, coriander and mint
Serves 4

For the fragrant chicken broth

2kg/4½lb whole chicken
6 cardamom pods, cracked
1 long stick cinnamon
3 star anise
5cm/2in fresh ginger, sliced
2 shallots, sliced

To serve

250g/9oz soba or udon noodles
2 tsp salt (or more to taste)
6 tbsp dark soy sauce or tamari
2 tbsp sugar
2 tbsp mirin
100g/3½oz/1 cup watercress leaves
6 spring onions [scallions], slashed into fine, short splinters
6 sprigs fresh mint
6 sprigs fresh coriander [cilantro]
6 tsp toasted sesame seeds
Japanese rice crackers
Japanese pickled ginger

Place all the ingredients for the fragrant chicken broth in a saucepan that will just hold the chicken, breast downwards. Cover with water, bring to a simmer, then cook for 30 minutes, skimming off all the fat and foam that accumulates on the surface.

Using a chef's fork, turn the chicken over and continue simmering for another 20 minutes. Turn off the heat under the pan and leave for 1½ hours or, ideally, until cool.

Remove the chicken from the pan. Strain the broth through a fine-meshed sieve, discard the aromatics, and use strips of paper towel to remove the eyes of fat from the broth's surface.

Remove the chicken meat from the bones, discard the skin and cut the flesh into bite-sized pieces. Set aside 500g/17oz for use in this dish, and store the remainder in the fridge or freezer for another occasion.

Bring a large pot of water to the boil, add the noodles in a blanching basket and boil for 2-6 minutes or until just cooked, stirring to prevent them sticking to the bottom. Drain and immediately rinse in cold water. Separate the strands gently with your fingers and keep in a little cold water until ready to serve.

Pour 2 litres/3½ pints/9 cups of the fragrant broth into a large saucepan and add the salt, soy, sugar and mirin. Trim the watercress and herbs. Bring the broth to a simmer, add the chicken pieces, spring onions and watercress and heat until they are piping hot.

Meanwhile, bring a kettle of water to the boil. Place the noodles in a sieve over the sink, and pour the hot water from the kettle through them to reheat. Divide the noodles between four large serving bowls.

Ladle the steaming broth over the noodles, sprinkle with the mint and coriander leaves, then the toasted sesame seeds. Serve, handing the rice crackers and pickled ginger separately.

Recipe notes Not only does this tasty recipe give you plenty of softly spiced chicken broth, you also end up with a chicken poached to silky, juicy perfection, with lots leftover for chicken salads and sandwiches.

Do try to spend some time on the broth, its quality naturally affects the flavour of the whole dish. It should be neither over-seasoned nor insipid.

Alternatively, you could start with a regular chicken broth, and add strips of char-grilled chicken or lean beef steak to the final dish.

Cellophane noodle salad with crisp greens and tiger prawns
Serves 4

8 asparagus spears, cut diagonally into 5cm/2in lengths
12 mangetout [snow peas]
12 sugar snap peas
125g/4½oz cellophane noodles
about 30g/1oz/¼ cup sweet, peppery salad leaves, washed and dried
2 tbsp groundnut oil
1 medium carrot, cut in strips
8 raw tiger prawns, peeled and deveined
salt and freshly milled black pepper

For the garnish
1 tbsp toasted sesame seeds
30g/1oz/½ cup coriander [cilantro] leaves, chopped

For the dressing
1 tbsp groundnut oil
1 clove garlic, crushed
15g/½oz fresh ginger, sliced
2 tbsp sherry vinegar
4 tsp balsamic vinegar
1 tsp caster sugar
100ml/3½floz/scant ½ cup soy sauce
5 tbsp sesame oil
3 tbsp olive oil
2 large red chillies, deseeded and finely chopped

To make the dressing, heat the groundnut oil, and stir-fry the garlic and ginger for about 3-4 minutes, over a high heat. Mix the two vinegars, sugar, soy sauce, the two remaining oils and the chilli in a bowl. Tip in the hot garlic and ginger and allow to stand for 3 minutes or more. Skim the oil from the top, and transfer to a large shallow dish.

Bring a large pan of salted water to a boil. Place the asparagus, mangetout and sugar snap peas in a blanching basket and dip them in the boiling water for almost a minute, or until bright green. Plunge into cold water to stop the cooking. Drain and dry the vegetables, then leave them to marinate in the dressing.

Bring a kettle of water to the boil. Place the noodles in a large bowl, and slowly pour the hot water from the kettle over them. Fork through gently and leave to rehydrate for about 4 minutes. Drain in a sieve and refresh under hot running water. Run your fingers through the noodles to smooth and disentangle them. Divide amongst four serving bowls, snipping them with scissors if you prefer, to make them easier to eat.

Begin assembling the salad in layers. Tuck the salad leaves underneath the noodles. Top with the blanched green vegetables and trickle over all but a few tablespoons of the dressing.

Heat a wok, then add the groundnut oil and quickly stir-fry the carrots. Add the tiger prawns and cook until they just begin to turn pink.

Place the carrots and prawns on top of the salad and sprinkle with the remaining dressing. Just before serving, garnish with the toasted sesame seeds and coriander leaves.

Recipe notes A recipe for a special occasion, this noodle salad features a variety of cooking methods, each bringing out the best in the ingredients. The result is unforgettable. If you can add the stir-fried element hot at the last moment, so much the better. Serve as a main course for lunch, or a lavish dinner party starter.

Rice noodles with shiitake mushrooms, tomatoes and quails' eggs
Serves 6

2 red peppers, halved and deseeded
2 yellow peppers, halved and deseeded
a little olive oil, for drizzling
3 tbsp groundnut or sunflower oil
6 small shallots, thinly sliced
5 tbsp Sri's Red Curry Paste (page 167)
225g/8oz shiitake or small chestnut
   mushrooms, sliced or quartered
150g/5oz cherry tomatoes, halved
6 quails' eggs
225g/8oz rice noodles
15g/½oz/¼ cup coriander [cilantro] leaves
salt

Heat the oven to 225°C/430°F/Gas 7½. Place the peppers in a small roasting pan and drizzle some olive oil over and around them. Roast for about 45 minutes, until they are toasted black in places. Remove from the oven, cool for a minute or so, then lift with tongs into a plastic bag. The steam generated in the bag will make the skins slide off easily. Cut each pepper into quarters and set aside.

To prepare the rice noodles, place them in a blanching basket. Bring a large pan of salted water to the boil. Remove the pan from the heat and plunge the basket into the steaming water. Cover with the lid and leave for 2-3 minutes, according to the thickness of the noodles. They should still be fairly firm after rehydration as they are cooked again later.

Drain in a sieve and immediately place under the cold tap. Hold the noodles under the cold running water for 2 minutes or so to stop the cooking. Set aside until required in a bowl with a small amount of water to prevent sticking.

Heat the groundnut or sunflower oil in a wok and stir-fry the shallots for 5 minutes until they are just starting to change colour. Add the red curry paste, stir well, then add the mushrooms and cook, stirring, for about 3 minutes. Gently incorporate the roasted peppers and adjust the seasoning to taste. Cover the wok, remove from the heat and set aside for about 30 minutes.

Meanwhile, in a saucepan fitted with a blanching basket, bring a quantity of water to a boil, and prepare a basin of ice-cold water. Plunge the quails' eggs into the briskly simmering water and time 3 exact minutes. Immediately lift and plunge them into the iced water, where they can remain until you are ready to peel and halve them.

Drain the noodles, then dress with the sauce and vegetables, slithering them about so they are well coated with the sauce. Season with salt again. Pile into a large serving bowl, or divide amongst individual plates, using tongs to scoop up the noodles in equal portions. Garnish with the cherry tomatoes, quails' eggs, and coriander leaves, then serve.

Recipe notes Sri Owen is a teacher of Indonesian and Thai cooking and an important source of my knowledge on these cuisines. On a few memorable occasions I have assisted her with some large parties, once within the Vatican. Sri has an engaging way of measuring her ingredients: a little more or less never seems to make any difference to her excellent results.

All components of this dish can be cooked in advance, and they all reheat beautifully. To prevent the noodles breaking, reheat them separately from the other ingredients.

Place them in a sieve or blanching basket and dip them briefly into boiling water, or pour boiling water from a kettle of boiling water through them, shaking off the excess water afterwards. Microwave or stir-fry (again) the mushrooms, peppers and cherry tomatoes and mix altogether lightly. I have reheated the entire recipe in the microwave for gratifying midweek suppers.

You have to be precise when cooking quails' eggs, because their tiny size means that 15 seconds over- or under-cooking makes a big difference to the result. Use a brisk simmer rather than a full boil, and plunge the cooked eggs into icy water to halt the cooking process as soon as the allotted time is up. This also has the advantage of making the quails' eggs easier to peel.

Use Chinese egg noodles if you prefer, boiling them lightly according to the packet instructions, then drain, rinse and set aside as above.

If you like, you can cook the cherry tomatoes, using my recipe for slow-roast tomatoes with garlic, thyme and basil (page 118), or use similar preserved tomatoes that you have bought from a shop.

Rice and grains

Make popcorn by heating 1cm/½in sunflower oil in a large saucepan until very hot. Scatter in enough dried corn kernels to cover the base and quickly replace the lid. You will soon hear the corn thudding against the lid.
Place two spoonfuls of rolled oats per person in a saucepan and cover with 3-4 times the volume of milk. Place on the stovetop at the lowest possible setting for 15 minutes. Stir and serve with fresh fruit, honey or brown sugar and light cream.
Boil grains of wild rice in a saucepan until they split slightly, then stir into white rice or pilafs at a ratio of 1:8.

Grains, sometimes called cereals after Ceres, the Roman goddess of agriculture, are the edible seeds of grass. They grow everywhere. Ears of wheat can be found nodding at the roadside, in city parks, as well as covering thousands of square miles of Canada, Russia and other countries with giant golden crops. Growing grain for food is far more economical than raising meat. Vast crops of barley, rye, wheat, corn, oats and rice can, like the potato, feed whole nations and their animals handsomely. How sad that many people now think that a cereal is a puffy, popped, flaked, extruded, processed, sugared and packaged breakfast 'meal'. In my view, a wasted eating opportunity.

Grains are simple to cook, and man has been cooking them since around 6000BC. All you have to do is boil them! But there are other exhilarating and simple ways of exploiting these tiny miracles of nature.

In the Northern hemisphere we tend to use our rich dairy products such as butter and milk, and rich meat stocks to add flavour and moisture to grains. Adding water alone makes a sustaining daily porridge ideal for breakfast though in some countries this is eaten three times a day. The Mexicans have made a striking success of preparing their native maize or corn in many imaginative ways, while its use as polenta and mamaliga in Europe, and as pap in Africa, is remarkably different.

The Chinese, Indian and Southeast Asian cultures invite us to cook rice with a fabulous heritage of exotic flavourings. It was the spice traders who brought rice from China to Italy. From there it was taken to Spain and subsequently to South America. Rice is often cultivated in water, with intense labour and terracing in mountainous areas.

It is grown across Asia, Europe and America, each country yielding different types and textures of rice, and typically cooking it in the manner most suited to the rice it produces.

What to look for and what to avoid

• The fresher the grain, and the better the conditions in which it was grown, and the less processing it suffers at the hands of the industrial miller, the better the results when cooking it and the better it is for your health.
• Grains look the same whether they are the new season's crop or four years old, so choose a source of supply you can trust. Use a store with a high turnover, and purchase organic varieties for preference.
• Wholegrain and semi-pearled grains contain a higher proportion of the grain's layer of bran and are therefore higher in nutritious fibre. Once you have acquired a taste for brown or wholegrain rice you are likely to enjoy a gentle addiction to its pleasantly chewy texture and sweet, nutty taste.
• For making risottos, it is essential to use authentic chubby

risotto rices such as arborio, carnaroli and vialone nano in order to achieve the right consistency in the finished dish. When cooked the rice should be creamy but with a firm core.

• The same is true of paella and medium-grain Spanish rices such as bomba and calasparra, which absorb the flavour of their tasty cooking liquid and have a juicy firmness when put in the mouth. Long-grain rices are not an acceptable substitute.

• Making sushi requires a sticky or glutinous rice, often labelled as sushi rice. It is usually grown in the US as the Japanese do not export their home-grown rice.

• Look for jasmine or Thai fragrant rice, a long-grain rice with an enticing aroma that enhances Thai meals. It is slightly sticky, which makes is easy to eat with chopsticks, or at buffets, where I find it paricularly useful. Rising like a graceful white cloud amongst colourful food and bold china, it holds its shape on the serving dish so guests can scoop up a serving easily.

• The deliciously fragrant basmati rice grown in India and Pakistan is one of the world's great grains and ideal not only for serving with curries but for making pilafs and Persian dishes. The grains are fragile and exceptionally quick to cook, making it my favourite of the quick-cooking rices.

• Par-boiled rices, also called easy cook rices, are part-cooked during processing. They are yellowish in colour, but this disappears on cooking. They are just about acceptable as an accompaniment to meals but are not suitable for making pilafs, risottos or paella.

• Instant rice has been completely cooked and dried before packing and requires only a short time in boiling water to rehydrate. Consequently it lacks the flavour and texture of other rices, and should be avoided.

• When buying wild rice, look for clear packs revealing long, black, unbroken grains.

• Whenever possible, check bags of wholegrains for any sign of infestation and avoid packs that seem to have a lot of dust in them.

Storing grains

• Grains and the meals or flours made from them store well in a dry, cool, dark cupboard. It is important to keep them well sealed in airtight plastic storage boxes or jars to prevent infestation from tiny beetles and rodents such as mice.

• Cooked grains and grain pilafs may be kept in a sealed plastic box in the fridge for a few days, though cooked white rice should be eaten as soon as possible.

The principles of cooking grains Our aim in cooking grains is to hydrate and make them tender and plump. After the starch cells gelatinze, making the grain soft, digestible and appetizing, the cells proceed to rupture, turning the grains into a creamy paste.

• To cook rices well it is not possible to follow one rule for all varieties. Look to the instructions on your packet, and in the recipe book. Always match the right type of rice to the dish you are making.

• When boiling wholegrains such as brown rice for salad or serving as a plain accompaniment, do not attempt to use the absorption method. It is best to use a large pan of water and allow the grains to bob about freely.

• Always use a fork to stir grains during cooking, not a spoon.

• To enjoy their textures to the full, grains must be drained thoroughly after boiling. The flavours are often subtle and not at their best when overcooked or waterlogged. Spreading the drained grains out on a tray lined with a clean tea towel will help the moisture evaporate fully. Place the tray in a cool draught for preference. This is also a useful technique if you have inadvertently overcooked rice and need to cool it quickly.

• Many grains benefit from a flavoured cooking water such as a stock, but rice to accompany spicy dishes is generally cooked in plain water.

• Most grains do not need to be routinely soaked or washed, though specific recipes may ask you to do this in order to achieve a certain textural result. Quinoa is an exception and should be thoroughly rinsed before cooking to remove the dusty remnants of its natural bitter coating.

How to tell when grains are cooked
Unless deliberately cooked to a porridge, such as Chinese congee, all grains should be tender after cooking yet retain some firmness of texture. In the case of quinoa, its equatorial band will also uncurl, while wild rice grains split to reveal their pale interior.

Simple boiled rice
Serves 4

225g/8oz/1 heaping cup jasmine,
basmati or other long-grain rice
salt

Bring a large pan of water to the boil. Stir in the rice, making sure no grains stick to the bottom of the pan. Add salt to taste (very little salt, if any, is used in Oriental rice cooking).

Return to the boil, stir briefly again, and cook for 10 minutes or so, until the rice is tender. Test for doneness by biting grains from all parts of the saucepan.

Drain, rinse the rice with hot water, then drain thoroughly and serve.

Recipe notes Jasmine rice will always be slightly sticky, which makes it easy to eat with chopsticks, but when cooked this way, other long-grain rice varieties will remain separate.

When cooking for a different number of people, simply allow 55g/2oz/¼ cup of rice per person.

For extra fragrance, place a few cracked cardamom pods in a muslin bag or spice ball and add to the rice while it's boiling.

To reheat the cooked rice from cold, place it in an ovenproof dish and cover. Lidded foil containers work best as they are thin and conduct heat very quickly. Place in an oven preheated to 180°C/350°F/Gas 4. Allow at least 30 minutes for rice in a covered foil container, and 40 minutes upwards for a porcelain dish – for the first 20 minutes the oven is simply heating the dish. If you have run out of time, and need to heat the rice very quickly, place it in a large sieve and pour the contents of a boiling kettle of water through it.

Basmati pilaf with fresh green herbs
Serves 4-6

225g/8oz/1 heaping cup basmati rice
2 tbsp sunflower oil
1-2 large cloves garlic, crushed
1 medium onion, chopped
15g/½oz/1 tbsp butter
450ml/15floz/scant 2 cups chicken or
vegetable stock, or water
3 tbsp chopped parsley
2 tbsp chopped dill
1 tbsp chopped mint or coriander
[cilantro]
salt and freshly milled white pepper

Place the rice in a sieve and rinse it thoroughly under cold running water. Set aside to drain for a few minutes or up to an hour.

In a shallow pan, ideally one that's 24cm/9½in diameter and 7cm/2¾in deep with a glass lid, heat the oil. Gently fry the onion and garlic for about 5 minutes or until soft. Add the drained rice and the butter and fry until opaque, about 2-3 minutes.

Pour in the cold stock or water, season well (this is the best time to do so) and bring the pan to the boil. Cover, then move the pan to your smallest flame or electric ring, and reduce the heat to a very gentle simmer. Cook for about 8 minutes.

Remove the pan from the heat and allow to stand for 5 minutes, still covered, during which time the rice will develop a few large holes. Use a fork to stir the fresh herbs through the rice, then adjust the seasoning to taste and serve hot or cold.

Recipe notes Roz Denny, my friend and one of Britain's most accomplished rice experts, taught me to cook rice and through her generosity, I have passed on her skills to others. This recipe uses a technique known as 'the absorption method', which has the advantage that no goodness is thrown down the sink with the cooking water. It is also easy and reliable.

You may need to practise to find the perfect low heat on your stovetop for the 8 minutes of simmering. If the rice is at all gritty or undercooked after the full 13-minute cooking period, simply repeat the two cooking processes – the simmering and steaming – adding just a little more liquid for simmering if the rice is dry.

This pilaf makes a perfect late night midweek supper, and is a good accompaniment to Asian and other spicy dishes. The combination of dill, mint and parsley, always eaten together in the Middle East to aid digestion, is optional. Instead, you could include nuts or seeds, or some ready-cooked pulses.

It is a good dish to make in advance of serving. To reheat the pilaf (or to keep it warm), place in a foil-covered dish in a low oven, but stir occasionally with a fork to keep the grains separate. Alternatively, place in a lidded foil container in an oven set to 180°C/350°F/Gas 4 and heat for at least 20 minutes. You could also reheat it gently in a microwave oven, using a few short bursts on the high setting.

Mushroom risotto – simmered, not stirred
Serves 6

about 1.5 litres/2½ pints/8¼ cups
chicken or vegetable stock
2 tbsp olive oil, plus extra for frying
1 small onion, finely diced
225g/8oz chestnut or shiitake
mushrooms, sliced
225g/8oz/1 heaping cup vialone nano,
carnaroli or arborio rice
150ml/5floz/⅔ cup white wine
30g/1oz/¼ stick butter
30g/1oz/¼ cup Parmigiano Reggiano
cheese, grated
about 2 tbsp white truffle oil
salt and freshly milled black pepper

Place the stock in a saucepan and bring to a slow simmer. Keep it steaming until you have finished making the risotto.

Heat 2 tbsp of olive oil in a wide, shallow pan and cook the onion over a low heat for 3-5 minutes or until soft. Meanwhile, in a separate pan, add enough olive oil to give a depth of about 1cm/½in of oil, and allow it to get very hot. Add the mushrooms and stir-fry for a minute or so, until the mushrooms are plump and juicy. Remove from the heat and drain in a sieve. Season well and set aside.

Back in the other pan, add the rice to the onion. Raise the heat and lightly toast the rice, stirring to ensure it is well coated with the oil. The rice will gradually become opaque.

Turn the heat up to medium and add 150ml/5floz/⅔ cup of the hot stock, stirring well with a wooden spoon. Poke all the grains under the liquid and leave it to cook. When the liquid has been absorbed, raise the heat a fraction, then add another 150ml/5floz/⅔ cup of the stock,

stirring well. Again, tuck all the grains beneath the surface of the liquid, adjust the heat to a slow simmer, and leave it to cook.

Continue this process until most of the stock is absorbed, and the rice is tender – about 20 minutes. When you notice a light cream appearing on the base of the pan as you stir it, just after absorbing a measure of stock, the risotto will be nearly cooked. The rice grains should be tender all the way through, not chalky or gritty, but not soft and mealy either.

Quickly add the drained mushrooms and season to taste. Remove the pan from the heat, and pour in the wine to halt the cooking. Vigorously stir in the butter and cheese, then trickle in a little truffle oil to taste. Check one last time for seasoning. If desired, add 3-4 tbsp of the remaining stock, or some water, to give a soupy texture and serve immediately.

Recipe notes It is not true you have to stir a risotto all the time. A chef from Gaultieri Marchesi restaurant showed me this method of simmering risotto so you don't have to stir it constantly.

For a deep flavour of wild mushrooms, soak a good brand of dried porcini (10g/⅓oz will do) in enough hot water to cover for 30 minutes, then strain through a fine-meshed sieve. Finely chop a few and add to the risotto when you fry the rice; add the remainder, sliced, at the end of cooking. The soaking water can be added to the stock.

As you are using the powerfully pungent truffle oil, it won't matter if the vegetable stock you use here is made from a reliable powder.

Wild rice blinis
Makes 10

125g/4oz/scant ¼ cup wild rice
175g/6oz/1 heaping cup plain [all-
purpose] flour
175g/6oz/1 heaping cup wholemeal flour
475ml/18floz/2¼ cups buttermilk
3 eggs, beaten
½ tsp salt
1 tsp baking powder
30g/1oz/¼ stick butter, melted
1 tsp bicarbonate of soda
1 tbsp hot water
groundnut or sunflower oil, for frying

Soak the wild rice in water for several hours or overnight. Meanwhile, in an electric mixer, mix the two flours and buttermilk together until smooth. Cover the bowl and keep in a cool spot for 8 hours to begin fermentation.

Boil the wild rice according to the pack instructions, or until it bulges and splits to show an oyster-coloured centre. Drain, rinse under cold running water and drain again. Place in a food processor, pulse to break it up a bit, then set aside.

Return the batter to the mixer and beat in the eggs, salt, baking powder and melted butter. In a jug, combine the bicarbonate of soda and hot water, then beat the mixture into the batter, followed by the wild rice.

When ready to cook, test the consistency of the batter. It should pour easily. Adjust as necessary with a little extra water.

Heat a large, round, non-stick pan and grease it lightly with a little oil. Have a ladle or spoon to hand that will give you the same amount of batter each time. The first blini is always your tester. Pour in just enough batter to cover the base of the pan, swirling it around to cover thickly and evenly. Quickly tip out any excess, then swirl again until the base is even and flat. Cook the blini until firm on one side (this will be its best-looking side), then flip it over and cook briefly on the other.

Stack the cooked blinis on a wire rack, with a square of parchment paper between each one, while you make the remainder. Pour off the burned oil in the pan from time to time and replace it with fresh.

Recipe notes Here wild rice gives the nutty flavour and colour traditionally supplied by rye flour in yeasted blinis. I think this recipe, given to me by Roz Denny, is an easier version, even though you need to start making the batter at least a day in advance of serving the blinis.

Watch the heat of the base of the pan. It must be hot enough to 'grip' the batter as soon as you swirl it into the pan, and you must tilt the pan to allow the batter to run right to the edges. When ready to flip, the blini should have large bubbles starting to appear and a dark rim.

If desired, you can use a cookie cutter to cut out tiny canapé bases from the large blinis. This is much quicker and less of a fiddle than making individual baby blinis. This mixture will give about 100 canape bases using a 3.5cm/1¼in round cookie cutter; if there is any surplus to requirements you can freeze the remainder for another time. The cooked blinis will also keep perfectly overnight, stored in a plastic box in a cool place. In both cases, interleave the blinis with parchment paper.

To serve as canapés, top with crème fraîche from the end of a teaspoon, a twist of smoked fish, a little caviar and a dusting of chives.

Millet cakes with chorizo, black olives and chilli
Serves 4

For the cakes
200g/7oz/1 cup millet
45g/1½oz/3 tbsp butter
5 tbsp creamy milk
3 eggs
salt and freshly ground black pepper

For the topping
3 tbsp extra virgin olive oil, or Thyme, Shallot and Garlic Aromatic Oil (page 166)
16 slices chorizo
3 spring onions [scallions], chopped
1 large red chilli, deseeded and sliced
16 small black olives, pitted
4 tbsp chopped flat leaf parsley

You will aso need
4 x 12cm/4½ inch diameter ovenproof frying pans

Place the millet in a fairly large saucepan with 450ml/15floz/2 cups of water and a pinch of salt. Bring to a boil, skim, then reduce the heat right down and cook for 20 minutes, until the water is absorbed. Remove the pan from the heat and leave to stand, still covered, for 10 minutes.

When you open the lid, you will find that some millet has stuck to the bottom, but don't worry about it, and don't try to scrape it off. Fork the butter into the millet, melting it into the hot grain so that the mixture becomes thick and gluey.

Warm the milk gently in a small pan. Briefly whisk the eggs in a small mixing bowl. Pour the eggs and milk into the millet, add some salt and ground pepper, and stir until creamy.

Heat the oven to 240°C/475°F/Gas 9. Heat the small frying pans on the stovetop, then add the oil and allow that to heat too. Divide the batter equally between the pans. Cook for about 3 minutes, until the edges firm up slightly. Transfer to the oven for about 5 minutes, placing the pans on a baking tray to prevent you burning your fingers. They are done when the sides of the cakes are brown and have shrunk slightly from the sides of the pan, and the tops are firmish.

Meanwhile, in a separate frying pan, heat the olive oil and gently fry the chorizo, spring onions and chilli for a few moments until softened. Add the olives and allow to warm through, then mix in the parsley. Serve on top of the hot millet cakes.

Recipe notes These millet cakes are clean-tasting, warming and satisfying as only grain recipes can be. They are simple to make and the mild sweetness of the millet is a perfect foil to the salty, spirited taste of the chorizo.

The cakes are from Jenni Muir's wonderful book, *A Cook's Guide to Grains*, where the idea is attributed to a chef named Didier Virot. They are ideal for people who believe, like my father, that small grains such as millet and linseed are only for birds.

If you do not have non-stick pans, you will need 1 tbsp sunflower oil to cook these cakes. Alternatively you could line your little pans with discs of Bake-O-Glide to prevent sticking.

Quinoa salad with grapes, celery and roasted cashews
Serves 4

125g/4½oz/⅔ cup quinoa
4 tbsp raspberry or apple cider vinegar
2 tbsp mirin
½ tsp salt
4 tsp chopped dill, rocket [arugula] or
*   mint leaves*
2 stalks celery, finely sliced diagonally
200g/7oz seedless red grapes, halved
110g/4oz/1 cup cashews, toasted and
*   roughly chopped*

To cook the quinoa, add the grains to plenty of boiling salted water, then boil rapidly until a tiny white thread appears around each grain, and the quinoa swells, becoming tender and juicy. Drain immediately in a sieve.

Fork out the cooked grains onto a baking tray in a shallow layer, and set aside to dry out thoroughly.

In a large bowl, combine all the remaining ingredients, mixing them in one at a time in the order listed above. Allow to stand for 1 hour or more to let the flavours mingle.

Recipe notes Quinoa is a tiny grain native to the Andes and packed with protein. Stripped during processing of its bitter coating (which in the field protects it from birds), quinoa is delicious, with a seductive texture and pearlescent appearance.

Serve this healthy dish chilled or at room temperature, as a starter, or a salad. For some reason it seems particularly good if you have over-indulged the day before.

To serve quinoa on its own, as a hot accompaniment to a meal, follow the cooking instructions above, then reheat it in the microwave, where it will become even plumper and juicier.

Sweet vegetable and quinoa pilaf
Serves 6-8

175g/6oz/heaping ¼ cup quinoa
1 shallot, finely chopped
1 stick celery, chopped
1 carrot, chopped
1 small fennel bulb, chopped
1 tbsp butter
salt and freshly milled black pepper

Rinse the quinoa a couple of times in a bowl of water until the water runs clear then drain in a sieve.

Heat the butter in a saucepan and gently fry the vegetables for about 10 minutes or until they are sweet but not coloured. Add the quinoa and cook, stirring, for about 2 minutes.

Add 350ml/12floz/1½ cups of water and some seasoning. Bring to the boil, cover and cook over a moderate heat for about 25 minutes. If the liquid has not all been absorbed by the time you remove the lid, stir the pilaf over a moderate heat for 5 minutes until the grain is shining, plump and pearlescent.

Recipe notes I recommend serving this gently flavoured pilaf with oily fish such as mackerel, salmon and tuna for a nourishing midweek meal.

As quinoa reheats so well in the microwave, it is a good idea to make more than you think is required for dinner, and have some leftover for lunch the next day.

Roast buckwheat pilaf
Serves 4

55g/2oz/4 tbsp duck fat
200g/7oz/1 cup kasha (pre-toasted)
*   buckwheat*
500ml/18floz/2¼ cups vegetable stock
a large pinch of salt

Heat the oven to 180°C/375°F/Gas 5. In an ovenproof pan, heat the duck fat, then add the buckwheat. Toast, stirring constantly, until the grains absorb the fat and begin to brown.

Meanwhile, in a separate pan, bring the vegetable stock to a boil and add the salt. Pour the liquid over the buckwheat – standing well back as the mixture of liquid and hot fat splutters. Cook over a low heat until the buckwheat begins to absorb the water, then cover the pan and place in the hot oven for 20-25 minutes, until the grain is dry and fluffy. Fork through before serving.

Recipe notes This recipe was given to me by my friend Ian Wisniewski, who introduced me to a fascinating book *Old Polish Traditions in the Kitchen and at the Table*.

Kasha is a term used in Poland for all groats and grains. Poles prefer the robust flavour of buckwheat, which they cooked instead of rice, with meat.

I like buckwheat cooked this way and served with steamed white fish fillets and the white wine and dill sauce (page 170), made pale green by the inclusion of plenty of fresh dill. It is also good with pan-roast salmon.

If you have no duck or goose fat, you can use lard or oil instead.

Potatoes

Nothing is simpler than cooking a potato. While you read this, place a large potato straight on the oven shelf, in the middle of an oven set to 220°C/425°F/Gas 7. Cook it for 1¼ hours. Now you have a baked potato with a soft, floury, comforting interior, and a delicious outer crust. Holding the hot potato in a cloth, cut in half lengthways, and across, about 2cm/¾in deep into the potato flesh. Then gently squeeze the base towards the middle. Up surge the crumbly nuggets of glistening potato, ready to be dressed with a nut of salted butter, a dollop of crème fraîche, or a large spoonful of thick yogurt.

Fast ways with potatoes

Microwave medium to large unpeeled potatoes on full power until tender. Crush lightly with a spoon, season and scatter with chopped soft herbs. Serve plain or dress with mayonnaise, yogurt, soured cream or hot melted butter.

Boil small new potatoes. When cold, scoop out some of the centre. Fill with a little sour cream and top with the best caviar you can afford.

Scrub rather than peel little potatoes such as Jersey Royals, so that they are tasty and nutritious. Dress with a wholegrain mustard vinaigrette, or herby mayonnaise thinned with a little warm water.

Boil small to medium potatoes such as Jersey Royals, Charlotte and fingerlings and serve with melted butter and chives or parsley scattered over.

Drain and rinse a can of pulses or sweetcorn and mix with a bottled sauce for a speedy baked potato filling.

A harvested potato is a well-wrapped package designed by nature – full of nutrients and with a good shelf life. It is an enlarged part of the stem of the potato plant, a tuber whose role it is to produce many new plants. These are first seen as dimples in the skin, later as little buds with plump sprouting stems.

The main constituents of a potato are water and starch and in a young new potato there is more water and less starch. In older, large potatoes there is more starch and less water. This is really all you need to know to cook potatoes successfully. The ratio of starch to water gives different results when cooked.

What to look for, what to avoid

• Now that superstores are able to store vegetables successfully for months, and produce potatoes of different sizes and varieties year-round, it is easy to buy by size and type for specific uses. You only need to remember a few names. The most important thing is the potatoes' size.
• If they are large, about 225g/8oz or 15cm/6in long, they will be old potatoes and contain less water. Use them for roast, mash, chips and gratins.
• If the potatoes are very small, use them for boiling, steaming and salad dishes.
• If they are in between, about 7.5cm/3in diameter, use them for ultra-fast 'crushed' potatoes.

Storing potatoes

• If potatoes come in earth, keep them that way. It protects them from bruising and developing black patches in the flesh.
• Store in a cool dark place at 7-10°C/44-50°F with air cirulating.
• Never keep them in polythene, which makes them sprout and sometimes sweat.
• Never put them in the fridge below 5°C/41°F as some of the starch will be converted to sugar. Too much sugar in a fried potato results in dark, streaky chips with a bitter taste.
• Do not store potatoes in the light or they will turn green and the solanine, present in small amounts in all potatoes, will increase to toxic levels. This is particularly dangerous to pregnant women.
• Properly stored potatoes keep for months. If you find them sprouting a little, rub off the buds then peel and cook as normal.

Preparing potatoes A potato peeler with a swivel blade is important to keep the potato looking smooth, round and in the case of Jersey Royals and Charlottes, kidney-shaped. Chunky edges on little peeled potatoes are usually caused by the wrong sort of peeler. Some people swear by the non-swivel kind. I always keep both with me at all times, so that I can gratefully accept offers of help when peeling potatoes.

If you find bruising (black patches) on the potatoes, winkle them out with the tapered end of the peeler. Leaving little holes is fine if you are puréeing them. If serving them whole, perhaps roasted or boiled, shave away at the black spots with the peeler so that the potatoes are smooth and retain their pretty, even shape.

Nutrients are often lost unwittingly by peeling and then cutting potatoes into small pieces (exposing lots of the surface area) followed by soaking and then cooking in plenty of water.

Place the peeled potatoes in water while you check them over, or they will go grey from contact with the air. Rinse and drain them quickly, then store them closely wrapped in a dry, clean tea towel, where they will keep for up to 2 hours.

The principles of cooking potatoes

• In most cases it is important to ensure that all the potatoes or pieces of potato being cooked are of even size, so that they are tender at the same time.
• Chips demand accuracy. It is difficult to cook big chips outside a restaurant as they frequently become sodden with fat. Old Maris Pipers, about 15cm/6in in length, are best. Make sure the fat or oil covers the raw chips by 7-8cm/about 3in, and that the fat and chips together are only one-third to half the capacity of the saucepan, otherwise it will boil over. Place the chips in a blanching basket and test one – if it bubbles vigorously in the oil, the oil is hot enough. Quickly plunge in the chips and fry for 7-10 minutes until they are golden and soft in the centre. Watch them. Remove them from the fat as soon as they stop bubbling and spread them out on a tray lined with crumpled kitchen paper to drain.
• I find it easier to make small fine game chips or straw potatoes at home, rather than big chips. They are lighter on the waistline, easy and quick to do successfully without a custom-built deep-fat fryer. Small ones can also be kept hot successfully in a low oven until ready to serve.
• Any large old potatoes can be used for baking but the fluffy ones are best, especially King Edward, Maris Piper and Idahos.
• Traditional roast potatoes are best made from large old Maris Pipers and King Edwards. They should be peeled, quartered, placed in cold water and brought to the boil for 10 minutes before draining. Then you can either scrape the outside of the potatoes with a fork, or roll them a few at a time in a large sieve. This helps them to pick up the fat while roasting, making them crunchy.
• Mash requires large old floury potatoes that do no collapse on boiling. Maris Pipers and Desirées are ideal, but not King Edwards. Cut the potatoes in even slices and simmer them gently. Be careful not to overcook the potatoes or they will disintegrate and result in a gummy mash. Do not try to mash potatoes in a food processor, as this will make them sticky too.
• For gratins you want Maris Piper, mature Jersey Royals or any large waxy yellow potato. Always use large ones to cut down on peeling. Don't soak the potato slices in water, as the starch will flow away. This prevents the gratin from setting as you cook it, and you want it to set so that you can serve it elegantly from the gratin dish.

How to tell when potatoes are cooked

When potatoes are raw they have an appley texture – the French still call them *pommes de terre* (apples of the earth).

To test if potatoes are cooked, pierce them in the centre with a skewer. If the centre is soft and unyielding, they are cooked. If it feels crisp, it is not. A boiled little potato should drop from the skewer as you try to lift it. Never serve potatoes al dente.

The texture of cooked potato differs according to the variety. Waxy and yellow varieties such as Charlotte, Jersey Royals, Pink Fir, La Ratte, Belle de Fontenay and fingerlings will be firm, yellowish, creamy and waxy rather than crumbly when you cut into them. Large old starchy potatoes such as Maris Piper, Desirée and Idaho should be mealy, soft and fluffy once cooked, perfect for mash, chips and baking.

Velvet mash
Serves 4-6

800g/1lb 12oz old boiling potatoes,
*   peeled and quartered*
60g/2oz/½ stick butter
about 200ml/7floz/¼ cup milk
15g/½oz/5 tbsp chives, finely cut
salt and freshly milled black pepper

Place the potatoes in a saucepan and cover with water. Season with salt, bring to the boil and boil gently until the potatoes are very soft and squash easily when pressed with the back of a spoon against the side of the pan.

Drain off all the water, then return the potatoes to the pan and place on the stovetop over a gentle heat to steam them dry, shaking the pan to prevent sticking. Put the potatoes through a vegetable mill (mouli-legumes) set over a mixing bowl.

Heat the butter and milk in a small saucepan until boiling. Whisk this mixture into the potato until it is creamy and frothy, then season to taste. Either serve immediately, or keep warm in a low oven, in a serving dish, covered by a film of milk. Scatter with the chives just before serving.

Recipe notes It is important to use a floury potato for this recipe. The several other keys to perfect fluffy mash are contained in the method given here. For best results, you must steam dry the potatoes, mill them, and ensure you whisk hot, buttery milk onto hot potatoes. Do not allow the potatoes to cool until you have finished the recipe, and be sure to cover the surface with a thin layer of milk to prevent the mash crusting while it waits to go to the table.

Mash can be successfully reheated in a microwave oven or double-boiler.

Olive oil mash
Serves 4-6

150ml/5floz/²⁄₃ cup creamy milk
2 cloves garlic, peeled and crushed
2 sprigs of rosemary
2 sprigs of thyme
800g/1lb 12oz old boiling potatoes,
*   peeled and quartered*
225ml/8floz/1 cup extra virgin olive oil
salt and freshly milled black pepper

In a small saucepan, heat the milk with the garlic, rosemary and thyme. Remove from the heat, cover and set aside to infuse.

Meanwhile, place the potatoes in a saucepan and cover with water. Season with salt, bring to the boil and boil gently until the potatoes are very soft and squash easily when pressed with the back of a spoon against the side of the pan.

Drain off all the water, then return the potatoes to the pan and place on the stovetop over a low heat to steam them dry, shaking the pan to prevent sticking. Put the potatoes through a vegetable mill (mouli-legumes) into the bowl of an electric mixer.

Strain the flavoured milk, then return it to the saucepan and reheat, adding the olive oil.

Fit the mixer with a mixing blade. Switch it on to slow speed and add the hot liquid in a steady stream. When all the liquid has been added, and the mash is glossy, adjust the seasoning to taste and keep warm in a low oven until ready to serve.

Recipe notes If you do not have an electric mixer, beat the potatoes vigorously with a spatula.

Never try to mix or purée potatoes in a food processor or blender – the result will be gummy and sticky.

Pommes au diable
Serves 4

2 cloves garlic, halved
2 shallots, peeled
900g/2lb small waxy potatoes, unpeeled
1-3 bay leaves

Heat the oven to 220°C/425°F/Gas 7. Rub the inside of an earthenware crock with the cut surface of the garlic. Arrange the potatoes inside the crock, nestling the shallots and bay leaves amongst them.

Cover and place in the oven for about 1½ hours, or until the potatoes are tender. The exact length of the cooking time will depend on the size of the potatoes.

Recipe notes A diable is an earthenware crock, usually with a handle on one side. With one of these, you can say farewell to potato preparation forever because you simply place the ingredients in the diable, close it, and bake. Never wash the diable, as the charred interior gives the potatoes a wonderful baked, earthy flavour. Simply rub the inside clean after use.

You can also cook this dish on the stovetop, over a low heat, using a metal heat diffuser if possible. Serve the potatoes with roasts and grills.

New potatoes with mint and chives
Serves 4-6

900g/2lb small new potatoes
4 sprigs mint
2-3 tbsp Basic Vinaigrette Dressing
   (page 162)
3 tbsp mint, chopped
2 tbsp parsley, chopped
2 tbsp chives, finely cut
4 small spring onions [scallions], very
   finely chopped
sea salt flakes and freshly milled black
   pepper

Wash and scrub the potatoes, but do not peel. Place in a pan with a pinch of salt and the mint sprigs, then pour in enough water to come only half way up the potatoes. Cover with a tight-fitting lid and simmer the potatoes for 20-25 minutes, or until very tender, being careful not to overcook. To test, insert the point of a small knife in the potatoes – they should offer no resistance and should fall off the knife when lifted.

Drain the potatoes in a colander, then place in a bowl. While the potatoes are still warm, pour over the vinaigrette dressing, season with salt and pepper and mix thoroughly. Set aside until the potatoes have cooled, then mix in the chopped herbs and spring onions, taste and season again if required. The salad will increase in flavour as it stands. Do not put it in the fridge.

Recipe notes This essential recipe will take you right through the summer. It can be served hot or cold. I think a hot potato salad always livens up a party table of cold food. Add the herbs just before serving so they do not discolour.

Choose Jersey Royals, Charlotte, La Ratte, Belle de Fontenay or fingerling potatoes for this recipe. Keep them in a cool spot, but never in the fridge as the starch changes to sugar, and they never cook the same afterwards. Don't scrape little new potatoes because a lot of the flavour lies in the skins. Never put potatoes in cold water after cooking as it affects their texture and flavour.

You can use creamy vinaigrette (page 162), if desired. In this case, wait until the potatoes have cooled a little before adding it, otherwise the egg in the dressing might set.

Worth noting too: new potatoes reheat beautifully in the microwave.

Roasted rosemary potatoes
Serves 4-6

670g/1lb 9oz very small potatoes
1-2 tbsp fresh rosemary leaves, very
   finely chopped
3-4 tbsp extra virgin olive oil
salt and freshly milled pepper

Heat the oven to 230°C/450°F/Gas 8. Peel the potatoes and, if they are larger than 5cm/2in across or deep, cut them into quarters. Rinse well, then drain, dry and wrap them up in a terry cloth towel – they must be perfectly dry to get crisp. Keep them in the towel until ready to roast.

On a heavy baking tray, combine the potatoes, rosemary and oil and use your fingers to turn the potatoes so they are evenly coated with both rosemary and oil. Spread the potatoes out in a single layer.

Place the baking sheet in the oven and roast for about 30 minutes, until the potatoes are golden brown and tender when tested with a fork. Once the potatoes start to brown, shake the baking sheet from time to time so that they colour on all sides.

When the potatoes are completely soft inside when pierced with a skewer and have lost their appley texture, drain in a sieve. They will rustle if cooked and crisp.

Line a tray with paper towel and tip the potatoes onto it. Season with salt and a little pepper and serve immediately in a hot serving dish.

Recipe notes This is a wonderfully reliable recipe. Just slip the potatoes into the oven 35 minutes before you want to serve them.

Choose a variety such as Jersey Royals, Charlotte, La Ratte or fingerling. Be sure the potatoes are rinsed and completely dry before cooking, and do not salt them until they have finished cooking. Salting only encourages them to give up their liquid, making them limp and pale during the cooking process. Resist the urge to turn the potatoes too often, allow them to brown first.

Roast potatoes cannot be kept warm. If they have to wait, pour off the oil, and gradually decrease the heat of the oven. However, the raw peeled potatoes can wait in the thick towel for several hours before cooking.

Roast potatoes go best with roasts and grills.

Gratin dauphinois
Serves 6-8

*500g/1lb red potatoes, peeled and sliced
    3mm/⅛in thick
1 clove garlic, halved (optional)
280ml/10floz/1¼ cups double [heavy] or
    whipping cream
about 100g/3½oz/scant 1 cup gruyère or
    emmental cheese, finely grated
softened butter, for greasing
salt and freshly milled white pepper*

Heat the oven to 150ºC/300Fº/Gas 2. Butter a gratin dish lavishly and rub with the cut surface of the garlic if you wish. Quickly rinse and dry the potatoes; do not soak them in cold water. Arrange the potatoes in even layers in the gratin dish, seasoning as you go with salt and pepper.

Pour the cream over the potatoes and sprinkle with the cheese. Place the dish on a baking tray and bake for about 1½ hours. The potatoes are done when a fine skewer inserted in the centre meets no resistance.

If necessary, shortly before serving, flash the gratin under a hot grill, or turn the oven up to high, to give the top a golden crust. Let the dish stand for a few minutes before serving.

Recipe notes If dishes had a temperament, this would be one of the sweetest. Quickly assembled, the gratin is slipped into a slow oven, where it bubbles gently without any attention. If you cover the surface completely with cheese, it can be prepared a few hours ahead, and kept in the fridge or a cool place.

To make a fennel dauphinois, steam 1-2 small bulbs of thinly sliced fennel until softened. Drain and dry the fennel well, then layer it with the potato and proceed as above.

Candied sweet potatoes
Serves 6

*6 sweet potatoes
2 tsp salt
75g/2½oz/8 tbsp brown sugar, or
    160ml/5½floz/⅔ cup maple syrup
a little softened butter
salt*

Heat the oven to 190ºC/375ºF/Gas 5. Butter a baking dish or roasting tray measuring 23x35cm/9x14in, or line it with a sheet of Bake-o-Glide or a Teflon-liner and dab that with butter.

In a large saucepan, boil the whole unpeeled potatoes in plenty of salted water until tender. Drain and set aside until cool enough to handle. Peel and cut lengthways into slices not less than 1cm/½in thick. Alternatively, if they are not too large, cut them into quarters.

Arrange the sweet potatoes in the baking dish. Sprinkle with the brown sugar or drizzle with maple syrup. Dot with butter and add a touch of salt. Place them at the top of the oven and bake for 30 minutes, or until nicely glazed and lightly browned.

Recipe notes This recipe works best with the readily available orange-fleshed sweet potatoes that are longish and pointed.

The dish can be made in advance and reheated. Serve it with roasts, especially of chicken and turkey, or jambonettes of duck (page 86).

Hot potato cakes with smoked salmon, sour cream and caviar
Serves 4

1 large old floury potato, about
340g/12oz, peeled and quartered
2 eggs
30g/1oz/4 tbsp self-raising flour
5 tbsp whole milk
5 tbsp double [heavy] cream

To serve
150ml/5floz/⅔ cup thick, solid soured
cream or crème fraîche
200g/7oz smoked salmon or smoked
trout slices
50g/1¼oz salmon eggs or caviar
4 heaped tbsp finely cut chives
a little sunflower or groundnut oil

You will also need
4 x 12cm/4½inch diameter frying pans,
preferably non-stick

If your pans are not non-stick, line them with discs of Bake-O-Glide or Teflon, and then rub them with oil.

Heat the oven to 240°C/475°F/ Gas 9. Cook the potato in boiling, salted water until just tender. Drain and return to the cleaned out pan to steam dry, shaking the pan over a medium heat to prevent it sticking. Put the potato through a vegetable mill (mouli-legumes) into a medium bowl and set aside to cool.

Whisk the eggs in a small jug, then use an electric beater to whisk them and the flour into the potato. In a small saucepan, heat the milk and cream together until they are just below boiling point, then whisk the hot milk into the potato mixture.

Heat the four small pans on the stovetop. Ladle equal quantities of the mixture into each and cook over a moderate heat for 1-2 minutes to

give the cakes a golden, toasted base. Transfer to the hot oven shelf and bake for about 10 minutes or until the potato cakes are softly firm.

Turn the cooked potato cakes out onto hot serving plates. Top with the soured cream or crème fraîche, a twisted furl of smoked fish, and the salmon eggs. Scatter with the finely cut chives and serve immediately.

Recipe notes Serve this as a hot starter before a special winter dinner party, or for lunch or brunch with a good mix of spicy, peppery and sweet salad leaves. At brunch, top it with slow-roast tomatoes (page 118) and fried speck or bacon, or with poached eggs and chives, and hollandaise sauce (page 168) if desired.

The batter can be prepared a couple of hours in advance, but the potato cakes are much fluffier if cooked immediately. Alternatively, bake the cakes in advance, and just before serving cover with a sheet of foil and reheat them in the oven, at the same temperature, for about 5 minutes. The milled potato will keep in the fridge for about 24 hours.

It is actually important to make the twisted furls of smoked salmon in advance. Keep them in the fridge, loosely covered with plastic wrap. Use a fish slice or spatula to lift them into place on top of the potato cakes. The hotter the potato cake and the colder the cream, salmon and caviar, the more delicious they are to eat.

Bacon and potato cake layered with cheese
Serves 8

50g/1¼oz/4 tbsp unsalted butter,
softened
400g/14oz smoked or unsmoked bacon
rashers [slices], middle cut or streaky
1.2kg/2lb 8oz potatoes, peeled and
sliced into discs about 3mm/⅛in thick
100g/3½oz/scant 1 cup gruyère cheese,
grated
freshly ground black pepper

You will also need
an ovenproof frying pan, 24cm/9½in
diameter, with a lid

Heat the oven to 220°C/425°F/Gas 7. Brush the frying pan thickly using some of the softened butter. Cover the bottom and sides of the pan with the bacon, so that the rashers overlap the sides of the pan.

Place a thick layer of sliced potato in the base and season with pepper. Add a layer of cheese, then another of potatoes and season again. Dot the potato cake with the remaining butter, then fold the hanging flaps of bacon up over the potatoes and cover with the remaining rashers.

Cover the potato cake with a sheet of foil, then the lid, and bake until the potatoes are tender, about 1½ hours.

Remove the pan from the oven and press down on the cake with a slotted spoon. Allow to cool for 15 minutes. Using a round-bladed knife, loosen the bacon from the sides of the pan, then turn the cake out onto a plate. Cut into portions with a serrated knife.

Recipe notes Inspired by a Joël Robuchon technique, this is good with roast beef, as a winter's lunch with a large salad, or at a barbecue.

Sauces, dressings and marinades

Trickle fine olive oil or balsamic vinegar on a grill, roast or salad.
Make a large batch of creamy vinaigrette or white wine sauce and blend small quantities with a different herb to give a different sauce.
Deglaze a pan with water after frying a steak for an instant gravy.
Pound basil, garlic and salt in a mortar, then add lemon juice, olive oil and black pepper and use the mixture to marinate lamb, pork, beef or white fish.
Marinate vegetables and sea bass in a mixture of extra virgin olive oil, lemon juice, finely sliced garlic and fennel seeds before char-grilling.

A sauce has the miraculous ability to change something simple into something special. Just think of the unpretentious poached egg when sitting beneath an elegant swathe of hollandaise sauce. Sauces provide an essential liquid, juicy element to a meal, and come to the rescue if something tastes a bit dry. They can also bring another layer of taste to a dish, such as in a delicious, carefully made gravy sauce, which features not just a meaty notes but herby fragrance and flavours.

Colour, texture and shine are important to most things prepared in the kitchen, but never so much as when making sauces. A sauce is not an extra, it is often the first thing we see and taste. A luxurious cut of meat is easily ruined by a badly made sauce: puckeringly sour with red wine, oversalted, indifferently coloured, or thin and watery.

As a self-taught cook, I produced all of these before I was allowed through the hallowed portals of some of the finest kitchens in the world, where I had the opportunity to learn where I was going wrong. When you have cooked a sauce successfully, as I hope you will do from the guidance in this book, you will find you are able to enhance an inexpensive chicken or pasta dish immeasurably and with ease.

It is important to use the best ingredients for sauce making, and shopping for them allows us to visit a variety of exotic shops. I would never think of buying my garam masala, onion seeds, spices and spice pastes from anywhere but an Indian shop, and I use Southeast Asian and Chinese retailers for ingredients such as nam-pla (fish sauce) and sesame seeds. Japanese ingredients are sold not only in specialist Japanese and Chinese stores but also in many delis, food halls and supermarkets. It is now quite easy to find tamari, the rich tasting wheat-free soy sauce, as well as mirin, rice vinegar, and wasabi.

What to look for, what to avoid

• Nowhere is it more important to choose fine ingredients than in a salad dressing. There are so few that every single one makes an impact. Using only a few drops of top-quality oil or vinegar each time will soothe any feelings of extravagance you may have had regarding their price.
• Search out estate-bottled olive oils from wine merchants as well as specialist independents and online suppliers. Read the label carefully – much of the 'Italian bottled' olive oil on sale actually comes from Spain.
• Experiment with various oils to find one you enjoy. Olive oils from Greece, Italy, Spain and France will each have different characteristics and it is good to get to know them if you like cooking food from these countries.
• Avoid oils infused with ingredients such as lemon or basil. These flavourings are often synthetic and taste disappointing.
• Avoid cheap vinegars in favour of a small but powerful range including aged balsamic vinegar

from Modena, PX quality Spanish sherry vinegar, and good quality rice and wine vinegars with clear colours and mellow flavours.

• Make sure you have fine, granulated sea salt, plus a packet of salt flakes or crystals on hand for making sauces and dressings.

• Purchase black and white peppercorns and keep separate mills for each. They have slightly different flavours, the black being more aromatic, and flecks of ground black pepper can look unattractive in some sauces.

• Butter should be unsalted, made from the finest quality cows' milk, and ideally produced in France, where sauces such as hollandaise were invented. The French ferment the milk to increase its flavour, and its nutty, delectable taste is part of the charm of a rich sauce.

• When buying ready-made sauces, avoid those with labels listing lots of E-numbers, gums and stabilizers, which give the sauce a nasty gloopy consistency.

• Decent ready-made pasta sauces can be purchased in specialist Italian delicatessens, but choose those made from a minimum of ingredients.

• It is not a good idea to buy commercially-produced salsas.

• Hollandaise sauce cannot be chilled successfully, and cannot be sold in a jar or packet.

Storing and freezing

• Salsas and sauces made with brightly coloured fruit and vegetables should not be stored. Their whole *raison d'être* is their exhilarating freshness.

• Vinaigrette and other olive oil based sauces and dressings keep exceptionally well, though the flavour of the extra virgin oil will gradually dissipate.

• Egg dressings will keep for up to a week in the fridge, stored in a clean, sealed jar.

• Cooked egg sauces such as hollandaise should not be stored in the fridge, or frozen.

• Rich cream sauces freeze well. Defrost them overnight in the fridge, and blitz them with a stick blender to remove any graininess.

• Flavored butters are ideal for freezer storage and very handy to have on hand. Keep them frozen for up to six months.

• Clear gravy sauces freeze perfectly. Make a large batch and keep them in the freezer in convenient portions. Heat them quickly and chill them quickly to prevent the growth of bacteria. Defrost in the microwave if you are in a hurry. Try not to throw an ice-block of sauce into a hot pan, as it will spoil the flavour.

• Asian sauces, like their ingredients seem to keep almost indefinitely. Keep sauces in the fridge and curry pastes in the freezer for up to six months.

• Fresh herb sauces such as basil pesto store well in the fridge providing the top is completely covered with a film of oil. Stir the oil into the paste before use, then seal the remainder with more oil and return to the fridge.

How to tell when a sauce is done A
sauce is ready when it is the correct consistency. Most should coat the back of a spoon, be viscous or, in the case of a salsa, should hold its shape on a spoon. The taste should be strong and clear. Many sauces need to be glossy and shining, some should be limpid and transparent as well. In some cases the right consistency is achieved through reduction by boiling, and/or thickening:

• Reduction by boiling should thicken a clear gravy. However, this can be helped by a little starch such as cornflour [cornstarch] or arrowroot. The latter gives a more transparent, lighter thickening. Combine equal quantities of the starch with water and stir to give a paste. This is called slaking. Then add the slaked mixture gradually until the sauce only just thickens enough to coat the back of the spoon. If the sauce becomes too thick, thin it again with a little water or stock.

• Intensely flavoured sauces and stews can be thickened using beurre manié, a paste of butter and flour. This is whisked into the hot sauce a little at a time until it is the desired consistency.

• A simple dusting of flour on the raw meat and poultry used for stews will thicken the sauce over a long cooking period.

Quick fixes for sauces

• Judicious use of salt and pepper will help a sauce more than you think possible.

• A squeeze of lemon juice in a rich sauce cuts through the fat, and allows other flavours in the mixture to come to the fore.

• You can adjust a non-commital flavour with sugar and salt.

• Add a teaspoon or less of balsamic vinegar to a gravy.

• Try a teaspoon each of honey and soy sauce to boost the flavour of Southeast Asian dishes.

Clockwise from top left: Creamy vinaigrette,
Watermelon salsa, Lime butter and
Roquefort butter, Pickled cucumber sauce

Lime butter
Serves 12

225g/8oz/2 sticks unsalted butter,
softened
finely grated zest of 6 limes
juice of ½ lime, plus extra to serve
a few drops of Tabasco Sauce, to taste
salt

In an electric mixer, beat the butter until it is soft, white and fluffy. Add the lime zest and juice, Tabasco and a little salt and mix until combined.

With a rubber spatula, scrape the butter from the mixing bowl and lay it in a straight line on a sheet of kitchen foil. Roll the foil round the butter, then twist the ends as though the foil was a large toffee wrapper, to make the cylinder nice and plump.

Chill the butter until almost firm, then twist the ends of the foil again and roll the sausage backwards and forwards on the worktop to give a well-rounded shape. Place in a small Ziploc bag and store in the freezer.

To serve, remove the butter from the freezer to soften a little before slicing, otherwise it will crumble when you try and cut it. Run a fine knife under the hot water tap, then slice through the butter, foil and all, cutting it into thick slices. Peel off the foil and place one slice of butter on top of each portion of your piping hot food, then squeeze over a little extra fresh lime juice. The butter should start to melt just as it is served.

Return the remaining butter to the freezer for use on another occasion.

Recipe notes Flavoured butters are best kept in the freezer, with the advantage that they are then always on hand when you need them. Give them a good day or so in the freezer before using. This one works especially well with grilled [broiled] or pan-roast fish, chicken or veal.

It may seem strange to choose unsalted butter then add salt to the recipe, but when there are only a few ingredients in a recipe, it tastes better if you have found the best possible ingredients. French varieties of unsalted butter and the Danish brand Lurpak have a superbly refined and fermented flavour, and I believe they are more carefully made. Without salt, there is nothing to preserve the butter or lengthen its shelf life.

The zest of citrus fruits contains pungent essential oils that makes them a more intense flavouring than citrus juice. To finely grate the zest from the limes most efficiently, use a box grater, or my favourite zesting tool, a Microplane fine grater.

You can vary this butter by adding 3 tbsp of chopped coriander [cilantro] leaves. This will have a shorter life in the freezer as the acid in the lime zest tends to discolour the herb. Another option is to add a small, deseeded chopped chilli along with the lime zest and coriander for a spicy flavour.

Roquefort butter
Serves 12-16

225g/8oz/2 sticks unsalted butter,
softened
225g/8oz roquefort cheese
2 tbsp finely chopped parsley
a few drops of Tabasco sauce

Place the butter in a bowl with half the roquefort, plus the parsley and a few drops of Tabasco. Mash together until the mixture is smooth. Crumble the remaining cheese into the bowl and gently fold it in.

Scrape the butter from the mixing bowl and lay it in a straight line on a sheet of kitchen foil. Roll the foil round the butter, then twist the ends.

Chill the butter until almost firm, then twist the ends again and roll the sausage backwards and forwards on the worktop, to make it smooth and round. Place the butter in a small Ziploc bag and freeze.

To serve, remove the butter from the freezer to soften a little before slicing, otherwise it will crumble when you try and cut it. Run a fine knife under the hot water tap, then slice through the butter, foil and all, cutting it into thick slices. Peel off the foil and place one slice of butter on top of each portion of your piping hot food. The butter should start to melt just as it is served.

Return the remaining butter to the freezer for use on another occasion.

Recipe notes Serve on grilled [broiled] steaks, accompanied by a green salad. For special occasions, I use chef Henry Harris' suggestion: Carve a grilled rib of beef into thick slices, put a couple of slices of the butter between each slice, then spoon over a clear gravy and serve with watercress.

Basic vinaigrette dressing
Makes about 50ml/2floz/¼ cup

½-1 shallot, finely chopped (optional)
1 tsp balsamic or sherry vinegar, or a
*   few drops of white wine vinegar*
½ tsp sea salt flakes
50ml/2floz/¼ cup extra virgin olive oil
freshly ground black pepper

In a salad bowl or mixing bowl, combine the shallot (if using) with the vinegar, salt and some freshly milled pepper. Mix thoroughly until the salt dissolves.

Whisk in the olive oil and use immediately, or store in a screwtop jar in the fridge for up to a week, in which case shake it well before dressing the salad.

Recipe notes Remember to always use only the minimum amount of dressing in a salad, or it makes the leaves lank and greasy.

While it is important to serve a salad as soon as it is dressed, you can prepare it in advance to an extent by placing the dressing in the bottom of your salad bowl, placing a set of salad servers in the bowl, then piling the leaves on top – this will keep the salad leaves free of the dressing until you start to toss them.

For a clear dressing, use a mild white wine or rice vinegar. For a warm and mellow flavour, add a little hazelnut or walnut oil to this basic dressing, which taste good with winter ingredients.

If you are really in a hurry, you can dress your salad with three drops of any vinegar, a trickle of extra virgin olive oil, and season with salt and black pepper. Turn the leaves in the dressing and serve immediately.

Creamy vinaigrette
Makes 570ml/16floz/2 cups

1 large egg
1 tbsp Dijon mustard
285ml/10floz/1⅓ cups groundnut or
*   sunflower oil*
4 tbsp extra virgin olive oil
3 tbsp hazelnut oil (optional)
3 tbsp tarragon or sherry vinegar
chopped fresh herbs such as chervil,
*   chives, dill, or parsley, as required*
salt and freshly milled white pepper

Whisk the egg in a bowl. Add the mustard then, using a steady dribble, add the oils and vinegar, whisking all the time. Alternatively, place the egg and mustard in a small food processor (not a blender) and trickle in the oil slowly and steadily, with the blade spinning. Add 100-150ml/ 3½-5floz/⅓-⅔ cup of warm water in a slow steady stream.

Store in the fridge for up to 1 week until ready to use. Then, for every 180ml/6floz/¾ cup of the mixture you wish to serve, add 2-3 tbsp of chopped fresh herb or herbs. Blend vigorously together, or pulse in a blender to give a pale cream sauce prettily flecked with green. Adjust the seasoning to taste, adding a drop more vinegar if required.

Recipe notes In this incredibly easy sauce you are making an emulsion (suspending fat in liquid), so warmth is essential. Warm the bowl by filling it with hot water before use, and warm the egg by placing it, still in its shell, in the hot water while you assemble the other ingredients.

The sauce will not freeze, but keeps in the refrigerator for up to a week. You can make a mayonnaise by simply leaving out the water.

Anchovy dressing
Makes 350ml/12floz/1½ cups

1 small clove garlic, crushed
1 large egg
3-4 anchovy fillets
6 tbsp sherry vinegar
200ml/7floz/¾ cup olive or sunflower
*   oil, or a combination of both*
about 6 tbsp vegetable stock
a few drops of Worcestershire sauce
salt and freshly milled white pepper

Make sure all the ingredients and equipment are warmed to blood heat. In a small food processor bowl, whiz the garlic, egg, anchovies and vinegar until smooth and creamy.

With the motor still running, add the oil slowly and gradually, until the sauce is thick. Thin the mixture with a little vegetable stock. Add the Worcestershire sauce and the seasoning, and a drop or two more vinegar if required, until the dressing is the consistency of single [light] cream. If you plan to use the dressing as a spread, add less stock.

Recipe notes Spread this mixture on toasted, garlicky croûtes for an instant appetizer, or drizzle it over hard-boiled egg quarters or grilled lamb chops. I use it when serving parmesan custards (page 90). You can turn it into a Caesar salad dressing by adding 1½ tbsp grated parmesan cheese.

The sauce can be stored safely in the fridge for a few days.

Warm tomato and herb vinaigrette
Serves 4-6

1 clove garlic, unpeeled
8 coriander seeds, crushed
6 tbsp extra virgin olive oil
2 tbsp sherry vinegar
450g (1lb) sweet, ripe, firm tomatoes
15g/½oz/¼ cup mixture fresh chervil, chives, tarragon and thyme
salt and freshly milled black pepper

Place the garlic, coriander seeds, olive oil, and vinegar in a small saucepan. Add 4 tbsp water and heat very gently for about 30 minutes to allow the flavours to mingle.

Bring a kettle of water to the boil. Lightly score the base of each tomato with a cross and place in a large bowl. Pour the water from the kettle over the tomatoes and quickly retrieve them with tongs as soon as the skin starts to peel away. Plunge the tomatoes into cold water. Peel, quarter and deseed the tomatoes, then cut the flesh evenly into small dice.

When ready to serve, add the diced tomato to the vinaigrette and allow to warm through. Season to taste, then remove from the heat. Tear or chop the herbs and add them to the sauce.

Recipe notes Varying the fresh herbs in this vinaigrette allows it to take on new flavours and colours.

The recipe can be prepared a day in advance, just keep the tomato and vinaigrette separately in the fridge.

Serve with goats' cheese mousselines (page 92), poached and steamed fish, grilled [broiled] pieces of chicken, fish or white meats, pan-roasted or poached salmon, and ravioli or other pasta.

Watermelon salsa
Serves 4

150g/5oz/1 cup watermelon flesh, diced and deseeded
2 heaped tbsp finely chopped red onion
4 tbsp rice vinegar
1 tbsp chopped fresh coriander [cilantro]
1 tbsp chopped flat-leaf parsley
1 small medium-hot red chilli, deseeded and finely chopped
1 tbsp olive oil
salt and freshly milled black pepper

Combine all the ingredients in a mixing bowl and season to taste. Chill thoroughly before serving.

Recipe notes This lovely salsa gives a sharp, bright accent to summer meals. Use it for grills and barbecues, and other al fresco eating. It is especially good with fresh tuna.

The beauty of a salsa lies in the careful cutting and chopping of the ingredients. For the best effect, try to chop the red onion and chilli into dice: little evenly shaped cubes.

Pickled cucumber sauce
Serves 10

30g/1oz/½ cup fresh dill
200g/7oz sweet pickled [dill] cucumbers, plus 100ml/3½floz/scant ½ cup liquid from the jar
1 large shallot, about 50g/1½oz, finely chopped
200ml/7floz/¾ cup extra virgin olive oil
1 heaped tsp grain mustard
a little sugar, to taste
salt and freshly milled white pepper

Place all the ingredients in a blender or a food processor and whiz for 30 seconds. Season to taste, aiming for a good balance of sweet and sour.

Recipe notes A large jar of pickled [dill] cucumbers is one of the store cupboard ingredients I would never be without. Each bottle I buy has the same trusty balance of pleasant sweet-sourness. The cucumbers are reliably crisp and crunchy, the colour is true, and they make a fulsome snack with rich high-fat foods such as melted cheese on toast, or potatoes with a creamy dressing.

Alas the same cannot be said of the little pickled gherkins that can also be used in this recipe. Although one of the humble highlights of French cuisine, cornichons, when sold in England, can be viciously sour and disappointingly flabby – so do taste them before using in this recipe.

This sauce is wonderful with salmon, cooked in any way, and with most other fish. It is also good served with new potatoes. Mix it with some plain low-fat or Greek yogurt for a creamier texture. Another bonus: the sauce keeps for weeks in the fridge.

Green coriander and coconut chutney
Serves 6-8

90g/3½oz creamed coconut block,
chopped
60g/2oz/1 cup fresh coriander [cilantro],
including stalks, roughly chopped
1 tsp ground cumin
1cm/½in piece fresh ginger, chopped
2 cloves garlic, crushed
2-4 green chillies, deseeded and chopped
grated zest and juice of 1 lime
½ tsp salt, or to taste
200g/7oz/¼ cup Greek yogurt

In a food processor, process the coconut, coriander, cumin, ginger, garlic, chillies, lime zest and juice and salt to a fine paste.

With a rubber spatula, scrape the mixture into a mixing bowl. Stir in just enough yogurt to make it thick and creamy. If the mixture becomes too stiff, thin it with some more yogurt. Serve at room temperature.

Recipe notes Refrigerated, this chutney lasts about a week, but alas, not in my home, where it is always consumed within the day. It makes a refreshing dip garnished with herb leaves and served with celery or carrots, prawn crackers or Japanese rice crackers. It is also a good filling for baked potatoes.

Peter Gordon's sweet chilli jam
Makes about 500ml/18floz/2¼ cups

10 cloves garlic
4 large red chillies, stems removed
100g/3½oz fresh ginger, roughly
chopped
2-3 lemongrass stalks, outer leaves
removed
50g/2oz/1 packed cup fresh coriander
[cilantro] leaves
285g/10oz/1½ cups caster [superfine
granulated] sugar
100ml/3½floz/scant ½ cup cider vinegar
50ml/1¼floz/3½ tbsp Asian fish sauce
(nam pla)
50ml/1¼floz/3½ tbsp tamari or soy
sauce

Put the garlic, red chillies, ginger, lemongrass and coriander in a food processor and purée to a coarse paste.

Place the sugar in a saucepan and add just enough water to cover. Heat gently, stirring until the sugar dissolves. Remove the spoon from the pan and raise the heat to a high setting. Bring the mixture to a boil, brushing down the sides of the saucepan with water from time to time to keep them clean. Boil for 5-8 minutes, or until the syrup turns to a caramel the colour of tea.

Meanwhile, prepare a basin of cold water. When the caramel is ready, plunge the base of the hot saucepan immediately into the basin of cold water to stop the cooking. Beware: it will steam and hiss. Set the saucepan aside to cool slightly.

Stir the spice paste into the caramel, return the pan to the heat and bring to a boil. Add the vinegar, fish sauce and tamari or soy sauce. Simmer for 1 minute. If the sauce stiffens at this stage, don't panic, just heat and stir it gently and the toffee threads will

melt. Remove the saucepan from the heat and set aside to cool before using or storing the jam.

Recipe notes Peter Gordon is one of the few chefs who can combine Western and Eastern ingredients with great skill and imagination. This chilli jam is one of his famous signature recipes, from the days when he was at the Sugar Club and served seared scallops with chilli jam and crème fraîche – you should try the combination, it's fantastic.

The base of this utterly delectable sauce is a caramel, and it perks up just about everything it comes into contact with, from steamed fish and broccoli to seared meat, noodles and rice. Stirred into chilled cellophane noodles, it will become fantastically crunchy in the fridge. I like to serve it as a canapé topping with Japanese rice crackers, steamed scallops and fresh coriander [cilantro] leaves.

Alternatively, add a little of this chilli jam to some finely chopped membrillo (quince paste) and serve on thin biscuits made from sweet shortcrust pastry (page 176). Top with a little crème fraîche if desired, and serve either as a canapé, or with a fruit salad made from pears and a light ginger syrup (page 200).

The chilli jam keeps indefinitely in the fridge. If you do not have fish sauce (nam pla) and tamari to hand, try a combination of Worcestershire sauce and mushroom ketchup.

Thyme, shallot and garlic aromatic oil
Makes 700ml/1¼ pints/3 cups

570ml/1 pint/2½ cups groundnut oil
3 shallots, chopped
3 large cloves garlic, squashed
45g/1½oz/¼ cup thyme
100ml/3½floz/scant ½ cup extra virgin olive oil

Heat the groundnut oil, shallots, garlic and thyme together in a saucepan until just below smoking point. Remove the pan from the heat and set aside to cool.

Pour in the extra virgin olive oil, then transfer to a bottle, seal and store in the refrigerator.

Recipe notes Use this superbly fragrant oil for frying, and in place of regular olive oil in vinaigrettes and other salad dressings.

To squash the garlic cloves, simply flatten them with the broad side of a knife blade, pressing down firmly using the heel of your hand, then peel off and discard the skins.

Roast garlic oil
Makes 250ml/9floz/about 1 cup

225g/8oz whole heads of garlic
250ml/9floz/1 cup extra virgin olive oil
salt and freshly milled black pepper

Heat the oven to 190°C/375°F/Gas 5. Slice off the top third of each head of garlic, trim away the root and rub off any excess papery skin.

Place the heads close together with the cut-side uppermost in a shallow baking dish small enough to hold the garlic snugly. Pour the olive oil over the garlic and season generously.

Cover tightly with foil and bake, turning the heat down gradually every 15 minutes or so, so that after about 1 hour the temperature is at 150°C/300°F/Gas 2. Cook until the cloves begin to pop out of their skins, then uncover and bake for another 15 minutes, or until the garlic is golden brown but not at all burnt.

Place a fine-meshed stainless steel sieve over a jug and strain the garlic oil through it. Leave to cool then store in a clean, tightly covered glass jar in the fridge for up to 1 week.

Recipe notes A clear, citrine-gold oil with an intoxicating aroma, this can be used to stir-fry vegetables, trickled over fish, steak, pasta, baked potatoes, char-grilled vegetables, or added with discretion to salad dressing.

To make roast garlic paste, press the garlic through a strong stainless steel sieve. Discard the debris. Trickle a little of the garlic-flavoured oil into the paste, and stir well. The paste will keep in the fridge for a few days.

Food writer Nigel Slater combines the paste with a tub of double [heavy] cream, boils it briefly, then stirs it into cooked pasta – the result is sublime.

Smoked paprika and rosemary marinade
Makes enough to marinate 1kg/2lb 4oz fish or meat

200ml/7floz/¼ cup extra virgin olive oil
1 heaped tbsp spicy smoked pimenton
2 heaped tsp rosemary, finely chopped
1 small onion, finely diced
1 tsp salt

Combine all the ingredients in a large bowl and mix well. Transfer to a large, shallow porcelain, glass or stainless steel dish (or a Ziploc bag), and add your meat or fish.

Cover (or seal) and leave to marinate for at least 6 hours in the refrigerator, turning the food gently in the marinade every so often.

Recipe notes Originally the purpose of a marinade was to tenderise and/or add flavour to food. Old fowl, goat, wild game and animals that had worked on the farms were marinated to make the flesh tender before cooking. Now most meat is farmed in such a way to make it very tender, but the result is often lacking flavour, so marinades are still important.

Remember to wipe off any excess marinade before cooking. When roasting, pan-roasting or frying, the excess marinade can burn and become bitter. On a barbecue it can easily flare up and blacken the meat or fish.

The remaining marinade can be lightly cooked by boiling, and served as a sauce if desired.

This recipe, from New Zealander Peter Gordon, works well with chicken legs and breasts, lamb loins, large chunks of cod fillet and salmon. Peter has also used it successfully with field mushrooms, pumpkin and courgettes [zucchini].

North African chermoula
Makes enough to marinate 1.5kg/3lb 6oz fish or meat

1 large onion, finely chopped
4 cloves garlic, finely chopped
½ tsp ground cumin
¼ tsp sweet paprika
⅛ tsp chilli powder
1 heaped tsp saffron threads
6 heaped tbsp coriander leaves
6 heaped tbsp flat-leaf parsley
6 tbsp extra virgin olive oil
juice of ½ lemon
salt

Combine all the ingredients in a small bowl, mix well, then pour into a shallow china, glass or stainless steel dish (or a Ziploc bag). Add your fish, poultry or meat and rub the mixture all over the food. Leave to marinate for at least 30 minutes.

Recipe notes This rub is excellent with baked or roasted whole salmon trout, sea bass, poultry, lamb and beef. For a whole fish, loosely wrap in foil and bake in the oven. If using the chermoula on fish fillets, cook them by shallow-frying in groundnut or sunflower oil.

To turn the chermoula into a marinade, add 125ml/4floz/½ cup olive oil and 2 tbsp mild vinegar. Marinate the food for at least 2 hours, and preferably overnight, in which case the dish should be covered and placed in the refrigerator.

Sri's red curry paste
Makes about 600ml/1 pint/2½ cups

3 tbsp coriander seeds
3 tsp cumin seeds
5-10 large red chillies, deseeded and
* chopped*
1 red pepper, deseeded and chopped
8 small shallots, chopped
1 stalk lemongrass, outer leaves
* removed, chopped*
4cm/1½in piece fresh ginger
3 kaffir lime leaves, shredded (optional),
* or the grated zest of 2 limes*
3 tbsp tamarind water, or lime or lemon
* juice*
3 tbsp sunflower or groundnut oil
1 tsp salt
1 tsp brown sugar

Roast the coriander and cumin seeds in a dry frying pan over a gentle heat for about 3 minutes or until deeply aromatic, being careful not to let them smoke and burn. Crush them using a mortar and pestle, spice mill, or in a strong plastic bag using the base of a saucepan for crushing.

Place the spices in a blender or food processor with all the remaining ingredients and 125ml/4floz/½ cup cold water. Blend until smooth.

Transfer the mixture to a saucepan and bring to a boil. Reduce the heat and simmer gently for 40 minutes. Set aside to cool before use or storage.

Recipe notes This recipe, from Sri Owen's book *Noodles The New Way*, makes more than you will usually need at one time. To serve six people, use about 200ml/7floz/scant 1 cup of paste. Sri suggests freezing the rest in an ice-cube tray, so that the cubes are ready to be used at any time. In the freezer the paste will last 3 months; in the fridge it will keep 10 days.

Pea pesto
Serves 6

85g/3oz/1½ cups basil
450g/1lb shelled peas
5 tbsp single [light] cream
about 4 tbsp grated Parmesan cheese
2 tsp sugar
300ml/10floz/1¼ cups mild extra virgin
* olive oil*
salt and freshly milled black pepper

Reserve a few good basil sprigs and leaves to garnish your dish.

In a saucepan of boiling salted water, cook the peas for 10 minutes or until tender. Drain and return one-third of them to a small pan of unsalted water and keep them simmering very gently until ready to serve.

Transfer the remaining cooked peas to a blender. Add the cream, cheese, basil and sugar. While the blade is whizzing, add the olive oil slowly, in a steady stream. Stop adding oil when the mixture is the consistency of double [heavy] cream. Season with salt and pepper and adjust the other ingredients to your own taste, adding more cheese or basil as desired.

Drain the reserved peas. To serve, pour the sauce over hot cooked pasta, garnish with the reserved peas and basil and serve immediately with extra freshly milled black pepper.

Recipe notes Taught to cookery teacher Anna Venturi by her Milanese grandmother, this sweet, seductive sauce is ideal for short, sharp pasta shapes such as penne. You can use frozen petit pois rather than fresh peas if desired – simply cook until tender.

The sauce is best made and eaten immediately. I would not recommend it for a party as it is inclined to go sticky after a short while.

Hollandaise sauce
Serves 6

7 tbsp white wine
3 tbsp white wine vinegar
2 shallots, finely chopped
4-6 peppercorns, cracked
225g/8oz/2 sticks unsalted butter, cubed
3 large egg yolks
juice of 1 lemon
about 150ml/5floz/²⁄₃ cup whipping or
   double [heavy] cream (optional)
salt and freshly milled white pepper

In a small stainless steel or enamelled saucepan, combine the wine, vinegar, shallots and cracked peppercorns and boil hard until the volume of liquid has reduced to 2 tbsp.

Meanwhile, melt the butter in a small saucepan, then heat it until it is boiling. While the wine and shallot mixture is still hot, press it through a fine sieve into a small food processor bowl. With the blade spinning, add the egg yolks, then the lemon juice, and some salt and pepper.

Pour in the hot butter, very slowly to begin with, until the sauce is thick, smooth and creamy. If you can, leave behind in the saucepan the white, milky solids that have separated from the melted butter fat, as these will thin the sauce.

Check the seasoning again, and add extra lemon juice, salt and pepper as required. If the sauce is too runny, transfer it to a very shallow saucepan and heat gently for 2-3 minutes or until thickened. Use straight away, or pour immediately into a warmed thermos flask and set aside until required.

To serve the reserved sauce, place the cream in a clean, medium-sized saucepan and boil hard until the volume of liquid has reduced by about two-thirds. Remove from the heat and allow the cream to cool slightly. Then whisk the egg mixture into the cream in a smooth, steady stream. Allow the sauce to warm through, but do not heat it. Whisk well, and adjust the seasoning and lemon juice to taste for the last time. Serve immediately.

Recipe notes Hollandaise has an unfair reputation of being difficult to make. The only problem you might encounter with this gorgeous sauce is that if it gets too hot, it will separate or curdle. However there is a safety clause built into this version, which takes care of that eventuality, leaving you to relax and enjoy the cooking process. Whisking the hollandaise into warm thickened cream just before serving allows you to make the sauce in advance, and has the advantage of giving warmth, colour and shine to the finished sauce.

Serve your hollandaise with grilled [broiled] beef steaks, steamed fish and chicken, asparagus, broccoli, or dishes featuring poached eggs. For a lemon-flavoured hollandaise to serve with hot broccoli mousses (page 90), simply add extra lemon juice to taste when you make the final adjustment of seasoning. The flavour should be refreshing but not too sour.

Sauce Choron
Serves 8

450g/1lb medium-large tomatoes
7 tbsp white wine
3 tbsp white wine vinegar
2 shallots, finely chopped
4-6 peppercorns, cracked
225g/8oz/2 sticks unsalted butter, cubed
3 large egg yolks
juice of 1 lemon
about 150ml/5floz/²⁄₃ cup whipping or
   double [heavy] cream
salt and freshly milled white pepper

Bring a kettle of water to the boil. With a small, sharp knife, lightly score the bases of the tomatoes with a cross and place them in a large bowl. Pour the boiling water from the kettle over the tomatoes then, as soon as the skins start to peel away, remove the tomatoes with tongs and plunge them into cold water.

Peel and and quarter the tomatoes, then remove and discard the seeds. Cut the tomato flesh into small dice and set aside until needed.

In a small stainless steel or enamelled saucepan, combine the wine, vinegar, shallots and cracked peppercorns and boil hard until the volume of liquid has reduced to 2 tbsp.

Meanwhile, melt the butter in a small saucepan, then heat it until it is boiling. While the wine and shallot mixture is still hot, press it through a fine sieve into a small food processor bowl. With the blade spinning, add the egg yolks, then the lemon juice, and some salt and pepper.

Pour in the hot butter, very slowly to begin with, until the sauce is thick, smooth and creamy. If you can, leave behind the white milky solids that have separated from the melted fat in the pan, as these will thin the sauce. >

Check the seasoning again, and add extra lemon juice, salt and pepper as required. If the sauce is too runny, transfer it to a very shallow saucepan and heat gently for 2-3 minutes or until thickened. Pour immediately into a warmed thermos flask and set aside until required.

When almost ready to serve, place the cream in a clean medium-sized saucepan and boil hard until the volume has reduced by about two-thirds. Remove from the heat and allow the cream to cool slightly.

Whisk the egg mixture into the cream in a smooth, steady stream, then add the diced tomatoes and allow the sauce to warm through gently. Whisk well, and adjust the seasoning and lemon to taste for the last time. Serve immediately.

Recipe notes Sauce Choron is one of several possible variations of hollandaise and named after a renowned French chef of the 1800s. I love the coral translucency of the tomato in this rich, luscious sauce and serve it with white crab meat and other seafood, with pan-roast, poached or steamed salmon, salmon trout and trout, or baked white fish.

The recipe requires tomatoes that are red and ripe but firm. Once peeled, deseeded and diced, they will keep for about a day in the fridge.

White wine and dill sauce
Serves 4-6

900ml/1½ pints/4 cups fish stock
1 shallot, finely sliced
15g/½oz/1 tbsp unsalted butter, plus about 50g/2oz/½ stick extra (optional)
75g/3oz/1 cup white button mushrooms, finely sliced
150ml/5floz/⅔ cup medium-dry white wine
about 150ml/5floz/⅔ cup whipping [heavy] cream
1 tbsp cornflour [cornstarch]
15g/½oz/¼ cup fresh dill, finely chopped
salt and freshly milled white pepper

Place the stock in a saucepan, bring to a boil and boil hard until the volume of liquid has reduced by half to give 450ml/16floz/2 cups.

Meanwhile, in a very small pan, sweat the shallot in 15g/½oz/1 tbsp of the butter without letting it colour. Cut the extra butter into cubes, if using, and place in the fridge to chill. Add the mushrooms to the shallot, cover and cook gently for 10 minutes or until the shallot is sweet.

Add the white wine to the vegetables, bring to the boil and boil hard until the volume of liquid in the pan has reduced by at least half. Then add 100ml/3½floz/scant ½ cup water and 300ml/10floz/1¼ cups of the reduced stock. Return to a boil and simmer slowly, until the volume has reduced by two-thirds.

Once the sauce has reduced, add the cream and simmer for 10 minutes, until it tastes strongly and clearly of fish. Add a little more cream if you wish to lighten the colour.

In a small dish, combine the cornflour with 1 tbsp cold water and stir to a smooth paste. While the sauce is boiling, add the slaked cornflour gradually, whisking constantly, until the desired thickness is achieved and the sauce is thick enough to coat the back of a spoon.

Use a paper towel to skim off any eyes of fat from the surface of the sauce. At this stage it can be frozen, or stored for 1-2 days in the fridge.

If desired, just before serving, whisk in the reserved butter, one cube at a time, taking care that the sauce steams but does not boil. It is ready when it has a smooth, velvety consistency and is silky on the tongue.

Gently pass the sauce through a sieve. Stir in the dill, season to taste again and serve immediately.

Recipe notes An ideal recipe for an important event, this elegant, smooth and beautifully balanced sauce goes particularly well with food that has been matched with a very good bottle of white wine. Try serving it with little smoked haddock custards (page 50), or fish that has been poached, steamed or grilled [broiled].

For a plain white wine sauce, simply leave out the herbs. To make a white sauce for chicken, use a pale chicken stock instead of fish stock and serve with steamed chicken, vegetables or hot vegetable mousses.

Saffron shrimp sauce
Serves 4-6

½ tsp saffron threads
about 225ml/8floz/1 cup whipping or
* double [heavy] cream*
juice of ½ small lemon
15g/½oz/¼ cup chives or dill, finely cut
* (optional)*
60g/2oz/½ cup cooked baby shrimp
salt and freshly milled white pepper

Place the saffron in a small bowl, cover with 2 tbsp boiling water and set aside to infuse for about 30 minutes.

In a saucepan, boil the cream slowly and carefully, whisking from time to time to keep it smooth and prevent it burning on the bottom of the pan. When the cream has reduced enough to coat the back of a spoon, strain the saffron infusion into the pan and simmer for a few minutes.

Strain the sauce into a clean pan, season to taste with salt and pepper, then set aside until needed.

When almost ready to serve, add lemon juice to sharpen the flavour, then add the herbs and shrimp and allow them to warm through.

Recipe notes You can make this sauce in advance and keep it in the fridge for up to 2 days. Serve it with little smoked haddock custards (page 50), and grilled or steamed fish, or chicken. Blanched strips of peeled, deseeded and thickly sliced cucumber make a refreshing (and vegetarian) alternative to the shrimp.

Quick cream pasta sauce
Serves 4-6

285ml/10floz/1¼ cups whipping or
* double [heavy] cream*
2 tbsp chopped parsley, chives or
* marjoram (optional)*
salt and freshly milled black pepper

In a wide pan, not too shallow, bring the cream to the boil, taking care it does not boil over. Boil until the cream has thickened and the volume has reduced by half.

Add the herbs, if using, and season to taste. If the sauce seems too thick, thin it with a little of the cooking water from your pasta.

To serve, pour the sauce over freshly cooked pasta and toss until each strand or shape is lightly coated.

Recipe notes When served with cooked pasta, fresh or dried, this makes a comforting supper. The sauce can also be stirred into cooked leeks or mushrooms, and poured over boiled broccoli or cauliflower.

Wild mushroom sauce
Serves 6-8

30g/1oz dried porcini mushrooms
2 tbsp olive oil
85g/3oz/¾ stick butter
2 cloves garlic, crushed
450g/1lb chestnut mushrooms, sliced
150ml/5floz/⅔ cup single [light] cream
15g/½oz/¼ cup fresh parsley, chopped
salt and freshly milled black pepper

Soak the porcini for 1 hour in a small bowl of 150ml/5floz/⅔ cup hot water.

In a large frying pan, heat the oil and butter and gently cook the garlic. When it is sizzling, add the chestnut mushrooms and stir-fry 3-4 minutes.

Strain the porcini through a fine-meshed stainless steel sieve, reserving the soaking water. Slice the porcini and add to the pan, then pour in the soaking water. Cover and simmer for 10 minutes, until all the water has evaporated. If this is not the case, remove the lid and simmer briskly.

Mix in the cream and bubble until the mixture has a sauce consistency. Season to taste and, just before serving, add the chopped parsley.

Recipe notes Another recipe from Anna Venturi and her Italian grandmother, this mushroom sauce goes beautifully with pasta. I also like to fill little tartlet cases with it and serve them as canapés, or simmer the mixture until it is very thick and use it as a rich topping for thick-cut slices of beef fillet.

When serving this sauce with fresh pasta, choose tagliolini and tagliatelle or, ideally, some dried penne. The sauce should not drown the pasta, but barely coat the pieces, so you can still taste the wheatiness.

Clear brown gravy
Serves 4-6

1 litre/1¼ pints/4¼ cups brown beef,
lamb or chicken stock
400g/14oz beef, lamb or chicken bones,
cut small
about 3 tbsp tomato paste
about 3 tbsp honey
80g/3oz/½ cup mixture of chopped
celery, carrot and onion
2 cloves garlic
about 1 tsp butter
200ml/7floz/¾ cup dark Amontillado
sherry, sweet Madeira or ruby port
60g/2oz dark mushroom caps
30g/1oz/3 tbsp deseeded tomato flesh
1 bouquet garni
30g/1oz/½ cup fresh herbs such as
rosemary or thyme
2-3 tsp arrowroot or cornflour
[cornstarch]
salt and freshly milled black pepper

You will also need
about 1 metre/1 yard of muslin
[cheesecloth]

Bring the stock to a boil in a large
saucepan and simmer briskly until
the volume of liquid has reduced to
750ml/1¼ pints/3 cups. Meanwhile,
preheat the oven to 220°C/425°F/
Gas 7. Paint the bones lightly with
tomato paste and honey, then roast
until dark brown, turning once or
twice during cooking. Pour off any
liquid that accumulates on the base
of the roasting pan and reserve.

Melt the butter in a non-stick pan
and gently fry the mixture of celery,
carrot and onion, plus the garlic,
until the celery and carrot are a rich
brown colour and the onion is
almost black but not burned.

Transfer the roasted bones to a
wide saucepan. Add the alcohol and

boil vigorously until there is barely
2cm/¾in of liquid left in the pan.

Add the reduced stock, browned
vegetables, mushrooms, tomato,
bouquet garni and three-quarters of
the bunch of herbs. Remove any fat
from top of the reserved bone cooking
juices and add the cooking juices to
the saucepan. In total, there should
be only enough stock to barely cover
the bones and vegetables. Bring to
the boil and simmer for 45 minutes,
carefully skimming off any froth that
accumulates with a spoon.

After 45 minutes of simmering, the
flavour should be strong and delicious.
Use a skimmer and tongs to remove
the bones and vegetables from the
pan, trying not to disturb the clear
sauce. Strain the sauce carefully, one
ladle at a time, through a double
layer of muslin placed in a sieve over
a deep bowl. Clean the saucepan.

Return the strained sauce to the
clean pan and add the remainder of
the rosemary or thyme. Bring to a
boil and reduce a little more. If
desired, thicken the sauce with a little
arrowroot or cornflour slaked in an
equal quantity of cold water. Use
strips of paper towel to skim off any
remaining eyes of fat from the top of
the sauce. Keep skimming any froth
from the surface as it simmers. When
the sauce is clear and glossy, season
carefully to taste. Keep the sauce
warm in a small pan on the stovetop.

To serve, heat the sauce to a rolling
boil, then immediately pour it through
a fine-meshed sieve into a gravy boat.

Recipe notes You may find it easier to
make double or triple this quantity of
gravy, and freeze it in tubs for use on
other occasions – and are right to do
so as increased volume when cooking
sauces often produces better results.

Sweet-sour cherry sauce
Serves 4

300g/10oz fresh cherries
225g/8oz/¾ cup redcurrant or rowan
jelly
2 tsp French mustard, or more to taste
3 tbsp wine vinegar
salt and freshly milled black pepper

Stone the cherries and, if they are
large, halve them. Set a heatproof
bowl over a pan of boiling water.
Add the jelly to the bowl and allow
it to melt gently.

Sieve the warmed jelly into a small
saucepan. Working over a gentle
heat, stir in the mustard, then the
vinegar, and a little pepper. When the
sauce is liquid and smooth, add the
cherries, and season thoroughly.

Allow the fruit to heat through and
serve warm or at room temperature.

Recipe notes Serve this delicious sauce
with pan-roast duck breasts, lamb
cutlets, venison steaks, loin of
venison, or haunch of venison. For
the best flavour, it should be made
and served within the day.

Pastry, bread and biscuits

Fast ways with pastry

Make canapé cups of filo pastry by brushing three layers lightly with olive oil and sprinkling with tiny thyme leaves, sea salt flakes and freshly ground black pepper before shaping.

Boost filo pastry for sweet tart cases by brushing with melted unsalted butter then dusting lightly with a mixture of caster [superfine granulated] sugar and cinnamon.

Cover a tray of buttered filo pastry with finely sliced fruit, or a mixture of colourful raw Mediterranean vegetables, then bake.

Fill pastry cases with a melange of char-grilled or roasted vegetables.

Whip double [heavy] cream and flavour with brandy, vanilla, and icing [confectioners'] sugar, then use to fill a sweet pastry case before topping with fruit.

Drain set yogurt in a sieve for 30 minutes, then mix with honey for a tart filling with a Mediterranean note.

Combine whipped double [heavy] cream and luxury lemon curd for a rich, citrussy filling.

My happiest moments are when I get down to making pastry. Will it by sweet or savoury? Shall I bake a quiche brimming with a soft, wobbly custard, or a crisp vanilla tart filled with summer berries? Perhaps I shall just stock up the freezer and leave those pleasant decisions for another day, when I plan a good bout of entertaining. Homemade pastry is a luxury. We bake it only to give us pleasure. As the aroma of baking the golden, buttery, crisp crust fills the house, I remember my grandma and her Cape apricot pie, made specially to welcome us after our long journey south. I believe it is easier to bake successfully than it is to cook meat or fish. Let me show you how to make pastry, the quality of which you will not find in the shops, neither in its flavour and shortness, nor its melt-in-the-mouth appeal.

I fell in love with pastry making when working in the small hours at the Lenôtre factory outside Paris and the Roux patisserie in London. I like the fact that there is no guesswork involved in making pastry. I love the sensation of the cool flour slipping through my fingertips, and am deeply satisfied by the economy of the measured ingredients. Once the pastry is made, I am excited by having a clean worktop and a smooth ball of dough in may palm, with the possibilities of over a hundred delicious things to bake, and happy faces around a table encouraging me to do so.

At the beginning of the 21st Century, pastry seems to have stepped out of the culinary limelight. Perhaps it is the fear of saturated fats and excessive calorie intake which has dampened the enthusiasm of learning to make pastry. Or is it the lingering legacy of sodden pastries, erroneously filled with damp, cold and compacted vegetables that has diverted us from mastering the simple and

rewarding skills of pastry making? The mastering of dozens of pastry recipes is not required. It is the variety of fillings and the ways pastries are baked, cut and served that make it appear to your friends and family as though your repertoire of pastry recipes is inexhaustible.

There are cooks who write recipes for pastry made with oil and wholemeal flour, to make pastry more 'healthy'. My logic is this: rich pastry is a treat, not a regular item in normal diets. Given the infrequent occasions I eat pastry, and the small amount consumed in the serving, I feel perfectly safe eating a portion made from just 1-2 tbsp butter, flour and egg.

The best pastries are made when you are relaxed. When I feel tense, I get my measurements wrong, my hand get hot, and my shoulder muscles are tight, making the pastry uneven when I roll it out. You need to relax, get the kitchen as cool as you can, and follow a trusted recipe. Most important is to follow the recipe and the steps it gives you in sequence. There is no point, for example, in turning on your oven and letting the room get hot when you need a cool temperature in which to make and roll out your pastry.

What to look for, what to avoid

- The regular 'strong flour' sold in British stores is not particularly strong. It makes fine, crisp pastry. British 'plain flour' makes a soft pastry and should be avoided.
- Fresh butter gives the finest flavour to pastry but is prone to darkening and burning.
- Lard and white vegetable shortening are 100 per cent fat and produce the shortest pastry. However, made with them alone, a cooked pastry would be white and tasteless, so they are often mixed half and half with butter.
- Hard margarine is a mix of unspecified ingredients which always makes me slightly nervous, but mixed half and half with butter it produces wonderful pastry.
- Granulated sugar crystals are too large for pastry making and do not dissolve in the mix. Use caster sugar [superfine granulated] or icing sugar [confectioners' sugar] where directed.
- If you have neither the time or inclination to make your own pastry, or your diet forbids hard fats and eggs, filo pastry is a brilliant option. Buy it from the freezer or chiller cabinet, or from specialist Greek or Turkish shops where it is sold fresh.

The principles of making pastry

- The right kit is essential when making pastries, especially when starting out. Good equipment smooths the way.
- Apart from making pastry more quickly, machines actually make better pastry. The faster pastry is made, the better the result, and machines require you to use less liquid than making by hand, so the result is a better, shorter pastry.
- It is sensible to assemble and measure all ingredients before you begin and return all jars and packets to your cupboards before your hands become buttery and floury. Then you will have the space, especially in a small kitchen, to collect your equipment and to roll out. Modern machines work so fast that it is essential to have everything to hand.
- Temperatures are vital in pastry making, and if you get them right consistently you will find the whole process is streamlined. Most ingredients need to be chilled, exccept the eggs, which should be warmed slightly to prevent curdling when added to a creamy butter and sugar mix.
- No matter how imaginative, hurried or confident you are, I urge you to follow recipes closely for optimum succeess.
- It really pays to measure and weigh accurately, and ultimately speeds up the process of making pastry because you are getting it right and not creating pitfalls.
- Dry ingredients are best measured and sifted onto sheets of silicone paper so you can easily move them around. Lift the paper by closing two opposite ends and making a chute down which to gently slide the dry ingredients into the mixing bowl.
- Choose your oven shelf while the oven is still cold. Shuffling about with hot racks just prior to baking your pastry means the heat is lost from the oven and it is easy to burn yourself.
- Many pastries are baked in the middle or upper part of the oven. The top is generally hotter. But nothing beats the crisp pastry baked on the hot floor of an Aga.
- A tough, leathery pastry may be the result of using too much liquid, or liquid soaking from the filling into the cooked pastry. It is also frequently due to too much handling of the pastry.
- Rolling pastry out again and again not only means it is being handled too much, it results in extra flour being incorporated in the mixture, which also causes toughness. Using too many scraps and trimmings from rolled and rerolled pastry will produce a leathery result as well.

The best advice I can give The

reason I believe pastry is quick to make is that I never need to wait for pastry to rest and chill until it is firm enough to roll out, because I always keep some in the freezer and automatically replace it with fresh each time I use a batch of it.

Pastry is exceptionally fast to make, especially in a machine, and unlike some other foods, pastry is never spoiled by storage in the freezer, whether as a dough, or formed into empty pastry shells, or part-baked.

You should refresh all baked or part-baked pastries or cookies taken from the freezer in an oven of 180°C/350°F/Gas 4 for 10-15 minutes, to drive out all the accumulated moisture and crisp up the items before serving.

Rich shortcrust pastry
Makes 900g/2lb

1 medium egg
450g/1lb/3 cups strong flour, plus extra
for dusting
1 tbsp caster sugar
a large pinch of salt
145g/5oz/⅔ cup hard margarine, chilled
and cubed
145g/5oz/⅔ cup salted butter, chilled
and cubed

Whisk the egg in a jug, adding 5 tbsp cold water if making the pastry in a machine, and 6 tbsp if making it by hand. Place in the fridge to chill.

Sift the flour, sugar and salt into a large mixing bowl, or whizz them together in a food processor. Add the margarine and butter. Cut the fats into the flour with a pastry scraper or table knife, if making by hand, otherwise whizz until the mixture resembles loose breadcrumbs.

Give the chilled egg and water a brief whisk and add it in a steady stream to the fat and flour.

If using a machine, stop mixing when the pastry clumps round the blades. If making by hand, squeeze the dough into a crumbly ball.

Transfer the pastry to a cool clean work surface. Using the heel of your hand (the coolest part), press the ball away from you, smearing it in a straight line about 10cm/4in long, then scrape it back together in a ball using a table knife or pastry scraper. Do this a few times until all the distinguishable bits of fat disappear and you have a homogenous paste.

On a cool worktop lightly dusted with flour, shape the dough into a sausage, wrap in plastic wrap and chill for 1 hour. Alternatively, label, chill and freeze in useful batches.

When the pastry has chilled, roll out what you need in a minimum dusting of flour to line your oiled or buttered baking tins and flan cases. Prick the pastry and chill.

To bake blind, which is necessary for this rich pastry, line the pastry shell with foil, fill it with baking rice and set aside to rest for 30 minutes.

Preheat the oven, and a baking tray, to 190°C/375°F/Gas 5. Place the tart tin on the hot baking tray and cook for 15-20 minutes or until the pastry has set. Remove the foil and baking rice and return the shell to the oven for a few minutes more to dry out, decreasing the oven temperature, and covering it with foil to keep it pale. The pastry shell should be crisp and still blonde at this stage. Cool on a rack until ready to fill.

Recipe notes An American friend once commented that my pastry was not as crisp as hers. Ahem. As a result, I always use strong flour, which makes quite a difference to this rich pastry. Don't use the 'very strong flour' now found in some shops, as it is only suitable for breadmaking.

This pastry can be used for apple tarts, and all savoury tarts, tartlets and quiches. By all means make it with all butter, which will taste fantastic, but take extra care so it does not burn. Cover with foil if necessary. Or you could substitute half lard and half butter, which will make it paler, less tasty, but more 'short' and melt-in-the-mouth.

Once you have made this pastry once or twice, you will find you can roll it out almost paper-thin for lining tiny tartlet tins. For larger, deeper pie tins, roll out the pastry slightly thicker, or the shell will not be able to support the contents.

Sweet shortcrust pastry
Makes 900g/2lb

450g/1lb/3 cups plain [all-purpose]
flour, sifted, plus extra for dusting
140g/5oz/1¼ cups icing [confectioners']
sugar
salt
225g/8oz/1 cup unsalted butter, chilled
and cubed
1 egg, beaten in a jug

Put the flour, icing sugar, salt and butter in a food processor and pulse 7-8 times to give a mixture the consistency of fine breadcrumbs.

Tip these into a mixing bowl, add the egg and 1 tbsp cold water, and mix together with a table knife. Knead and squeeze the dough lightly to give a firm paste. Wrap in plastic wrap and rest in the fridge for 30 minutes.

Roll the pastry out thinly on a cool worktop lightly dusted with flour and use it to line your tart tins.

Meanwhile, place a baking tray in the middle of the oven and preheat the oven to 190°C/375°F/Gas 5. Place the pastry shell on the hot baking tray – it does not need to be lined with foil and filled with rice.

Part-bake the shell for 20 minutes, decreasing the oven temperature every 5 minutes so that the shell bakes at 160°C/310°F/Gas 2½ for the final 5 minutes. The pastry should then be blonde and crisp.

Remove to a wire rack and set aside in a cool place until required.

Recipe notes Voted by many of her readers to make the best and most wonderfully easy mince pies, this recipe is from Lorna Wing's book *Party Food*. I use it for open fruit tarts, and the fig and fennel tart (page 198) pictured here.

Sweet almond pastry
Makes 1.235kg/2lb 12oz

*150g/5oz/⅔ cup caster [superfine
   granulated] sugar*
100g/3½oz/¾ cup ground almonds
*500g/1lb 1oz/3⅓ cups plain [all-
   purpose] flour, plus extra for dusting*
a pinch of salt
*380g/13oz/3¼ sticks unsalted butter,
   chilled and cubed*
1 tsp dark rum
1 egg, plus 2 egg yolks
½ tsp finely grated lemon zest

Place the sugar, almonds, flour and
salt in a food processor and whizz
for a few seconds. Add the butter
cubes and process again until just
blended. The mixture will resemble
fine breadcrumbs.

Whisk the rum into the egg and
egg yolks, then add to the processor
with the lemon zest and process
again until the mixture forms a ball.

With floury, cool fingers scrape the
mixture out of the processor and
divide it into convenient batches for
your tins. Place on sheets of plastic
wrap and shape each portion of
dough into a cylinder of about
5cm/2in diameter. Mark each pack
with the pastry type and date.
Chill for at least 2 hours, then freeze
those not required immediately.

This dough is impossible to roll
out, so use a sharp knife to cut thin
discs off the end of the dough
cylinder and use these to cover the
bottom and sides of the tart tin.
Overlap the discs slightly and push
down lightly with your fingers and
knuckles to make the surface of the
shell as even as possible. Be careful to
press the pastry right into the
corners, curves and flutings so there
is no air between the tin and the
pastry. Fill the pastry shell with your
desired filling (see below) – it does
not need to be baked blind.

Place a baking tray in the centre of
the oven and preheat the oven to
190°C/375°F/Gas 5. Sit your tart on
the hot baking tray and cook for
25 minutes, then decrease the heat to
150°C/300°F/Gas 2 and continue
baking for another 20 minutes or so.
The pastry is done when it is golden
and has started to shrink from the
sides of the tart tin.

Recipe notes In addition to its superb
flavour, this pastry freezes well and
can be filled and cooked straight
from the freezer. I simply fill it with
soft fruit and frangipane (page 198),
and it cooks beautifully.

Because of its high butter content,
this pastry can be kept in the fridge
for a month, or frozen as directed in
the recipe. This quantity of dough
covers 2 flan tins 24cm/9½in
diameter and 6cm/2½in deep. In deep
flan tins such as these, the pastry
should be solid around the sides to
support the filling, and pushed right
up to the top of the fluting as it will
shrink slightly during baking.

Huff pastry
Makes 1kg/2lb 4oz

15g/½oz/2 tbsp dried milk powder
*10g/⅓oz/1 heaped tbsp salt, plus extra
   to glaze*
*675g/1lb 8oz/4⅔ cups strong [bread]
   flour, plus extra for dusting*
1 tbsp sunflower or groundnut oil
*about 310-340ml/11-12floz/1¼-1½ cups
   water*
*7g/¼oz fresh yeast, or 3.5g/⅛oz/1¼ tsp
   active dried yeast*
1 egg plus 1 egg yolk

Make the dough ideally with a dough
hook on an electric mixer, or the
plastic blade of a food processor. It is
possible to make by hand (of course,
that's how it was made traditionally)
but requires a lot of muscular work.

First sift the milk powder, salt and
flour together into a large mixing
bowl, rubbing any large milk powder
granules through the sieve. Add the
oil to a jug of 310ml/11floz/1¼ cups
water, then add the yeast. Stir the
mixture to smooth out all the lumps,
then whisk it briefly.

With the machine running, add the
liquid to the dry ingredients. There is
no need to be gentle: the dough
should be firm, tight and hard.
However, if it does seem terribly dry
and tough (probably due to a very
high gluten content in the flour), add
an extra 2 tbsp of water.

When the dough loses its stickiness
and forms a smooth ball, place it in a
large plastic bag. Leave it to rest for
30 minutes in the fridge to allow the
dough to soften and become pliable,
and allow the yeast to work.

Roll the pastry out firmly on a
cool, flour-dusted surface, using
plenty of pressure on your rolling pin
to obtain a thin sheet of pastry.

Just before baking, whisk the egg and egg yolk together in a jug with a pinch of salt and use the mixture to glaze the pastry lightly and gently.

Recipe notes Huff paste was the name originally given to the unleavened dough that was used to protect food from the heat of the fire. Clay was once employed for the same purpose. To this day pastry such as this is used to seal the lids of cooking pots for stews and braises in traditional English and French recipes. My version includes a little yeast, as it causes the pastry to rise during baking and form beautiful shapes with the trimmings.

Measuring out such small amounts of ingredients may seem fiddly, but therein lies the success of pastry in general, and this one in particular. The yeast and salt measurements are especially critical. If you own a balance scale, note that a British two pence piece weighs 7 grams.

The dough can be made 1-2 days in advance, and it will prove while chilling. Periodically remove it from the fridge and, with the palms of your hand, squeeze the dough out flat and firmly on the worktop.

The quantity here makes enough huff paste to cover a 1.8kg/4lb joint of meat and provide plenty of trimmings for decoration.

Smoked salmon scones
Makes 15

225g/8oz smoked salmon, finely chopped
3 spring onions [scallions], finely chopped
grated zest of 1 lemon
300g/10½oz/2 cups plain [all-purpose] flour, plus extra for dusting
2 tbsp baking powder
30g/1oz/¼ stick salted butter
2 eggs
150ml/5floz/⅔ cup milk or cream
salt and freshly milled black pepper

For the glaze
1 egg yolk
2 tbsp cream

You will also need
a plain round cutter of 6-7cm/2½in diameter

Preheat the oven to 200°C/400°C/ Gas 6. Combine the salmon, spring onions and lemon zest in a small mixing bowl and set aside.

Sift the flour and baking powder together twice into a large mixing bowl. Rub or cut the butter into the flour until the mixture resembles fine breadcrumbs. Fold in the salmon mixture and make a well in the centre.

Whisk the eggs together in a jug with the milk or cream, then pour the liquid into the flour mixture. Gently mix to a dough with a knife or spatula. Season well.

Turn the dough onto a floured board and pat it out with the palms of your hands until it is about 2cm/¾in thick. Cut it into rounds with the cutter, adding a little more flour if the mixture seems too sticky.

To make the glaze, combine the egg yolk with 2 tbsp cream in a small dish. Place the scones on a baking sheet and brush the tops very lightly with the glaze. Transfer to the oven and bake for 10-15 minutes or until the scones are golden. Serve warm on their own, or split and filled.

Recipe notes If the scones are too sticky to move onto the baking sheet, you have not incorporated enough flour. Simply add a little more.

This is a good recipe to serve as canapés. Using a 3.5cm/1¼in diameter cutter will give 35 baby scones, and for that quantity you will need ½ cucumber, 150g/5oz/⅔ cup cream cheese, 5-6 tbsp of finely chopped chives and seven slices of smoked salmon.

To fill, split each little scone in half and place a thin slice of cannelled cucumber on the base of each one. Mix the cream cheese with some of the chives and season with salt and pepper. Spoon this mixture over the scones, then add a disc of smoked salmon. Place the top of the scone at an angle, then dip the exposed cream cheese into a dish of the remaining finely chopped chives to decorate.

Chilli corn bread
Serves 4

2 eggs, at room temperature
400g/14oz can corn kernels, drained
4 tbsp olive oil or sunflower oil
5 green or red chillies, deseeded and
  chopped
125ml/4floz/½ cup soured cream
150g/5oz/1 cup coarse cornmeal
1 tbsp baking powder
a large pinch of salt
250g/8½oz/2 cups mature cheddar
  cheese, grated
butter, for greasing

You will also need
a square cake tin of 22cm/8½in diameter

Preheat the oven to 180°C/350°F/
Gas 4. Make sure the eggs are at
room temperature. Use the butter to
grease the tin, then line it with
buttered parchment paper.

Place the corn kernels in a food
processor and whizz to a textured
but creamy paste. In a large mixing
bowl, whisk the eggs and oil together
until blended. Add the creamed corn,
chillies, sour cream, cornmeal,
baking powder, salt and all but a few
tbsp of the grated cheese. Mix well.

Pour the batter into the prepared
tin and sprinkle the remaining cheese
over the top. Bake for 1 hour, then
remove from the oven and serve warm.

Recipe notes This recipe from Sonia
Plenderleith of South Africa is good
served with chunky tomato-based
soups, beef steaks and at barbecues
with a side dish of chopped avocado,
sweet ripe tomato, coriander
[cilantro], red onion, Worcestershire
sauce, and Tabasco.

Black olive and red onion quick bread

1 large red onion, sliced
4 tbsp extra virgin olive oil
225g/8oz/1¼ cups plain [all-purpose]
  flour
60g/2oz/scant ½ cup cornmeal
1 tbsp baking powder
1 tsp salt
2 eggs
200ml/8floz/1 cup buttermilk or soured
  milk
1 large red chilli, deseeded and chopped
400g/14oz can pitted black olives in
  brine, drained thoroughly and roughly
  chopped
60g/2oz/½ cup parmesan cheese, grated
softened butter, for greasing

You will also need
a loaf tin measuring 22 x 11 x 6cm/
  8½ x 4½ x 2½in

Butter the tin and line the long sides
with a sheet of buttered parchment
paper, leaving a little hanging over
each side to act as handles when you
lift the cooked bread from the tin.
Heat the oven to 200°C/400°F/Gas 6.

Fry the onion in 2 tbsp of the olive
oil until soft. Sift the flour, cornmeal,
baking powder and salt together into
a large mixing bowl. In a jug, beat
the eggs with the buttermilk or
soured milk, and the remaining
2 tbsp of olive oil.

To the dry ingredients, add the chilli,
olives and half the Parmesan cheese.
Stir, then add the cooked onions,
scraping any oil from the pan into
the bowl. Pour in the egg mixture
and mix well. Spoon the mixture into
the prepared tin and sprinkle with
the rest of the Parmesan cheese.
Bake for 40-50 minutes or until the
loaf is well-risen and golden brown.

Remove from the oven and place on
a wire rack, leaving the bread to cool
in the tin for 5 minutes, before turning
it out and serving in thick slices.

Recipe notes I particularly enjoyed
The Telegraph's Saturday food page
when it featured 'The Weekend Bake'
by Thane Prince. Coming home from
a walk or a jog to the aroma of
baking, then eating something warm
and crumbly straight out of the oven
with family or friends, are good
weekend memories.

As ingredients have such a mild
flavour after their long journeys to
London, I sometimes try to make up
for it by serving them twice in the
same course – cooked and uncooked
– to get the most out of them. So, in
summer I would serve this with a feta
cheese salad, crisp cos lettuce hearts,
finely sliced red onion, black and
green olives and vine tomatoes. In
winter, I'd simply spread it with
butter and serve with a soup. In both
cases, serve the bread warm.

Parmesan crisps
Makes 10

*100g/3½oz/scant 1 cup parmesan
    cheese, grated*
*25g/1oz/¼ cup dry, mature cheddar
    cheese, grated*

You will also need
*a round cookie cutter of 6.5cm/2½in
    diameter*

Heat the oven to 180°C/350°F/Gas 4.
Mix the grated cheeses together in a
bowl. Place the cookie cutter on a
non-stick baking sheet or one lined
with a flat silicone mat. Using a
1 tbsp measuring spoon, scoop up
the cheese, level it off, and distribute
it evenly in the cookie cutter. Use the
point of a knife to tickle the cheese
evenly into a circle.

Remove the cutter and repeat the
process across the tray, leaving plenty
of space between the rounds for the
cheese to spread while baking.

Place the tray in the oven carefully,
keeping the circles of cheese in shape.
Cook for 8 minutes or until golden.
Remove from the oven and leave the
cheese discs to cool on the tray.

Using the point of a knife, remove
the crisps from the tray and store
them in an airtight tin or plastic box,
interleaved with paper towel.

Recipe notes As light as a feather, as
lacy as brandy snaps, these cheese
crisps could not be easier to make
and contrast beautifully with the cool
silkiness of parmesan custards (page
90). They are a perfect and elegant
nibble served on their own with
drinks and make a wonderful canapé
when used to sandwich fresh crab
that you have just moistened with
creamy vinaigrette (page 162).

Alternatively, make it a combination
of crab meat and diced avocado, and
flavour the creamy vinaigrette with a
little balsamic vinegar.

If preferred, you can use only
parmesan, and leave out the cheddar.
This gives a slightly crisper result,
but I find the cheddar seems to hold
these fragile biscuits together better.

To grate parmesan easily, throw
little chunks of it onto the whizzing
blade of a food processor, then store
it in plastic tubs in the freezer. You
can use it from almost-frozen for
cooking. However, you should never
buy ready-grated parmesan, because
it tastes quite foul.

If you already have some grated
parmesan to hand, simply combine
both cheeses in the food processor
and whizz to a fine crumble.

The secret of making them exactly
the same size is to ensure all the
measured tablespoons of cheese are
levelled off evenly. The secret of the
golden colour and lacy holes is the
right oven temperature: it is worth
experimenting in your own oven if
you are disappointed with the results
achieved at the temperature given here.

When stored interleaved with paper
towel in an airtight container, these
crisps will keep for several days.

Sesame sablés
Makes 25

*10g/⅓oz/2 tbsp sesame seeds, plus 2 tsp
    extra for sprinkling*
1 egg white
*60g/2oz/½ cup icing [confectioners']
    sugar, sifted*
a large pinch of salt
*135g/4¾oz/1¼ sticks salted butter, very
    soft*
*175g/6oz/1¼ cups plain [all-purpose]
    flour*
¼ tsp sesame oil

Ideally, you should make this recipe
in a warm kitchen, or warm the
ingredients and equipment to body
heat before you begin. Preheat the
oven to 180°C/350°F/Gas 4.

Toast the sesame seeds by placing
them all on a tray and roasting for
about 8 minutes (but watch!) until
they are golden. Set aside 2 tsp for
sprinkling over the sablés.

Place the egg white in a jug and
whisk it lightly until a few bubbles
appear. Sift the sugar and salt
together into a large mixing bowl.
Add the butter and beat together,
using an electric hand whisk or a
wooden spoon, until the mixture is
very pale, soft and fluffy. Gradually
beat in the whisked egg white.

Stir in the flour, sesame oil and
toasted seeds to give a smooth paste.
Using a teaspoon, drop equal
quantities of the dough onto a heavy
non-stick baking tray and flatten
each mound with your finger.

Lightly sprinkle the sablés with the
reserved toasted sesame seeds and
bake in the oven for 10-15 minutes
or until they are golden.

Remove the sablés from the oven
and leave to cool on a cake rack
before storing in an airtight tin.

Recipe notes Sablés take their name from the French word for sand, and biscuits and pastries of this type should have a pleasantly crisp, sandy, and friable texture, which is achieved in part thanks to the process of creaming the softened butter and sugar together. Although they are essentially a savoury biscuit, the icing sugar helps make them very light and crumbly, and I love their combination of sweet and salty savouriness.

They make an unusually good contrast to plain and oatmeal crackers when served with cheese, and are especially delicious alongside creamy blues such as Dolcelatte or Cambazola, where a note of sweetness is welcome. I think these sesame flavoured sablés would be gorgeous too with firm Nashi pears and a light sugar syrup flavoured with chilli and ginger (page 200).

Toasted sesame seeds are useful to have on hand in the kitchen and store well in an airtight box in a cool, dark cupboard, so don't hesitate to toast some extra while you have the oven on. Sprinkle them over Chinese and Asian dishes, or salads.

Ginger cookies
Makes 50-60

290g/10½oz/2 cups self-raising flour, plus extra for dusting
115g/4oz/⅔ cup caster [superfine granulated] sugar
10g/⅓oz ground cinnamon
4 tsp ground ginger
a pinch of ground cloves
75g/3oz/¾ stick salted butter, chilled and cubed
4 tbsp golden syrup [light corn syrup]
4 tsp black treacle [molasses]
1 egg, beaten

You will also need
a round cookie cutter of 6.5cm/2½in diameter

Sift the flour, sugar, cinnamon, ginger and cloves together into a large mixing bowl. Cut the butter into the flour and rub together until the mixture resembles breadcrumbs.

Add the syrup and treacle and begin to knead the mixture. Pour in the beaten egg, which will bind everything into a large ball of dough. Roll into a cylinder, wrap in plastic wrap and place in the fridge to chill until the mixture loses its stickiness.

Preheat the oven to 175°C/330°F/Gas 3½. Roll out the dough on a cool worktop lightly dusted with flour. Use the cookie cutter to cut the dough into discs, then use a fish slice or spatula to help you transfer them to non-stick baking trays.

Bake for 15 minutes then remove from the oven. Slide the cookies onto a wire rack to cool before storing them in an airtight tin.

Recipe notes Serve these cookies with ice-creams, mousses, or with cups of coffee after a meal. You certainly don't have to use only round cookie cutters – I stamp them into heart shapes and gingerbread men, though the mixture is perhaps too strongly flavoured for children.

The cookies are ideal served as part of the festive fare at Christmas but they are rich and buttery and meant for eating, unlike the decorative ginger cookies one normally sees at that time of year. Don't try and make a gingerbread house or tree ornaments from the dough, however you might want to consider topping them with royal icing and little silver or coloured balls. The decorated cookies look fabulous when tied in cellophane bags and are so much nicer to take to a party as a gift for the hosts than the predictable bottle of wine.

If you would like to make large gingerbread men, roll out sections of the dough on your work surface then slide the dough onto silicone paper. Continue to roll the dough on the silicone paper until it is thin, then cut out the figures using a gingerbread man cutter. Slide the gingerbread men, still on their paper, onto the baking trays to cook.

It is essential that the measurement of syrup and treacle is accurate in this recipe. To achieve this, rub your measuring spoon first with a little oil, and cut off the treacle or syrup with a small knife as it pours from the jar. The treacle and syrup will slip easily off the measuring spoon.

Both the dough and the biscuits store well in the freezer.

Oatmeal crackers
Makes 40

225g/8oz/1⅔ cups plain [all-purpose]
flour, plus extra for dusting
1½ tsp salt
½ tsp bicarbonate of soda [baking soda]
85g/3oz/scant ½ cup caster [superfine
granulated] sugar
225g/8oz/1⅓ cups medium oatmeal
85g/3oz/¼ stick butter
85g/3oz/6 tbsp lard
a little milk

You will also need
a plain or crinkled round cookie cutter
of 4cm/1½in diameter

Preheat the oven to 200°C/400°F/
Gas 6. Sift the flour with the salt,
bicarbonate of soda and sugar into a
large mixing bowl. Stir in the oatmeal.
Dice the butter and lard and drop
them into the dry ingredients. With
the tips of your fingers, rub the flour
and fat together until the mixture
looks like fresh breadcrumbs.

Add a little milk, 1 tbsp at a time,
adding only just enough to enable
you to clump up the dough into a
ball. If the dough feels too sticky at
this stage, place it in the bowl in the
fridge for 20 minutes or so.

Dust a cool work surface with a
little flour and roll the dough out
thinly. Cut into rounds with the
cutter and place on a heavy non-stick
baking tray. Bake for 6-7 minutes or
until pale golden. Remove the
crackers from the oven and slide
them onto a wire rack. They will firm
up a little as they cool. Store the
crackers in an airtight tin.

Recipe notes Perhaps it is the sensation
of 'shortness' – the melt-in-the-mouth
quality unique to lard – combined
with the nuttiness of the oats, and
the hint of salt and sugar that makes
these crackers so good.

They do keep exceptionally well,
but not in my home. I like to serve
them with a simple home-made curd
cheese, rolled in finely chopped fresh
chives and parsley. They make a
wonderful breakfast spread with
butter and some heather or orange
blossom honey, they're gorgeous with
home-made jams, and a great snack
to include in a packed lunch. In fact
I can't think of anytime when I
wouldn't eat them, which is why I
can't keep them in the house.

It is essential to use oatmeal for
this recipe, not rolled oats or porridge
oats, which are manufactured by a
different process and have a completely
different texture and flavour to the
traditional steel-cut oatmeal favoured
in Scotland and Ireland. The bonus is
that oatmeal is wholegrain, therefore
particularly high in fibre. It is also
exceptionally good for heart health
in helping to reduce cholesterol.

Almond thins
Makes 30

30g/1oz/3½ tbsp blanched almonds
70g/2½oz/⅓ cup caster [superfine
granulated] sugar
110g/4oz/1 stick unsalted butter
150g/5oz/1 cup plain [all-purpose] flour,
plus extra for dusting

Heat the oven to 180°C/350°F/Gas 4.
Spread the almonds out on a baking
sheet and toast in the hot oven for
about 10 minutes or until golden.
Remove from the oven and cool.

Place the nuts and sugar in a food
processor and whizz until fine, being
sure to stop before the almonds turn
oily. Slice the butter into the bowl
and process until light. Add the flour
and blend to a paste.

Turn the dough out onto a lightly
floured board and shape it into two
cylinders, or bricks. Wrap in plastic
wrap, flatten slightly and refrigerate
for several hours until firm.

Heat the oven to 190°C/375°F/Gas 5.
Line some baking trays with silicone
paper. Use a fine, sharp knife to slice
the dough into thin cookies and place
them on the trays. Bake for 10-12
minutes, or until beginning to brown.

Remove the cookies from the oven
and cool on the trays for 2 minutes
before transferring to a wire rack.
Store in an airtight tin, out of sight.

Recipe notes Katie Stewart taught us
to cook these at my old cookery
school and they were so admired in
one of my classes that Michel Roux
decided to put them in his guest
bedrooms at The Waterside Inn.

You can store the blocks of dough
in the freezer and cut and bake the
cookies as required. Use hazelnuts
instead of almonds if you prefer.

Desserts and cakes

Fast ways with desserts

Sandwich round shortbread biscuits with whipped cream and raspberries

Serve ripe, sweet fruit in perfect condition, or a fruit salad presented in half a melon.

Crush amaretti or almond macaroons and fold with chopped strawberries into vanilla-flavoured whipped cream.

Sprinkle a glass bowl of strawberries liberally with Grand Marnier.

Slice canned pears and steep in a little ginger syrup, reduced until it tastes hot and spicy. Serve with shiny chocolate sauce.

Fry cubes of pineapple until caramelized and served on toasted brioche, topped with passionfruit seeds and ice-cream.

Bake sliced bananas and passionfruit en papillote. Or use peaches or nectarines sprinkled with white rum and topped with a vanilla bean.

I see desserts as the thoroughly spoiling and loving part of a meal. If you are very fond of your guests, you find you will go to immense lengths to cook them something special. If you love cooking, it is the part of the meal where you can lose yourself in dreaming up imaginative, new, rich and evocative recipes, and making them a dazzling reality. It is the course in which you can indulge in fantasy and sensuality, where you can place hot on cold, contrast tart with sweet, match crisp and gritty with creamily soft, and make the most of the seductive hues of spices, caramel, chocolate, and the brilliant range of colours given to us by fruit.

In my home weekdays are usually spent trying to eat sensibly, and jogging to work off the calories consumed during dinner parties or recipe testing the weekend before. When I get late-night cravings for something sweet, ripe fruit is good. In fact, I'd say that finishing off a meal with perfectly ripe, fresh fruit is the ideal, except that living in England means it can be a struggle. Unless you have a greenhouse, it is just not the same wonderful conclusion to a meal that it is in Italy and the South of France. Instead, I might have some fine organic chocolate, either white or bitter, broken into shards and served with coffee, or finish off the week-end baking session by serving leftover cakes in small wedges with the smallest trickle of cream.

Producing desserts for mid-week dinner parties demands consideration for guests. I avoid all liqueurs and rum in sauces and fruit, and replace crème fraîche and double [heavy] cream with yogurt or egg custard. I try to make the dessert a feast for the eye, choosing jelly or a warm fruit dessert to round off the evening with panache, so that everyone feels delightfully spoiled even if the dish is fairly light and low in calories.

After a particularly jovial evening, I find dessert is often the only part of the meal guests remember with any clarity, and they certainly do so with genuine appreciation. I like to serve an ice-cream, which melts to form the sweet sauce, alongside a cake and something crisp. A few segments of fresh fruit, which glisten in the candlelight and provide a refreshing element to the dessert, are an important inclusion. Spices, the use of bright, deep colours, and contrasts of temperature such as vanilla ice-cream with a hot tarte Tatin can provide a sensual element.

What to look for, what to avoid

• Try to find a source of fresh, sweet nuts. Almonds and hazelnuts are especially useful for desserts. Nuts in shells are the freshest but can be too time-consuming to prepare. When using nuts in desserts and baking, refresh them by drying them out a little in an oven set to 160-180°C/310-350°F/Gas 2½-4.

- Choose pure unsalted butter, preferably one made by a French manufacturer.
- For the best flavour, chocolate should be a good quality dark variety with a cocoa solids content of around 70 per cent (this will be noted on the packet). Try not to mix brands of chocolate. It helps to become very familiar with one variety when striving for consistent results.
- Double [heavy] cream can be whisked, and boiled without curdling. It is the best cream to use for piping and decorating, and can be flavoured, though this should be done with restraint.
- Crème fraîche, a thick fermented French cream with a pleasant bite, can be served plain alongside desserts, or whisked into a crème chantilly, which is whipped cream flavoured with sugar and vanilla or brandy.
- Mascarpone, the rich Italian cream, makes a delectable accompaniment to cakes and tarts. It is similar to double [heavy] cream and although sold set firm in tubs, melts easily.
- I tend to favour Greek yogurt for cooking. Its rich flavour and texture can be intensified by straining through a sieve lined with paper towel or muslin [cheesecloth] for half an hour.
- Preserved stem ginger in syrup is an excellent store cupboard stand-by for use in desserts. Choose a reliable brand from China, or Australia, where the stems of ginger grown are especially tender and not fibrous.
- The best vanilla beans look plump and luscious and are generally grown in Madagascar.

Storing and freezing
- I keep all spare egg whites in the fridge in a spankingly-clean lidded glass jar for 10 days or so. They are good to have on hand for meringues and soufflés and are easily measured by weight into a beaker placed on a scale.
- Egg custards keep for about two days in the coldest part of the fridge. Always keep them chilled, and remember to heat and chill them quickly to prevent the growth of bacteria. Blitzing with a stick blender just before serving will infuse custard with light, frothy bubbles.
- Raspberry and chocolate sauces can be frozen for months. It is worth making much more than you need and storing them in the freezer in convenient portions. A 350ml/12floz/1½ cup tub of sauce will serve five to six people. You can blitz half-frozen raspberry sauce with a stick blender or in a blender to help it defrost quickly, and imbue it with bubbles.
- Sugar syrups store well in clean glass bottles in the fridge for up to two weeks, after which they will start to grow a little mold.
- Ice-creams and sorbets obviously store well in the freezer and are good to have on hand for quick desserts, or accompanying cakes and tarts. Vanilla is perhaps the most versatile flavour. I also like to make my own lemon ice-cream, and buy in mango sorbet made from the best alfonso mangoes.

How to tell when desserts are cooked
- Ripe fruit is so full of juice that special care needs to be taken when baking or poaching it. It should be cooked until it is soft but still holding its shape. Allow it to steep in the syrup until required. If baking, remove it gently from the oven and allow to cool a little before serving. Hot steaming fruit has little flavour.
- A sweet custard cooked in a mold in order to be turned out is done when the top is firm near the sides of the mold and spongy in the centre. A skewer inserted in the centre usually comes out clean. Sometimes it will start to shrink away from the sides, in which case it will come cleanly out of the mold, after a resting period of about 7 minutes, in or out of the bain-marie, depending on the recipe. When you shake the plate it is served on, the custard should shiver with confidence 'like a belly-dancer's tummy', as they say in Persia.
- A custard baked and served in ramekins, tea glasses, or shallow dishes should be set and firmish at the sides, with the middle wobbly. To check, protect your hands with an oven cloth and shake the cooking vessel. If you think it is undercooked, allow it to remain in the water bath, to soak up all the residual heat and continue cooking. If it is still a bit runny in the centre, chill it in a very cold fridge to firm it up.
- If you want to serve six perfect soufflés, make nine. The extras allow you to test for doneness easily. You can then reach right into the bottom of one of the soufflés with a spoon to check the consistency. They should have risen to their maximum expansion and be tender and creamy at the centre.

Orange and Campari jellies
Serves 4

350ml/12floz/1½ cups clear apple juice
100ml/3½floz/scant ½ cup Campari
11g/¼oz/1 sachet powdered gelatine
1 orange
4 sprigs mint
8 tbsp thick pouring cream (optional)

You will also need
4 molds or serving glasses of
150ml/5floz/⅔ cup capacity, chilled
a bag of ice (optional)

Combine the apple juice and Campari in a spanking-clean saucepan. Sprinkle the gelatine over the liquid and leave to soak for at least 5 minutes.

Heat the mixture gently, without boiling, and stir from time to time with a clean metal spoon to prevent bubbles forming. Meanwhile, rinse your chosen molds in cold water but do not dry them.

When the gelatine has dissolved and the mixture is perfectly clear, pour a little into the molds and set the remainder aside in the saucepan. Place the molds in the fridge to set, or nestle them in a roasting tray filled with ice and a little water and leave them until the jelly is firm.

Meanwhile, segment the orange. Reserve four segments for decorating the finished desserts, if desired.

When the jelly has set in the molds, place 1-2 orange segments and a mint leaf on top of each, then cover with a little more of the liquid jelly. Chill again until set. Repeat this layering process until you reach the top of the mold, ensuring that the fruit is completely covered by the jelly.

Chill the jellies for several hours or overnight, until they are completely set. Serve in the glasses, allowing the

jelly to soften a little at room temperature until it has a slight wobble. Alternatively, dip the base of each mold in hot water, or rotate it over a small gas flame. Invert onto a small serving plate and slide the jelly into position, using the mold to help you, before lifting it off.

Garnish with a sprig of mint, and the reserved orange segments, then either serve with a drizzle of pouring cream, or clean and fresh without.

Recipe notes It was one of the hottest ever days in London when I made this for the photograph, so I resorted to the fail-safe way of making jellies, with ice and a roasting tray. The small amount of jelly poured into the molds sets within minutes because the glasses are surrounded by ice and water, which are much colder than the cool air of the refrigerator.

If you have a large roomy fridge and plenty of time, simply chill the molds or serving glasses in the fridge as you go through the stages of layering up the orange segments and the rosy liquid jelly.

I am often asked if there is an easy conversion between the leaf gelatine often used in French and Italian recipes, and powdered gelatine favoured in many British recipes. The answer is no: keep both in the store cupboard, and use them as directed. The difference between success and failure in the conversion may seem to be only a cat's whisker but is horribly obvious in the result – a hopelessly collapsed jelly or a piece of rubber.

Fortunately, you can make this slithery, cool and refreshing dessert the day before serving. It is the ideal conclusion to a spicy or rich meal.

Summer berries with lemon custard
Serves 6

800g/1lb 12oz/7 cups very ripe, sweet
berries

For the custard
240ml/8floz/1 cup single cream
220ml/7½floz/scant 1 cup freshly
squeezed lemon juice
140g/5oz/13 tbsp caster [superfine
granulated] sugar
6 egg yolks

To make the custard, combine the cream and lemon juice in a stainless steel saucepan and add 5 tbsp of the sugar. Heat until almost boiling. Meanwhile, in a mixing bowl, whisk the egg yolks with the remaining sugar until the mixture is lemon-coloured, pale and sticky.

Pour the boiling cream carefully onto the yolk mixture, whisking constantly with a hand whisk but trying to create a minimum of bubbles. Clean the pan and pour the custard mixture back into it.

Cook gently, stirring continuously with a spatula and pressing it hard on the base of the pan, until the custard thickens. Strain into a jug, and stir from time to time as it cools, then cover and chill.

To serve, wash the berries quickly, hull and dry well. Sprinkle the fruit in a pretty shallow dish, pour over the custard and serve immediately.

Recipe notes This quintessentially summery recipe is a refreshing finish to any summer meal but the fruit must be ripe and sweet to form a contrast to the lemony custard. If you can, decorate the dish with a few leaves and berry flowers.

Spiced orange salad with star anise
Serves 8

*175ml/6floz/¾ cup light sugar syrup
    (page 200)*
8 star anise
1 cube fresh ginger, chopped
1 small piece cinnamon stick
*1 tsp orange flower water, or more to
    taste*
8 large oranges
5-6 mint sprigs or bay leaves
*seeds of 1 ripe red pomegranate
    (optional)*

Place the sugar syrup, star anise and ginger in a clean saucepan and bring to the boil. Simmer for 5 minutes, then set aside to cool. Add the cinnamon and orange flower water.

Take the oranges one by one, and with a sharp serrated knife, cut off the tops and bottoms so they stand stable on the worktop. Cut a strip down one side of each fruit, following its curve, to remove the peel and white pith in one piece, leaving the juicy orange flesh exposed beneath. Repeat all around each orange until there are no flecks of white pith.

Cut across the oranges then slice them into rounds, and place them in a bowl. Strain the spiced syrup over the oranges, reserving the star anise to use as a garnish.

Divide the orange salad and syrup amongst serving dishes, add the mint or bay leaves, star anise, and top with the pomegranate seeds.

Recipe notes Serve this on its own, or alongside chocolate cake (page 196), or a creamy cheesecake bought from your local patisserie or deli. If you can, make it well in advance, to give the flavours time to mellow and blend.

Plums with red wine
Serves 4-8

*110g/4oz/heaped ½ cup caster [superfine
    granulated] sugar*
1 large cinnamon stick
4 vanilla beans
*280ml/10floz/1¼ cups red wine such
    as Merlot*
900g/2lb large firm red plums
juice of 2 lemons

Preheat the oven to 160°C/310°F/ Gas 2-3. Place the sugar, cinnamon, vanilla, red wine and 280ml/10floz/ 1¼ cups water in a casserole [Dutch oven] and bring to a simmer on the stovetop, stirring constantly until all the sugar has dissolved.

Use a small, pointed knife to cut a cross in the base of each plum and plop them all in the wine mixture. Cover and maintain the heat at the slowest simmer for 5 minutes.

Transfer the pot to the oven and cook for about 15 minutes, until the plums are tender when pierced with a skewer. Be sure to stop before the skins split and the fruit begins to look manky or dishevelled.

Remove the pot from the oven and leave the plums to cool in the liquor if time permits, rolling them once or twice as they cool.

Use a skimmer to lift the plums carefully from the pan as they will have become quite fragile. Drain, dabbing the base of the skimmer on a wad of kitchen paper, and place the fruit in a serving dish.

Strain the cooking syrup into a clean saucepan, and boil until the mixture has reduced to a volume of around 400ml/14floz/1¾ cups.

Add enough freshly squeezed lemon juice to the syrup to make it taste pleasantly tart. Serve the plums hot or cold in bowls with plenty of the syrup poured over them, either on their own or accompanied by vanilla custard or ice-cream.

Recipe notes There is something about autumn and dark plums – those glowing, dusky, deep mulberry, burgundy colours – that I find really comforting and rewarding, especially having grown up in the tropics. It is a feeling akin to getting out that winter coat you love and snuggling up warm when that first icy breeze nips around your neck.

This is a quick, homely dessert that can be made the day before serving and seems to get better the longer you keep it. The plums can also be served with chocolate cake (page 196), or thick slices of almond or ginger pound cake, bought from a deli or patisserie.

Wash the vanilla beans under the tap after use here, then leave them to dry and return to the storage jar for use on another occasion.

Cherry whim-whams
Serves 8

16 amaretti, ratafia or sponge finger biscuits
8 tbsp cherry brandy, brandy or kirsch
16 brandied cherries (griottes), or fresh cherries, stoned
8 Crystallized Rose Petals (page 201)

For the custard
150ml/5floz/²⁄₃ cup whipping [heavy] cream
280ml/10floz/1¼ cups milk
8 large egg yolks
60g/2oz/5 tbsp caster [superfine granulated] sugar
½ tsp vanilla extract

For the syllabub
8 tbsp sweet muscat wine
2 tbsp cherry brandy or brandy
juice of ½ large lemon
60g/2oz/5 tbsp caster [superfine granulated] sugar, or to taste
280ml/10floz/1¼ cups double [heavy] cream

To make the custard, heat the cream and milk together in a heavy-based saucepan until almost boiling.

Meanwhile, whisk the egg yolks and sugar together until pale, creamy and lemon-coloured. Pour the hot cream mixture onto the yolk mixture, whisking constantly.

Clean the saucepan and return the custard to it. Cook until thick, voluptuous and silky, taking care not to overheat the mixture or it will separate. Remove from the heat and plunge the base of the pan into a basin of cold water, to stop the cooking. Set aside to cool, stirring occasionally, then flavour with the vanilla extract.

Divide the biscuits and cherries between eight serving glasses and

spoon over the cherry brandy, brandy or kirsch if using. Carefully spoon the thick custard into the glasses and set aside in a cold place for about 4 hours or overnight.

To make the syllabub, measure the sweet wine, brandy and lemon juice into a mixing bowl and stir in the sugar until dissolved. Whisking constantly (preferably with an electric whisk), add the cream and whisk until the mixture is thick enough to softly hold its shape. Spoon the syllabub carefully into the glasses and chill them for another hour.

Just before serving, decorate with the crystallized rose petals.

Recipe notes A thoroughly English pudding, this comes from an eighteenth century recipe for whim-wham, meaning a trifle. Rich, cool and creamy, it can be deeply alcoholic, fruity or dainty and is best made the day before serving as a long chilling allows the flavours to blend into something glorious.

In late summer, ripe, scented peaches, nectarines and soft fruit can be combined for a fresh flavour, in which case you should replace the cherry brandy with sherry or sweet muscat wine. Cherry brandy and kirsch are often most easily purchased as miniatures. If you prefer, you can also replace the syllabub topping with 300ml/10floz/1¼ cups of softly whipped cream.

Yogurt mousse with raspberry sauce
Serves 6-8

900g/2lb plain stirred yogurt, or 500g/ 1lb 2oz set or strained yogurt
125ml/4floz/½ cup double [heavy] cream
4 tbsp caster [superfine granulated] sugar
4 egg whites

To serve
vanilla sugar, sifted, for sprinkling
300ml/10floz/1¼ cups whipping [heavy] cream
200g/7oz/scant 2 cups fresh berries (optional)
8 sprigs of mint or lemon verbena
1 quantity Raspberry Sauce (page 201)

You will also need
6-8 perforated molds (optional)
6-8 small squares of muslin [cheesecloth], or 1 large piece of muslin

Line a sieve with paper towel and set it over a mixing bowl. Add the yogurt and leave to drain for about 3 hours if using stirred yogurt, and about 1 hour if using set or strained yogurt. After draining, weigh the yogurt and measure out 400g/14oz to use in this recipe.

Place the drained yogurt in a large mixing bowl and whisk in the cream and sugar. In a separate large bowl, whisk the egg whites until they form fairly stiff peaks, then lightly fold them into the yogurt mixture.

Dampen the muslin squares and use them to line the perforated molds. Alternatively, line a medium-sized sieve with a large piece of damp muslin. Pile the mousse mixture into the molds or sieve, and place in or on something to collect the moisture >

that will seep out. The mixture will sink slightly as the water from the egg whites drains away. Leave the mousses to drain overnight (if you have the time) or just for an hour or so in the fridge.

To serve, turn out the mousses or mousse and serve with a bowl of vanilla sugar, a jug of cream, fresh berries (if using), a sprig of mint or verbena, and the raspberry sauce.

Recipe notes This soft, luscious concoction began as a French dessert with a delightful fluffy texture called Cremets d'Anger, from the Loire Valley. You can still buy the special little heart-shaped porcelain molds with perforated bases designed for this dessert. By all means use them, but they are not essential to the success of the recipe.

If you are making the mousse in a sieve (or a small colander), serve it by turning the snowy mound of mousse out onto a very wide, round, coloured platter, and surround it with the fruit.

Fruit crèmes with cherries, raspberries and almonds
Serves 6

90g-150g/3oz-5oz/⅓-½ cup fruit cake or
*   plum pudding, crumbled, or drained*
*   mincemeat*
450ml/16floz/2 cups whipping [heavy]
*   cream*
60g/2½oz/6 tbsp caster [superfine
*   granulated] sugar*
4 large egg yolks
½ tsp vanilla extract
about 80g/3oz/¾ cup mixture of
*   cherries, redcurrants, raspberries*
*   and blueberries*
3 tbsp toasted flaked almonds
icing [confectioners'] sugar, for sprinkling

You will also need
a roasting tray bain-marie
6 small Moroccan tea glasses or heat-
*   proof tumblers of about 125ml/4floz/*
*   ½ cup capacity*

Heat the oven to 170°C/325°F/Gas 3. Put a kettle of water on to boil. Divide the cake, mincemeat or plum pudding amongst the glasses and press it firmly to the bottom.

In a saucepan, heat the cream and half the sugar until almost boiling. Meanwhile, in a mixing bowl, whisk the egg yolks with the remaining sugar and vanilla for 2-3 minutes or until the mixture is pale and lemon-coloured. Slowly and gently, pour the hot cream onto the yolk mixture, whisking constantly.

Fill a deep roasting pan with enough hot water from the kettle to come at least three-quarters of the way up the sides of the glasses when they are placed in the bain-marie.

Divide the hot custard amongst the glasses, filling each just over halfway, not more, and sit them in the water

bath. Place the roasting pan in the middle of the oven and bake the custards for 55 minutes.

Remove the roasting pan from the oven. Test the custards by pressing them in the centre with your finger. If they have set, put on your rubber gloves, lift the glasses from the hot water, and set aside to cool. If they are still wobbly in the centre when pressed, leave them to cool in the water bath so that they can continue cooking gently in the residual heat.

Cover the desserts with plastic wrap and chill in the refrigerator for at least 6 hours. To serve, pile the fruit and toasted almonds on top of the chilled custard and sprinkle with the icing sugar.

Recipe notes A clever recipe from Peter Gordon of New Zealand, where Christmas falls in the middle of summer, this dessert uses custard to form a wonderfully soothing combo with the fresh and dried fruits and crisp toasted nuts.

Check that the water comes well up the sides of the glasses to protect the delicate custard, otherwise the surface of the custards will overcook, turn grainy and separate.

You can make this dessert up to two days in advance, but decorate with the fruit only just before serving.

Little raspberry soufflés
Serves 4

175g/6oz/1½ cups raspberries
juice of ½ lemon
40g/1½oz egg yolks, about 2 yolks
125g/4½oz/11 tbsp caster [superfine granulated] sugar
25g/¾oz/1 tbsp plain [all-purpose] flour
220ml/7½floz/scant 1 cup milk
140g/5oz egg whites, about 4 whites
softened butter, for greasing

To serve

1 quantity Raspberry Sauce (page 201)
4 fresh raspberries
4 sprigs of mint

You will also need

4 china soufflé dishes

Heat the oven to 180°C/350°F/Gas 4. Butter the soufflé dishes twice, chilling them in between each buttering.

To make the soufflé base, purée the raspberries in a food processor or with a stick blender. Transfer the purée to a stainless steel saucepan and boil over a medium heat until it has reduced and thickened. Sieve the thickened purée to remove the seeds, then add the lemon juice.

Use an electric hand-held blender to whisk the egg yolks with 85g/3oz/ 8 tbsp of the sugar until pale and sticky. Slowly stir in the flour using a metal spoon. Bring the milk to a boil in a small saucepan. Carefully add a ladle of milk to the yolk mixture, using a hand whisk to whisk it to a smooth consistency.

Transfer the yolk mixture to a fresh, clean saucepan and heat gently, stirring constantly. Add the rest of the hot milk and let the mixture boil briefly over a moderate heat, so that it thickens and comes up the sides of the pan. Add the raspberry purée and cook for 2-3 minutes, then remove from the heat and set aside. Cover the surface of the custard with a buttered disc of paper if you are preparing it well in advance.

In a large, clean mixing bowl, whisk the egg whites with the remainder of the sugar to give a dense foam, using a large balloon whisk or electric whisk. Whisk a quarter of the egg whites briskly into the yolk mixture to loosen it, then use a rubber spatula to carefully fold in the remainder of the beaten egg whites. Lift the mixture up and over, to incorporate more air, and use the spatula in a figure of eight motion which cleans the side of the bowl.

Pile the mixture into the buttered soufflé dishes. Holding a palette knife or metal spatula at an angle, lightly press down the foam. Tap the dish on the counter to remove any large air bubbles. Use the palette knife to smooth the mixture flat, and wipe the dishes clean with a damp cloth to remove all mixture from the sides. Run your thumb round the inside rim of each dish to make a small groove that helps the soufflé to rise.

Place the soufflés in the centre of the oven and cook for 15 minutes, or until they still wobble a little and feel spongy when pressed in the centre. Meanwhile, heat the prepared raspberry sauce and heat some small plates. Remove the soufflés from the oven and quickly garnish with the berries and mint and serve immediately on the hot plates.

Recipe notes Although soufflés are renowned for being complicated to make, they aren't in reality. In fact, there are just two finite elements in sweet soufflés: the meringue and the soufflé base. Here the base is made of a custard containing a smidgen of flour, plus a strong flavour – in this case raspberry but it could be blackcurrant or chocolate. I favour this soufflé method as it is unfailingly reliable, and the soufflés stay risen until they reach the table.

Be careful not to overwhisk egg whites. Your guide is the all-important pointy peak at the top of the whisk. When it's lifted from the bowl, it should just flop over, which is the stage known as soft peak. If you overwhisk the meringue, it will stiffen to a dry, compact mass, making it difficult to mix softly and thoroughly into the flavoured base in the next stage of cooking.

The soufflé base can be made in advance and chilled, but it should be gently warmed to 37°C/98°F, or blood heat, before proceeding. The soufflés can be completed, chilled and cooked straight from the fridge, but you will need to lengthen the cooking time a little.

If there is a last-minute delay in serving the soufflés, you can keep them puffed and stable by standing them on an electric hotplate, or in a large empty frying pan over a low heat, for up to 15 minutes.

The raspberries can be fresh or frozen, although slightly better results come from fresh raspberries.

Pavlova roulade with passionfruit sauce

Serves 6-10

For the pavlova

1 tbsp sunflower oil (optional)
6 large egg whites
a pinch of salt
200g/7oz/1 cup caster [superfine
    granulated] sugar, plus 2 tbsp extra
    for dusting
1½ tsp cornflour [cornstarch]
2 tsp white wine vinegar
½ tsp vanilla extract

For the filling

400g/14oz/3 cups soft berries
300ml/10floz/1½ cups double [heavy]
    cream
1 tbsp crème de cassis or brandy
1 tbsp icing [confectioners'] sugar

For the decoration

5 strawberries or 10 sprigs of
    redcurrants (optional)
200ml/7floz/scant 1 cup double [heavy]
    cream
icing [confectioners'] sugar, for dusting
    (optional)

For the sauce

4 passionfruit
2 large firm mangoes, peeled, stoned
    and diced
2 nectarines, stoned and diced
10 strawberries, diced
about 200ml/7floz/scant 1 cup light
    sugar syrup (page 200)

You will also need

a 32 x 23cm/13 x 9in Swiss roll pan

Heat the oven to 170°C/325°F/Gas 3.
Line the Swiss roll pan with a sheet
of Teflon paper or silicone paper and
paint it lightly with the sunflower oil
if using silicone paper.

Whisk the egg whites and salt in a
large bowl until they stand in soft
peaks. Gradually beat in 100g/3½oz/
½ cup of the caster sugar, adding it
2 tbsp at a time in a steady stream.
Carefully fold in the remaining 100g/
3½oz/½ cup sugar, plus the cornflour,
vinegar and vanilla extract.

Spread the meringue over the
prepared tin, using a palette knife or
round-bladed knife to smooth the
surface. Bake at the centre of the
oven for 15 minutes. Turn the tin
around in the oven and continue
cooking for another 10 minutes or
until the meringue is just beginning
to colour on the top. Remove from
the oven and leave the pavlova to
cool in the tin for 10 minutes.

Place a large sheet of silicone paper
on a wire rack and sprinkle it evenly
with the extra 2 tbsp of caster sugar.
Carefully invert the pavlova onto the
sugar-dusted paper and peel away the
paper that lined the pan during
baking. Leave the pavlova to cool for
another 10 minutes, then trim the
short sides with a knife to neaten.

Make the filling. Hull the berries
as necessary, quartering any large
fruit such as blackberries or
strawberries. If using redcurrants, use
a fork to pick them from the stems.

Whisk the cream until very thick.
Add the crème de cassis or brandy,
and the sugar, and whisk until just
stiff. Spread the flavoured cream
evenly over the pavlova and sprinkle
with the prepared fruit.

Using the paper underneath to help
you, roll the pavlova lengthways to
create a log and pat into shape.
Leave it covered with the paper until
ready to decorate.

Make the sauce by scooping the
seeds and juice of the passionfruit
into a jug. Add the diced mangoes,

nectarines and strawberries and stir
gently, adding just enough of the
sugar syrup to moisten the sauce.

To decorate, gently transfer the
pavlova to a long serving dish,
pulling the paper away. Whip the
cream and pipe rosettes or other
shapes on top as desired. Decorate
with the red fruit, if using, halving
any strawberries. Alternatively, dust
the roulade with icing sugar. Slice
and serve with the sauce.

Recipe notes Despite appearances,
this dessert takes surprisingly little
time to make and much can be done
in advance to make it stress-free. The
filled pavlova can be left overnight in
the fridge while the fruit sauce can be
prepared entirely the day before
serving. The roulade serves six
people generously or can be stretched
to feed ten less hungry guests.

The inclusion of vinegar and
cornflour is the key to achieving a
snowy marshmallow centre that
contrasts beautifully with a golden,
sugar-sparkly crust. Don't worry if
the pavlova puffs up like a duvet in
the oven: it will sink a little as it cools.

Spiced Italian espresso cake with buttered chocolate pecan crust
Serves 6

150g/5oz/scant 1 cup pitted dates
1 tsp bicarbonate soda [baking soda]
*250ml/9floz/1 cup freshly brewed
    espresso coffee*
seeds of 3-4 cardamom pods, ground
*65g/2¼oz/5 tbsp unsalted butter, plus
    softened butter, for greasing*
90g/3oz/8 tbsp caster sugar
1 egg, lightly beaten
finely grated zest of 1 orange
*175g/6oz/1¼ cups plain [all-purpose]
    flour*
1 tsp baking powder

For the crust
3 tbsp muscavado or dark brown sugar
65g/2¼oz/5 tbsp butter
*120g/4oz plain dark chocolate, with
    70 per cent cocoa solids, chopped*
100g/3½oz/1 cup pecan nuts

To serve
250g/8oz/1 cup mascarpone
1 orange

You will also need
*a 22cm/8½in round, loose-bottomed
    cake tin*

Heat the oven to 180°C/350°F/Gas 4.
Butter the cake tin, then line it with a
circle of buttered silicone paper.

Place the dates in a mixing bowl
with the bicarbonate of soda, cover
with the freshly brewed coffee and
leave to soak for 15-20 minutes.
Meanwhile, melt the butter gently.

Use a pair of scissors to snip the
soaked dates until all are chopped
small. Add the ground cardamom,
then the melted butter, sugar, beaten
egg, orange zest, flour and baking

powder. Stir well, then pour the
batter into the prepared cake tin.
Bake in the middle of the oven for
25 minutes, until the centre of the
cake feels set when pressed with your
finger and a skewer inserted into the
middle comes out clean.

Meanwhile, make the crust. Heat
the butter and sugar together very
gently in a double boiler. Add the
chocolate and stir until the sugar has
dissolved. Add the pecans.

Remove the hot cake from the oven,
spread the topping over it, return the
cake to the oven and continue cooking
for 10-12 minutes. Remove the cake
from the oven and set aside to cool in
the tin for 20-30 minutes.

To prepare the garnish, cut the peel
away from the orange and slice it into
fine strips with no white pith. Place it
in a small pan of water, bring it to a
boil and, as soon as it starts to boil,
drain and rinse the orange zest in cold
water. Set aside while you segment
the orange flesh using a very sharp
serrated knife.

Turn out the cake. Using a spoon
dipped into hot water (preferably one
of those old-fashioned, egg-shaped
soup spoons with a pointed tip),
scoop a portion of chilled mascarpone
onto each serving plate. Cut the cake,
placing a piece alongside each scoop
of mascarpone, then decorate with
the orange zest and segments.

Recipe notes The crust of this cake is
crunchy and sweet, giving a seductive
introduction to the deep, dark, spicy
bitterness below. Try to make the
coffee with soft water, so that it is
not too aggressive in flavour.

The cake, orange zest and segments
can be prepared up to a day before
serving if desired.

Flourless chocolate cake
Serves 8

*250g/8oz plain dark chocolate, with
    70 per cent cocoa solids, finely
    chopped*
175g/6oz/¾ cup unsalted butter, cubed
*100g/3½oz/½ cup caster [superfine
    granulated] sugar*
3 large eggs, separated
a pinch of salt
softened butter, for greasing

To serve
*½ quantity Spiced Orange Salad with
    Star Anise (page 190), or fresh
    berries, or poached fruit*
500ml/18floz/2¼ cups thick cream
*a little Vanilla Custard or Raspberry
    Sauce (pages 200-201), or both*

You will also need
*a cake tin of 20cm/8in diameter, with
    a solid base*
*a roasting pan into which the cake
    tin fits*

Heat the oven to 180°C/350°F/Gas 4.
Brush the cake tin liberally with
softened butter and line the base with
a neat disc of silicone paper. Brush
again with butter.

Place the chocolate in the top of a
double boiler with 4 tbsp of water.
Fill the base section with steaming
water and keep at a moderate heat
while you melt the chocolate. Stir
gently with a rubber spatula until the
chocolate mixture is smooth. Stir in
half the butter, a little at a time, until
it has melted. Then stir in half the
sugar. Add the remaining butter one
piece at a time, stirring until melted.

Remove the double boiler from the
heat and stir in the egg yolks, allowing
them to cook a little in this gentlest
of temperatures. >

Using an electric hand-held mixer, begin to whisk the egg whites with a pinch of salt in a large, clean bowl. When the whites are just starting to form a foam, add the remaining sugar in a steady stream and whisk for 30-60 seconds to make a light and glossy meringue.

Add a quarter of the meringue to the chocolate mixture, stirring until smooth. Put this mixture back into the main bowl of meringue and fold together, up and over, using a figure of eight motion, as lightly as possible.

Pour the batter into the prepared cake tin. Set the cake tin gently in the roasting pan and pour hot water from a kettle around the tin, until it comes halfway up the sides of the tin. Place the water bath carefully in the oven and cook for 15 minutes. Then turn off the oven and leave the cake for 4-5 hours until quite cool.

Remove the cake tin from the water bath and leave to cool for another 30-60 minutes in the tin, on a wire rack. Carefully turn the cake out onto a serving plate and leave it to sit in a warm place for a while before serving, so that the butter in the mixture softens and the cake is soft, yielding and luscious.

Serve each portion with the spiced oranges in syrup, or other fruit, plus thick cream and vanilla custard or raspberry sauce as desired.

Recipe notes This recipe is a good example of why it is important to know how to whisk egg whites properly – they can form the base of so many luscious desserts, not just meringues and soufflés.

Ideally, use a clean metal or glass bowl, rubbed completely clean and grease-free with a cut lemon, vinegar or boiling water. Choose the largest possible whisk for your bowl, and begin beating slowly, increasing the speed gradually. When the egg whites are still slipping loose against the bowl and the bubbles are large on the surface, add a tablespoon of the sugar. Then start to beat faster, until the whites take on a sheen. The spoonful of sugar has helped to stabilize the whites, firm them up, and make them ready to receive more sugar. Add the rest of the sugar steadily, but not too slowly, so that you end up with a dense, satiny cloud that holds its shape on the end of the whisk.

Although this cake is easy to make, you should only do so if you feel in the mood to follow the method carefully. Chocolate is a complex ingredient. In this instance you are combining it with water, butter and egg yolks, which is a tall order for chocolate!

If, in the unlikely event that all the ingredients separate in the double boiler, fold the chocolate mixture into the egg whites anyway, because you will still wind up with a very respectable result.

Take care when preparing the cake tin, as the bottom becomes the top, and there is no decoration to hide any imperfections.

If all goes well, and I am sure it will, you will have an amazing chocolate cake with the delicate texture of silk, a lovely sheen and a rich, chocolatey flavour. Do not chill the cake, simply keep it in a cool spot, then transfer to a warmer place before serving. Cut it with a hot knife, wiping the blade clean after each slice.

Fig and fennel tart
Serves 8

1 x 25cm/10in diameter round sweet shortcrust pastry tart case, or a 35 x 10.5 x 3cm/14 x 4 x ⅛in rectangular tart case, half-baked (page 176)
500g/1lb 4oz black figs, quartered lengthways
2 tsp fennel seeds
about 225g/8oz/1 cup apricot jam

For the frangipane

1 large egg
50g/1¼oz/½ stick unsalted butter, softened
50g/1¼oz/5 tbsp caster [superfine granulated] sugar
50g/1¼oz/scant ½ cup ground or flaked almonds
35g/1¼oz/¼ cup self-raising flour
2 drops bitter almond essence (optional)

To serve

500ml/18floz/2 cups mascarpone, e xtra-thick double [heavy] cream, or clotted cream

Heat the oven to 180°C/350°F/Gas 4 and place a baking sheet in the oven to get hot.

To make the frangipane, beat the egg lightly in a jug, then place the jug in a basin of hot water to warm the egg through while you measure out the other ingredients.

In a food processor, whizz the butter briefly until creamy, then add the sugar and whizz until the mixture is pale and fluffy. Add the almonds and whizz until combined. Pour in the warmed egg in a slow, steady stream. Pulse in the flour, and the almond essence, if using. You should have a paste at this stage – it does not matter if the almonds are slightly gritty.

Spread the frangipane over the base of the pastry shell. Cover it with the figs, placing them cut-side up and as close together as possible, as they will shrink during cooking. Sprinkle with the fennel seeds.

Sit the tart on the preheated baking sheet in the middle of the oven and bake for 40 minutes or until the filling is a pale golden brown and set. Turn the tart around halfway through cooking to ensure even browning.

Remove the tart from the oven and set aside to cool on a rack.

In a small saucepan, heat the apricot jam until melted. Sieve it, then return it to the pan with 2 tbsp water. Boil the jam mixture until it falls from a wooden spoon in sticky drops. Keep the mixture warm while you paint it lightly over the figs to glaze them, then return the remainder to the jar for use on another occasion. Serve the tart within the day.

Recipe notes This fabulous tart works best with small, round black figs with a dense flesh and minimum of juice. Alternatively, it can be made with quarters of drained canned pears.

Frangipane is the name given to the almond mixture traditionally and effectively made to protect the pastry from the juice of the fruit which would make it leathery or tough. I love the way it puffs up between the figs. It is a good idea to make more frangipane than you need and store it in the freezer in small tubs for use on other occasions.

If using almond essence, it must be top quality. I make a special trip to Fauchon for essences and food colourings whenever I'm in Paris.

'La tarte' Desmoiselles Tatin
Serves 6-8

115g/4oz/½ cup unsalted butter
150g/5oz/⅔ cup caster [superfine granulated] sugar
8-9 firm dessert apples
zest of 2 lemons

For the sponge

150g/5oz eggs, beaten
a few drops of vanilla extract
100g/3½oz/½ cup caster [superfine granulated] sugar
100g/3½oz/⅔ cup plain [all-purpose] flour, sifted

You will also need

a tarte tatin mold, or a copper or non-stick ovenproof frying pan of 23cm/9in diameter

Heat the oven to 190°C/375°F°/Gas 5, placing a black oven tray in the middle of the oven to get hot. Cover the base and sides of the tarte tatin mold or frying pan with a thick layer of butter and a lavish sprinkling of sugar. Peel the apples, rub them with the cut surface of a lemon, then core and cut into quarters or eighths.

Arrange the apples in concentric circles around the base of the pan. Dredge them with the remaining sugar. Sprinkle with the lemon zest and dot with pieces of butter. Place the pan over a high heat on the stovetop and cook for 15 minutes, or until the apples are tender and the butter and sugar melted, thickened and caramelized to a deep golden brown colour. Move the pan around on the heat and adjust if one side is getting darker than another.

Remove the pan from the heat and allow to cool a little. Arrange the fruit more neatly in the dish if necessary.

To make the sponge, place the eggs in a double boiler over hot water, but do not place the double boiler on the stovetop. Using a hand-held electric mixer, whisk the eggs until you have a high, dense foam, which forms a thick firm trail over the top of the mixture as the blades are lifted from the bowl (whilst the machine is turned off!). Do not over-whisk them.

Lightly fold in the flour with a rubber spatula, lifting the mixture up and over. The foam will appear to shrink alarmingly – just be as gentle and quick as you can. Spoon the batter over the warm apples and use a palette knife to spread the surface of the mixture evenly, so that it is flush and flat with the rim of the pan.

Place the pan in the oven on the hot baking sheet and bake for 25-30 minutes, or until the batter is risen and golden and shrinking away from the edges of the pan. Remove from the oven and immediately place a round, flat serving plate over the pan and invert the tart. If you leave it any longer, the apples will stick to the pan. If this does happen, place the pan on the stovetop for 1-2 minutes to melt the caramel and free the missing parts of the topping.

Allow the tart to cool a little before slicing and serving, otherwise the apples will be so hot that their taste will be diminished.

Recipe notes The Tatin sisters originally made this dessert with puff pastry but this version uses a sponge cake mixture instead. The sponge benefits from the hot, buttery, appley juices soaking into it, whereas those same juices make the finest puff pastry tough and leathery after just a few minutes. Serve it with some chilled custard flavoured with Calvados.

Light sugar syrup
Makes 450ml/16floz/2 cups

225g/8oz/1 heaping cup caster
  [superfine granulated] sugar

Place the sugar in a saucepan with
450ml/16floz/2 cups water and stir
gently with a metal spoon over a low
heat until the sugar dissolves, taking
care that no granules stick to the
sides of the pan.

Stop stirring, raise the heat under
the saucepan and boil the syrup for
3 minutes. Then remove the pan
from the heat and set aside to cool.

Store the syrup in a clean sealed
bottle in the refrigerator, where it
will keep for about 2 weeks.

Recipe notes Sugar syrup is wonderful
for fruit salads and other desserts. It
can be varied in numerous ways. For
a vanilla syrup, add two split vanilla
beans to the mixture once the sugar
has dissolved. For ginger syrup, use
four slices of fresh ginger, or 3-4
slices of fresh ginger plus a mild red
chilli that you've deseeded and diced.

A mix of fresh herbs can be lovely,
such as a sprig each of mint, rosemary
and lemon verbena. Alternatively, add
three sprigs of a single sweet herb,
but do adjust the flavours to taste as
home-grown herbs are often much
stronger than shop-bought varieties.

In all these cases, you should strain
the syrup before use or storage.

To make lime syrup, add the juice
of half a lime, then taste and add
more as necessary to achieve a
refreshing balance of sweet and sour.
You can also combine sugar syrup
with equal quantities, or to taste, of
freshly squeezed orange, grapefruit
or passion fruit juice.

Shiny hot chocolate sauce
Makes 400ml/14floz/1¾ cups

150g/5oz plain dark chocolate, with
  70 per cent cocoa solids
½ tsp unsalted butter
200ml/7floz/¾ cup double [heavy] cream

Break the chocolate into pieces and
place in the top of a double boiler.
Fill the bottom section with steaming
water and set the top section over it.
Keep the heat at a medium
temperature while you gently stir the
chocolate until it is smooth and
glossy – chocolate loves to be stirred.

Add the butter, then stir in the
cream and serve the sauce hot.

Recipe notes If you have ever
wondered how restaurants achieve
those designer dots and squiggles on
plates, this is a good sauce with which
to try. It will firm up when cold, so
serve it from a squeezy bottle that
you have gently and carefully heated,
otherwise the plastic will melt.

Vanilla custard
Makes 500ml/18floz/2¼ cups

1 vanilla bean
5 large egg yolks
50g/1¾oz/4 tbsp vanilla sugar
375ml/13floz/1⅔ cups creamy milk
a few drops of vanilla extract

Place the vanilla bean in a good
saucepan, not too deep. Cut open the
bean and scrape out the tiny seeds,
trying to avoid getting them in your
finger nails (terrible waste!).

In a mixing bowl, whisk the egg
yolks and sugar together until the
mixture is pale and sticky.

Add the milk to the saucepan and
heat it slowly until almost boiling.
Remove it immediately from the heat
and pour the hot milk gradually onto
the yolk mixture, whisking all the
time with a hand whisk. Try to avoid
creating too many bubbles, as they
could prevent you spotting the
thickening process in the next stage.

Clean out the saucepan, return the
custard mixture to it and cook,
stirring over a gentle heat. Use a
wooden spoon to stir across the base
and sides of the pan, and press down
well to prevent any lumps and bumps
forming at the bottom of the
saucepan, the part which is hottest.

The sauce will gradually thicken.
Remove it immediately from the heat
as soon the sauce coats the back of
the spoon. The test is to draw a
horizontal channel with your finger
on the custard-coated spoon. If the
channel stays clean and dry, your
custard is ready. If the sauce becomes
too hot at this stage it will curdle or
separate. Don't expect a spectacular
change – thickening with egg yolks is
a subtle process. Remember the sauce
will thicken further as it cools.

Add the vanilla extract to taste, then tap the sauce through a fine-meshed sieve into a jug. Set aside in a cool spot until completely cold, stirring from time to time as it cools. Alternatively, on a hot day, cool it quickly by placing the jug of custard in a bowl filled with ice and water. To serve the custard warm, reheat it and keep it warm in a double boiler.

Recipe notes So simple, but one of the greatest sauces ever invented, a real egg custard is always welcome at the end of a meal, judging by the bent heads and little noises of pleasure that greet its appearance. This always reassures me that cooking for others is one of the greatest pleasures in life.

If the sauce should curdle, process or liquidize it until smooth, then reheat it carefully with about 4 tsp of cornflour [cornstarch] or custard powder slaked in a little milk. The famous Bird's custard powder is simply egg-flavoured starch, invented by Mr Bird for Mrs Bird, who loved egg custard but was allergic to eggs.

Vanilla beans are expensive but the good news is that you can re-use them for a long time. They should be flexible, soft and oily when fresh. Wash and dry them after cooking. Store them in an airtight jar, in a cool dark place, and place one or two in a canister of caster sugar to use for baking and custards.

To make vanilla sugar, I simply put used dry vanilla beans into a jar of caster [confectioners'] sugar. The jar must have a tight lid to seal in the aroma. Keep topping it up with sugar and used vanilla beans so it's an ongoing process. I use vanilla sugar for all desserts and puddings except meringues, for which it is too moist.

Raspberry sauce
Makes 300ml/10floz/1¼ cups

300g/10oz/2½ cups raspberries
70-90g/2½-3½oz/⅓-½ cup caster [superfine granulated] sugar, or vanilla sugar (see left)
a squeeze of lemon juice, to taste

Purée the raspberries briefly in a food processor. Then press the purée through a stainless steel mesh sieve to remove the tiny raspberry seeds.

Clean the food processor bowl and return the raspberry purée to it. Gradually add the sugar and lemon juice to taste, whizzing thoroughly for 5 minutes to achieve a glossy sauce that will stand proud on a plate and form a perfect circle.

Recipe notes This sauce freezes so well that it is one of the staples of my freezer. If you want to make it in advance but keep it fresh, it should be served within 24 hours.

Crystallized petals
Makes 24

a few full-blown unsprayed roses, violets or primulas
1 egg white
caster [superfine granulated] sugar

You will also need
somewhere warm to dry the petals, such as an airing cupboard
a small fine painter's brush

Separate the petals from the flowers. Stir 1 tsp water into the egg white. Sift a generous quantity of sugar into a shallow bowl or tray.

Working in batches of three petals at a time, use the painter's brush to carefully paint the egg white all over the petals. Then bury the petals in the sugar, tossing it over them, until they are completely covered. Carefully lift the petals from the sugar and sit them on parchment or waxed paper.

Repeat with the remaining petals, then leave to dry overnight in a warm place. Store in an airtight tin, in which they will keep well for months.

Recipe notes You need to make these at least one day before use.

There are some plastic boxes that keep their contents crisp, and many that don't – in fact, they actually soften cookies and breads. When I need a box to keep cookies and meringues crisp and dry, I prefer to use a tin left over from purchased cookies or sweets.

To make a tin airtight, take a large sheet of paper, larger than the surface of the tin, and place it over the base of the tin as you close it so that once the lid is on the paper shows all around. Add sachets of silica gel to the container too, if you have them.

PART THREE

Entertain

"When Lyn Hall goes down to the hotel kitchens to visit the chef, it is like Churchill inspecting the troops."
Len Deighton

Introduction

Entertaining is cooking on show, as simply or as extravagantly as you like. It is a numbers game, requiring that you have the right amount of food and tableware for your guests. It is an organizational exercise, so your guests eat reasonably soon after their arrival. It involves thinking long and hard about what you are going to do, cooking food with which you are comfortable, and editing the menu to fit your equipment, tableware and occasion. It is not the time to try out a batch of new recipes. Most importantly, entertaining is about giving and enjoying, and it is terrific fun. And towards having more fun, there are a few professional secrets I would like to share with you here.

The mise-en-place means 'everything in its place'. It is the collecting and measuring out of all the ingredients before you begin to cook – right down to the six coriander sprigs and pinch of paprika, that often come at the very end of the recipe.

Before you turn over the page with glazed eyes, please stop a moment and just think of the stress this will save you. No rummaging with chocolatey hands in the cupboard for a non-existent vanilla bean, no racing down to the corner shop at 11.05pm, five minutes too late.

Weigh the entire recipe out, put it all on a tray, and sit fresh ingredients back in the fridge as necessary. This process also includes getting out and carefully checking over all the equipment you need. It's time for dusting out any dead spiders from the roomy stewpot used once a year, scrubbing its rusty bottom, and discovering that someone has not returned the borrowed gratin dish. Relax! Performing the mise-en-place gives you the time to think again. Admittedly, mise-en-place takes longer than the actual cooking, but when you do come to cook, the process will be seamless and hugely enjoyable.

The time sheet Sometime before, preferably with a glass of wine, or a mug of tea, sit down with a sheet of paper and your recipes. Work out how long each recipe will take you and write a list. I do mine in hours and quarter hours. Don't forget to include the weighing out time (the mise-en-place) and the time that will need to be spent clearing away and washing up for each recipe. Add up the hours and see if it fits into your allotted time. Be ruthless. If you don't have time, don't do it! Instead, streamline the menu, or see if a quick dash to a cheese shop or delicatessen fits in.

Similarly, if you have a mishap such as a blocked sink (lamb fat on a cold day, fish bones in the U-bend, drat!) or an overflowing bath, and lose a precious hour or so, you can again boldly edit the menu and enjoy the relief it brings.

The kitchen prompt An action time sheet or kitchen prompt helps you to have everything ready at the time you need to serve it. If you are a natural cook, you will skip this, but many of us are not so confident. Towards the end of the food preparation, you will find you have finished with the recipes, but still need to know the time each dish goes in or comes out of the oven, and the temperature required, when things should go on or off the hob, in or out of the microwave, plus meat resting times, so that everything is ready at the right time. I make a basic timetable and stick it up in the kitchen. The bonus is that I can then get right into my guests' conversation the moment they arrive. The oven-timer, pingers and prompt list take care of the food.

Other aspects of getting ready When scheduling, allow time for getting the last dishwasher load in, out and unpacked, so it's empty and ready to help you with your dirty tableware once the food has been eaten. You will also need to fully clean the kitchen and its floor, so that the room then transforms into the streamlined surface required for arranging food on plates and pouring drinks.

Remember to build in time to feed children, dogs and cats, and get the children to bed. Do the flowers and move any furniture the day before – it takes more time and energy than you think. If your living room is your dining room, allow at least an hour and a bit to tidy, set the table, pull out serving platters, and organise the candles, drinks and music. For a special dinner party, you need a three hour break between the end of the main cooking tasks and welcoming guests. You are of course fully mise-en-placed for the finishing touches. I feel cheated if I don't have the pleasure of laying the food out carefully, so it looks appetising and beautiful. For many of my students, it's the part they enjoy most.

Favourite ways of entertaining

Having people round This is the kitchen supper, Sunday lunch, mid-week supper, for four to six people, generally informal. I love kitchen suppers. They have an element of spontaneity, of everyone being involved, of being right at the nerve centre of the meal. Guests help stir the risotto, toss the salad, top up the drinks, pass plates – everything you can't do at a formal meal.

Now is the time for small roasts, poultry and game cooked en cocotte, anything on the bone, seafood in the shell, dishes requiring immediate service or finger bowls, stews served straight from the pot, and large platters of pasta, so guests can freely help themselves to seconds. If you don't have time to cook, shop for a deli meal.

Although it seems spontaneous, behind every good kitchen supper is a clean, organized kitchen, with open spaces for the cooking, final preparation and serving to take place. If every inch of surface is taken up with telephone directories, pet-food, and the fax machine, no-one is going to feel very comfortable. Here are some more key points to remember:
• If the washing machine is in your kitchen, make sure it is off, empty and that the door is shut.

• Show off pedigree ingredients in designer packaging, plus any stunning kitchen equipment.
• Don't have a different glass for every wine. Give glasses a quick rinse and polish when moving from white wines to red.
• You want good inexpensive wine chilled in the fridge, reds out on the counter – but ready!
• Review and tidy your fridge before guests arrive. Throw away anything mouldy or slimy.

Formal dinner parties Heralded five to three weeks in advance by a regal white invitation, a formal dinner party is a real treat. One feels honoured and delighted to be invited, and there are bound to be fascinating guests, memorable wines and lively conversation.

You want to look as if you do it all the time, and it is absolutely no trouble at all, but this is a real challenge when starting out.

By the time you have polished all the glasses required for each wine, there is usually a friendly forest of them on the table. When serving fine wines, your ingredients should be of excellent quality, but prepared very simply. You want easy to recognise food, so everyone can concentrate on the conversation, and not feel uncomfortable that the food outstrips their interest in it.

Plate service is perfect for this occasion, as guests prefer their own space until they get to know each other better. Everything should be easy to eat, very tender, and barely need cutting with a knife. No bones, skin or gristle, definitely no small birds. Choose fillet of beef, breast of

chicken, or loin or breast of game. Even if you have not been fore-warned, make sure a vegetarian option is available. Have a cold starter and pudding, and buy fine chocolates for serving with coffee. Each portion should be ready to serve, without splattering your best frock or suit, so: no sizzling fat, no last minute sauce reductions, no aromatic char-grill smoke wafting into the dining room.

Drinks should offer no hidden surprises either. Select the best quality vintages and vineyards, dependable French wines, and champagne to begin.

Good standard tableware, such as white bone china or porcelain, is ideal. You should also:
• Have an electric hot plate in the dining room, if possible, keeping the plates hot. A sideboard is indispensable.
• Ensure your best cloth or linen napkins are pressed to perfection. Never offer paper napkins.
• Eschew anything too whacky or ostentatious. Aim for an image of pared-down elegance.
• Buy a flower arrangement. It need not be expensive, but should be low, so everyone can see each other over the top.
• Write a table plan.
• Ensure the bathroom is exceptionally clean and tidy.
• Farm out exotic pets. Small dogs and labradors can be seen, but not heard. Children should be with a nanny or baby-sitter.
• Place a bucket of water somewhere discreet, ready for flowers you may receive.
• Have a vodka if you feel a panic attack coming on.

Menu planning

A well-balanced, planned meal seduces the appetite gently and enticingly, course by course. None of these should be too large or too small, and should consist of just enough cream, butter and fat, protein, vegetables, carbohydrates and fruit cooked and presented in such a way to make everyone feel inwardly comfortable and outwardly delighted afterwards.

Enjoying the preparation First of all, not everything has to be cooked. Take advantage of the wonderful ingredients on offer in fine food shops and by mail order. Buying carefully selected items such as marinated grilled artichokes, fresh ravioli, kiln-roasted salmon, or a fresh cheesecake from your local patisserie can remove a whole course from your worksheet.

Never try three new dishes for the first time in one menu. I firmly believe in running the same menu past all my friends, until everyone has tried it. By the third time, you barely need a shopping list, you instinctively know the next step of each dish, and you will be loving it every inch of the way.

Be sure to split the cooking between the hob, oven, steamer and grill. Juggling five hot saucepans on a four-burner stovetop might be fine for a restaurant chef, but not for home cooks. Guests feel uncomfortable when a hot and flustered hostess totters out of the kitchen.

Make one of the courses the day before. Arrange your worksheet so that the dishes are not all finished at the same time. This will relieve both mental and physical pressure.

Choosing the dishes Begin with something tangible. If it is a birthday, what is the guest of honour's favourite dish? Let's say it is mushroom soup laced with truffle oil. Good. Now we know we cannot have a casserole to follow, or a 'wet' pudding. Budget-wise, the soup will not be expensive, so a roast, or something else a bit pricey, would be a perfect choice of main dish.

After the taupe-coloured soup, we will need brighter colours, and these can be found in vegetables. Zinging greens, tiny white turnips with a flash of violet, vibrant baby carrots in the summer, and a butternut purée in the winter, will do nicely. Then a starchy dish to round it off, such as little roasted potatoes or a gratin dauphinois.

With a moist vegetable purée, and an ultra-creamy gratin, you could get by without making a sauce for the main course. Otherwise, commit yourself to a lovely clear gravy sauce, and make a big batch so you can put some in the freezer for next time.

It's looking good. A cake for a celebration always hits the spot, and chocolate is a consistent winner. With a sparkler or candle, and dimmed lights, this will make a perfect birthday dinner, and one that will be remembered with huge affection.

Other ways to focus your menu Pick something in season. A basket of chanterelles calls for autumnal fare such as a roast pheasant with game chips, or haunch of venison, followed by plums or a fig and fennel tart.

If your guests regularly dine in the best restaurants, plump for something rustic, like Alsatian-style sausages. To start, choose something that will revive jaded palates, such as fresh coriander [cilantro] chutney with felafel. After seconds of sauerkraut, have mercy on your guests' failing digestions and finish with a sweet wine and a few almond cookies.

Menu watchpoints Beginning with a strongly-flavoured starter means the next course has to be equal, if not more powerful in taste. This is why mild-tasting fish and seafood make good starters.

The dessert or pudding must make its presence felt with panache. Sweet summer berries with lemon custard is a striking contrast in texture and colour, and will successfully conclude most meals. A cooling, slithery jelly will soothe tastebuds aroused by a spicy main course.

Do not repeat ingredients in a meal. A menu with salted toasted almonds in a starter should not have an almond ice-cream, pastry or cookies to finish. If you really are stuck, change the nuts on the salad to pine kernels. That's menu planning! You also need to avoid repeating garnishes. Swapping flat-leaf parsley for chervil is often a neat solution.

And finally... Remember to ask your guests for notice of potential problem foods well in advance. It may help eliminate several of your choices right way.

Menu planning

The following menus are a selection based on the recipe section of this book, and include some ingredients of the best possible quality sourced from delis and other fine food stores to widen your scope further. Remember, the more thought you give to your ability to prepare and serve the food in the environment available, the more successful the meal, and the more you will enjoy it too. If you cannot serve it, don't choose it! Wrestling with a guinea fowl for the first time on a polished sideboard in the near-dark is a misery. Watching the rest of the food go cold, hearing the conversation come to a hush...

Think of what your guests would enjoy, the kind of food that makes them feel comfortable. This is particularly important for formal occasions where guests can't escape and everyone is on show. Chillies and garlic are terrific in a Mexican restaurant with your friends, but some elderly people have trouble digesting strong, spicy ingredients.

Be sure to include something you love to cook too. A recipe cooked with love and joy is really special.

If things do go wrong, ask your children and partner explicitly not to mention dishes, recipes and ingredients that they have seen earlier but do not appear as part of the meal or celebration. Then none of the guests will ever know of what they missed, and you will be saved, all over again, the painful angst of the dish that went wrong. If, for example, your dog eats the main course that is cooling on the patio, try not to panic. Have a glass of wine, or a cup of tea. Raid the local shops. No-one except you will know that you have failed to achieve your personal best.

Formal occasions
Menu 1
- Fresh crab with avocado and parmesan crisps
- Fillet of fish with tarragon crust
- White wine and dill sauce
- Glazed vegetables
- Buttered noodles
- Flourless chocolate cake with raspberry sauce and vanilla custard

Menu 2
- Mushroom cappuccino
- Jambonettes of duck
- Glazed sugar snaps or baby turnips
- Char-grilled fennel
- Candied sweet potato
- Clear brown gravy
- Fig and fennel tart with vanilla custard
- Chocolates

Menu 3
- Little smoked haddock custards with saffron shrimp sauce
- Roast sirloin of beef
- Wild mushroom sauce
- Roasted rosemary potatoes
- Swede [rutabaga] purée
- Florentine fennel gratin
- Glazed French beans [haricot verts]
- Cherry whim-whams with crystallized rose petals

Intimate dinners
Menu 1
- Salmon and fennel ravioli with saffron sauce
- Roast chicken with honey, salt and cracked pepper crust
- Basmati pilaf with fresh green herbs
- Green salad with cherry tomatoes
- Little raspberry soufflés with hot raspberry sauce

Menu 2
- Baby clams with chilli, white wine
- and garlic
- Really fresh pasta with cream sauce and chives
- Violet artichokes in olive oil and white wine with sweet vegetables
- Green salad
- 'La tarte' Desmoiselles Tatin with vanilla custard

Menu 3
- Hot potato pancakes with smoked salmon, sour cream and caviar
- Venison with cranberry sauce
- Velvet mash
- Glazed green vegetables
- Vanilla ice-cream with chopped preserved ginger
- Shiny hot chocolate sauce
- Ginger cookies

Glamorous fork buffet

Menu 1

- Japanese rice crackers, steamed scallops and Peter Gordon's chilli jam
- Mushroom cappuccino, served in espresso cups
- Persian-style chicken pilaf with pistachios and barberries
- Fillet of salmon Bois Boudran
- New potatoes with mint and chives
- Puy lentils with chilli, cumin and coriander
- Orange and Campari jellies
- Summer berries with lemon custard
- Spiced Italian espresso cake with buttered chocolate pecan crust and mascarpone

Menu 2

- Wild rice blini canapés, smoked salmon and sour cream
- Soufflé roulade with crème fraîche and caviar
- Roast fillet of spiced beef
- Chinese rainbow salad
- Jasmine rice
- Fish baked with potatoes, olives, tomatoes and Mediterranean herbs
- Flourless chocolate cake
- Yogurt mousse with raspberry sauce
- Spiced orange salad with star anise

Family meals

Menu 1

- Green salad, fried pancetta, poached eggs
- Pot-roast poussin with olive oil and herbes de Provençe
- White bean and basil mash
- Poached plums, vanilla custard or cream

Menu 2

- Courgette [zucchini] and parmesan soup
- Char-grilled ciabatta
- Pork chops baked in spices, herbs and garlic
- Kettle-wilted glazed spinach
- Steamed carrots
- Fruit salad with ginger syrup

Menu 3

- Penne pasta with pea pesto
- Roast racks of lamb with Provençale white beans, tomatoes and rosemary
- Velvet mash
- Mixed salad
- Fruit crèmes with cherries, raspberries and almonds

Menu 4

- Char-grilled Mediterranean vegetables
- Steamed trout with baby leeks, ginger, spring onions [scallions], and little potatoes
- Sesame and soy dressing
- Greek set yogurt swirled with raspberry sauce

Kitchen suppers

Menu 1

- Pasta shells with ricotta and spinach, in a tomato sauce with thyme and garlic
- Guinea fowl with lemon, juniper and bay rub
- Roasted rosemary potatoes
- Stir-fried savoy cabbage with little crisp bacon strips
- Pear and almond tart with vanilla custard or shiny hot chocolate sauce

Menu 2

- Mushroom risotto – simmered not stirred
- Lamb shanks, with mustard, rosemary, chickpeas and caramelized onion
- Glazed courgettes [zucchini] stir-fried with mint
- Green salad
- Cheese with oatmeal crackers and flat-breads
- Greek set yogurt with toasted, cracked hazelnuts, blueberries and runny honey

Menu 3

- Mussels with chilli, white wine and garlic
- Alsatian-style sausages
- Steamed baby potatoes
- Sweet wine with almond thins

Book Club, Bridge Lunch, Girls' Night

Menu 1
- Goats' cheese mousselines
- Warm tomato and herb vinaigrette
- Duck khoresh with bitter orange and pistachios
- Basmati pilaf with fresh green herbs
- Char-grilled courgettes [zucchini]
- Raspberries topped with lemon syllabub
- Hazelnut florentines

Menu 2
- Asparagus with hollandaise sauce
- Whole baked salmon
- New potatoes with chives and parsley
- Slow-roast tomatoes with garlic, thyme and baso;
- Peas with mint
- Orange and Campari jellies

Menu 3
- Parmesan custards
- North African fish bake with fennel and pickled lemons
- Whim-whams with crystallized rose petals

Barbecue, al fresco

Menu 1
- Quinoa salad with grapes, celery and roasted cashews
- Thai spiced pork with coriander [cilantro] and coconut dipping sauce
- Bobotie in iceberg lettuce with bay skewers
- Char-grilled rib-eye steaks, lamb cutlets and Merguez sausages
- Char-grilled aubergine [eggplant], with yogurt and dried mint
- Peeled and sliced fresh mango, papaya, kiwi-fruit, with lime syrup

Menu 2
- Chlodnik with dill, cucumber, beetroot and prawns
- Vitello tonnato
- Yogurt-marinated char-grilled lamb leg steaks
- Char-grilled tuna
- Mixed salad
- Sweet yellow peppers with capers and crumbs
- Cheeses and breads
- Watermelon

Sunday night, friends around, easy entertaining

Menu 1
- Char-grilled figs with taleggio fondue
- Pan-roast duck breasts with cherry sauce
- White bean and basil mash
- Glazed broccoli
- Yogurt mousse with raspberry sauce

Menu 2
- Spicy Chinese tofu salad with dried shrimp and ginger
- Soba in chicken and soy broth with wilted watercress, coriander and mint
- 'La tarte' Demoiselles Tatin with vanilla ice-cream

Barely cooking

Menu 1
- Green coriander [cilantro] and coconut chutney with shrimp crackers
- Slow-cooked lamb with Baharat spices
- Baked potatoes with set yogurt and chives
- Green salad
- Spiced orange salad with star anise

Menu 2
- Smoked eel, smoked cod's roe, lemon wedges
- Rye bread
- Cold roast beef, horseradish sauce
- Green bean salad
- New potatoes with mint and chives
- Mild goats' cheese, Wensleydale cheese, celery and flat breads

Menu 3
- Tuna, red onion, and cannellini bean salad with basic vinaigrette
- Salad of smoked chicken, flageolet beans, toasted flaked almonds, and creamy vinaigrette
- Steamed new potatoes
- Dolcelatte with fresh pears

Presentation

Essential plateware

Seated dinner party

For a 4-course meal for
eight including canapés,
cheese, biscuits and coffee
you will ideally need:

45 very small plates
    (including 8 starter
    course liners, 8 side
    dishes, 8 pudding dishes,
    3 sauceboat liners,
    2 chocolate plates,
    8 coffee saucer liners)
2 large canapé plates
8 medium dinner plates
8 large dinner plates
2 large serving platters
3 vegetable dishes
3 sauceboats
2 bread baskets
2 butter dishes
1 large cheese platter
8 coffee cups and saucers
2 small teapots
2 sugar dishes
1 milk jug

Crowded buffet party

For a 4-course buffet for
20 people including soup,
canapés, coffee and tea
you will need:
5 large flat plates
22 large dinner plates
42 medium dinner plates
32 teacups for soup
22 coffee cups and saucers
10 saucers for tea

Presentation starts with the basic good cooking of a meal and extends to the subtle details you wish to employ in serving it. Life is not a photo shoot, with exquisite tableware, a table groaning with flowers, and a professional chef-cum-stylist in the kitchen. But there are many cooks I know who love to dream, to plan ahead, to formulate details for presenting their menu in the best possible way.

Presentation is good cooking It's about browning the meat all over, and I mean all over, holding it firmly, pressing even the difficult curvy edges against that smoking pan, using rubber gloves to protect yourself, so the outside or skin is dark, caramelized and shining. It's about taking every single droplet of fat off a sauce to reveal the lustrous gravy beneath. It's about blending a raspberry sauce so full of fruit that a tablespoon dropped on a plate naturally forms a perfect circle, without a trace of watery, leaky juice.

I shall do my best to explain the sleights of hands that make food look special. Much of it comes from within, and is difficult to put into words. One needs to be able to sense that something does not look quite right, that the colours are jarring, that once striking ingredients have been muted by the colour of the crockery, or that something can be too flat, and another too high.

Good presentation of dishes takes a little extra time, but those of us who like to arrange food on the plate as appetisingly as possible feel cheated and distressed if we have been too slow to get the cooking finished in time to indulge in this activity. To get a well-presented multi-course meal on the table, on time, and in sequence, every single element must be considered, pampered if required, and kept literally waiting in the wings. It is yet another reason why you need to be very familiar with your recipes before serving them on special occasions. Getting to know a recipe helps you show it at its ultra-best.

Cutting, chopping and selecting You need a few assiduously honed, sharp knives. Watch the chefs on television, practise as much as you can. Good knifework comes along brilliantly, once you get the knack and you will be thrilled at your progress.
• Cut all vegetables and fruit to the same size – near enough is not good enough.
• Ruthlessness is required when selecting your uniform cubes, dice, matchsticks or strips. Save those that don't make the grade for a salad. When selecting herb leaves to use as a tiny garnish for canapés, only pick those of exactly the same size and shape.
• Slash vegetables on an acute slant for Oriental dishes.
• Peel small potatoes and fruit such as kiwi fruit carefully. Echo the smooth, curved sides of the ingredient with your peeler, helping nature if necessary.

Greens add freshness Salad leaves, herbs and leafy vegetables should look so vital and healthy, that it seems as if they were picked only an hour ago.

• In a salad, include frisée for curl, baby beet leaves for colour, rocket [arugula] and curly lettuce for a swirl and distinction. Clear dressings give the greatest impact.

• Use a salad-spinner only for leaves that do not tend to bruise.

• Pinch out as many crushed stems, blackened edges, and stalky sprigs as you can.

• Spray leaves with a water spritzer to keep them fresh and moist, and store in a large plastic box with dry paper towel on top.

• Pinch to the correct size the required number of herb sprigs or leaves for garnishing, plus a few extra for accidents. Spritz a folded square of paper towel with water, place it in a plastic container, and pile the herbs on top. Give them a final spritz. Seal and label, and keep in the fridge – they will appear even more fresh and lively the following day.

• Avoid tarragon and watercress, which wilts after a few moments on the table. Use chervil straight from the bunch and basil straight from the plant. Coriander [cilantro] will never look as vigorous as flat-leaf parsley. Use coriander leaves only to float on Asian broths and curries, and to toss over the food at the last moment.

• For glistening vegetables, tip the cooked vegetables into a bowl, drizzle with olive oil, and tip and tilt them gently with your finger tips, using clean rubber gloves if the vegetables are piping hot.

• To brighten cooked spinach before serving, move it around a pan with a little hot olive oil (not smoking, or it will burn the leaves).

Other watchpoints

• Use a good fishmonger and butcher who cut and fillet neatly.

• When you fry, char-grill, pan-roast or brown, it is the first side down in the pan that will look best. Make sure this side is uppermost when you serve.

• To make meat shine, brush it with a little olive oil.

• Drain fried food on paper towel before serving, to prevent any fat or oil spoiling the presentation.

• Although acid enhances and brightens red fruits and vegetables (for example lemon with raspberries), it will destroy greens, such as mint sprigs used as a decoration for apple juice, or green beans in a salad.

• Whipped cream sags overnight, and has to be whisked again before use to achieve full volume.

• Beware ingredients with a high salt content, as they will draw the natural juices from others. What looked like a delightful melange the night before, can be a slimy puddle the next day. Prepare them in advance, but store separately in plastic tubs covered with damp paper towel, until ready to serve.

The plate wardrobe Most cooks, including myself, are smitten by gorgeous plates and tableware. They are probably the most powerful means of setting the scene for a well-cooked meal. Make sure yours fit your table, and form the right background for the food you love to cook. The plate forms your all-important frame, so don't fill it too full when arranging the food.

Some plates come and go with fashion. For a stylish opening to

your meal, serve canapés and nibbles on the latest vogue. I believe porcelain or bone china are most practical and I am more comfortable with neutral colours and white plates, preferring the food to be the most colourful element on the table. However, it is a good idea to collect coffee cups like jewels – all the same size, but in different colours, silvers and golds – to finish the meal as richly as you began.

Do keep your good tableware and glasses to hand. Travelling up ladders or down into the cellar for weighty piles of plates, and bringing silver out from under the bed, is exhausting.

Plating food, or not Food photographs and television programmes tend to give the impression that all dishes should be individually plated before serving, so that every portion of food is carefully arranged on each plate, and carried to the table without disturbing the arrangement.

In a good restaurant, to serve a hot main course to eight guests, there will be four chefs, running from various parts of the kitchen, bringing the meats, fish, sauces, starchy ingredients and the vegetables. Piece by piece, in a few minutes, the plates are dressed in a pre-ordained, precise pattern, on a heated bench, beneath hot lights, watched over by the eagle eye of the head chef. Are you really sure you want to try this at home?

If so, you will need space in the kitchen, or nearby, where plates can be smoothly laid out. Also, you will need the right number of hands to help, so the plates and the food don't get cold before they reach the table. Here are a few tips for times when you want to plate dishes individually:

• Think of threes and fives when laying out food. They look more interesting than even numbers.

• When plating a main course, avoid the centre of the plate, unless you are particularly artistic.

• Place the meat, poultry or fish on the plate so that it sits right in front of the guest. This helps them to eat it neatly, especially if they have to negotiate bones.

• The potatoes or rice go at 2pm, as most people are right-handed, and will go to this part of the plate to mop up juices and gravy.

• Add a trickle of sauce if you must, but take care not to soften or soak any ingredient that you have spent time making crisp and dry, such as pastry or roasted potatoes. Serve the remaining sauce in a sauce boat or bowl, so your guests can take as little or as much as they like.

Taking large dishes to the table This method of serving food to guests is the most practical for many people, however you still need to make the food look appetising, keep it hot, and make it easy for guests to recognise the food and serve themselves if required.

The key look of today is natural presentation, arranged-but-not-arranged, and fairly easy. In any case, many guests steer clear of food that looks as if it has been over-handled.

Your main consideration is to have enough plates, platters and bowls in various shapes and sizes to show your food off gracefully. You do not want to be making decisions about what looks best on the night. Here are some more things to bear in mind:

• Food casually piled on a plate looks more appetising than that lurking in the bottom of a huge plate. It keeps food hotter too.

• Aim for a wide, undisturbed rim of plate around the food, to act as a frame and help people focus on its intrinsic beauty.

• If the colour of your food is the same or near to the colour of your plate, line the plate with green leaves – anything non-wilting and non-poisonous.

• Grind black pepper over bland-looking savoury food – this helps crisp up the definition.

• If cinnamon sticks and bay leaves have been used in the cooking, pull them out, wash, and lay them semi-wildly, across the top of the dish. Remember that odd numbers look better than even.

• Two items on one plate is quick to serve, and can look gorgeous. For example, line a platter with mash, couscous or risotto, and top with lamb cutlets, lying flat, their little bones criss-crossed down the centre.

• If you are serving mussels and clams, quickly arrange them with the open shells looking upwards, so that they look fresh and lively.

• To avoid carved meat looking flat and ordinary, contrast it with some curvy, crisp parsnips, game chips, or sprigs of flat-leaf parsley.

• Run canapés in straight, precise lines on round and oblong platters.

• Tumble semi-shelled nuts and dried fruit around a cheese platter for a quick autumnal look.

• Cakes do not have to be flat. Try cutting a plain cake into squares and build it up, with lots of angles, castle-style. Drizzle with a syrup or sauce and scatter with edible flower petals, which are very useful to keep on hand for making desserts look special.

Consideration However funky your meal or your friends, consideration for your guests remains most important. If serving noodles in a broth, lay the table with a fork and spoon. Don't expect guests to toil with knife and fork in a tiny Japanese bowl, or cut a perfectly good steak with a blunt knife.

Most importantly, presenting a meal should be fun for you and uplifting for your guests. Be practical. Let your storage dictate your capacity for tableware, or lovely objects will get broken. Serve food piping-hot where applicable, using tableware that keeps it hot, and serve it on time. The rest will come naturally when you combine imagination with planning, and practice.

What to drink

Even though I've enjoyed making the most complicated dishes throughout my years of teaching, I've always said that all you need to make a dinner party is a good loaf of bread, a gorgeous piece of cheese and a decent bottle of wine. Nevertheless, there are times when you want to make more fuss, and will enjoy doing so.

Liquid assets Cocktails always get a big party off to a sparkling start. Unusual, colourful, and with an exhilarating combination of spirits, they slip down a treat. Too many, however, and many guests may suffer the following day, so keep them short and simple, before moving on to some good wine.

Long gone are the days when wine was a simple matter of white, red or rosé. There has never been such a great choice of wine available, but it can seem difficult to know where to begin. The key points to remember are:
• Any bottle too cheap can produce a headache.
• If in doubt, choose a wine that comes from the same country as your recipe – French wine with French dishes and Italian with Italian. If you can match the two from the same region, even better.
• Get to know your wine supplier and give them plenty of information. Tell them what you are cooking and you will be surprised at the expert free advice and help you will receive. It also makes shopping more fun.
• If someone brings wine along to your party, it is important to read the label with interest and

comment on the wine. Then judge whether to serve it or keep it for another occasion. Fine, old wines should certainly be kept for another day as they need to settle after the journey. Don't worry: it will be seen as a mark of respect.

When it comes to mineral water, for special occasions I buy the most stylish glass bottles with a minimum of branding that I can find. They may cost more, but they add grace and chic to a table. If you can only buy large plastic bottles of water, decant it into glass jugs before serving.

Soft drinks are best bought from the chiller cabinet, for optimum quality and flavour. Cloudy apple juice or a mango fruit cocktail is generally more appreciated as an all-night tipple than acidic orange juice. Another option is elderflower cordial, topped up with sparkling water, served with ice and lemon.

Glasses There is something about sparkling glassware that really does it for me. Rows of glasses, shimmering in candlelight, and I am as excited as a child on Christmas morning because I know the party is moments away.

Buy cheap glasses rather than very expensive sets, because after a while you won't be able to replace them. Don't choose any so tall they cannot go in the dishwasher – unless you enjoy, as I sometimes do, washing glasses by hand whilst pleasurably mulling over the details of the party and intriguing fragments of conversations picked up during it.

For meals you need clear glasses, except for water tumblers

which can be made of coloured glass such as blue or amethyst if desired. Always buy one or two more than your maximum table setting. If in doubt, choose tulip-shaped glasses, which concentrate the aroma of the wine enticingly right under your nose. Start out with a set of large goblets for red wine and another slightly smaller for white, which you only half-fill with wine. Then you need small glasses for sweet wine after a meal, or a cold fino sherry before, plus a set of champagne glasses – I love tall flutes. Classic cocktail glasses give you a chance to be wild and creative, and enjoy that ever-so-dry Martini cocktail. For spirits with mixers, such as gin and tonic, you need tall, straight-sided glasses (these can double as soft drinks glasses) and, if you plan on serving vodka, little shot glasses.

Although the dishwasher does a valiant job, you should polish all glasses before special occasions. To do this, pour water from a boiling kettle into a dish. Hold each glass downwards by its base or stem for a few seconds, and the rising steam will loosen any marks in the bowl of the glass. Polish well with a linen, or a linen-cotton mix, cloth. Then hold the glass up to the light to check for any remaining blemishes.

Other useful items are trays in neutral or vivid colours (avoid anything in between), glass jugs for soft drinks, ice-buckets, and cloth napkins, to blot the base of bottles that have been sitting in ice-buckets, and grip the corks of sparkling wine bottles so you can twist them open.

Champagne cocktail For 20 glasses you will need a small box of white sugar cubes, 4 large oranges, some Angostura Bitters, no less than 350ml/12floz/1½ cups Grand Marnier, and 4 bottles of chilled champagne or dry sparkling wine. For each glass, rub each side of a sugar cube against the side of an orange. Drop the flavoured sugar cube into a tall champagne glass, splash the cube with the bitters, then add a generous tablespoon of Grand Marnier. When ready to serve, top up each glass with the sparkling wine.

Vin d'orange To serve six people, you will need 2 oranges, half a lemon, 350ml/12floz/1½ cups dry French rosé wine, 4 tbsp rum, 4 tbsp sugar, a camomile teabag, plus garnishes such as lemon knots or small strips of lemon peel. Pare the rind from the oranges and lemon half and cut it into strips. Place the peels in a jug with the wine, rum and sugar and leave to infuse overnight. A couple of hours before serving, add the camomile teabag, which gives a welcome astringency. Strain through a very fine stainless steel mesh sieve, or muslin [cheesecloth], and serve chilled in generous stemmed glasses with a tiny strip of lemon zest, or a lemon knot, in each.

Garnishes

Lemon and lime slices Water, vodka and gin all look the same when they are in a glass. To distinguish them easily, use lemon slices for glasses of water and lime slices for vodka and gin (or the other way around). Cut the fruit into thin slices, cover with plastic wrap and sit them at your bar area with a few cocktail sticks ready to lift into glasses when serving.

Lemon and orange peel strips Peel the fruit using a vegetable peeler. You want to shave off the zest only, so there is no white pith. Cut the zest into strips and, as you place a piece in each glass, squeeze it to release the oil and fragrance.

Citrus peel knots These store well overnight. Take a cannelle knife and pull it carefully down the side of the fruit to make the longest possible fine strip of zest. Tie it in a knot and keep moist by storing it in an airtight plastic box on damp paper towel. Repeat as often as you can on one piece of fruit before going onto the next.

Party ice cubes In a regular ice-cube tray, place sprigs of mint and cherries that still have their stems on the fruit. Fill with water and freeze for use in vodka cocktails and fruit punches.

Estimating quantities
From each bottle of still wine you will get 3 large, or 5 smaller glasses. From each bottle of sparkling wine, you will get 6 glasses.

Dinner for six
2.7kg/6lb ice
3.6 litres/6 pints/16 cups mineral water
1 bottle champagne or sparkling wine
2 bottles white wine
2 bottles red wine

Buffet parties
450g/1lb ice per person
½-¾ bottle wine per person
500ml/18floz/2 cups mineral water per person

Roasting chart

Roasting meat is not an exact science, but I have tried to make up a roasting chart that will help you roast loins and legs of pork, legs and shoulder of lamb, beef on the bone and the Christmas turkey and goose to perfection. Do remember to make the necessary adjustments to the timing and temperatures of fan ovens.

I have found that the safest way of estimating the cooking time is to take the meat or bird out the fridge, weigh it, estimate the cooking time, allowing a good measure of time generally, especially if it is an expensive cut, and then use other tests of doneness that are mentioned in the recipes, such as wobbling the bones and pressing the meat to see the colour of the juices. Back-up tests are invaluable. A meat probe thermometer may seem expensive in the shop, but it takes so much of the guesswork and fear out of roasting meat and poultry that, considering the premium price of the food you are cooking, it is an excellent and very worthwhile investment that will last many years.

Large poultry

	Preheat oven to	Then reduce the temperature to	and cook for X min per 450g/1lb	Internal temperature when done
Turkey up to 6.3kg/14lb	190°C/375°F/Gas 5	170°C/325°F/Gas 3	15 min	80-82°C/176-180°F
Turkey over 6.3kg/14lb	190°C/375°F/Gas 5	170°C/325°F/Gas 3	17 min	80-82°C/176-180°F
	Sear for 30 min at	Then reduce the temperature to	and cook for X min per 450g/1lb	Internal temperature when done
Goose 3-4kg/9-11lb	200°C/400°F/Gas 6	180°C/350°F/Gas 4	10-12 min	76-80°C/170-176°F
Goose 9kg/20lb	200°C/400°F/Gas 6	180°C/350°F/Gas 4	15 min	76-80°C/170-176°F

In the UK, add about 45 minutes to the total cooking time for turkey on Christmas Day to compensate for the drain on the national power supply.

Roast goose on its side for 30 minutes, turn the bird over for 30 minutes, then turn it breast-side up for the remainder of cooking.

Take the thermometer reading in the deepest part of the thigh.

For roast chicken, see page 78.

Large cuts which cannot be browned in a roasting tin, weighing up to 2.25kg/5lb

	sear for 15 min at	then reduce the temperature to	and cook for X mins per 450g/1lb	internal temperature when done
Beef (rare)	250°C/480°F/Gas 10	190°C/375°F/Gas 5	12 min	51°C/125°F
Beef (medium)	250°C/480°F/Gas 10	190°C/375°F/Gas 5	15 min	60°C/140°F
Beef (well done)	250°C/480°F/Gas 10	190°C/375°F/Gas 5	20 min	70°C/160°F
Lamb (pink)	250°C/480°F/Gas 10	200°C/400°F/Gas 6	15min	60°C/140°F
Lamb (medrare)	250°C/480°F/Gas 10	200°C/400°F/Gas 6	17 min	62-65°C/145-150°F
Lamb (well done)	250°C/480°F/Gas 10	200°C/400°F/Gas 6	20 min	70°C/160°F
Pork (cooked)	200°C/400°F/Gas 6	180°C/350°F/Gas 4	30-35min	75-82°C/170-180°F

Small roasting cuts that can be browned first in a roasting tin

	sear for 15 min at	then reduce the temperature to	and cook for X min per 450g/1lb	internal temperature when done
Beef (rare)		190°C/375°F/Gas 5	12 min	51°C/125°F
Beef (medium)		190°C/375°F/Gas 5	15 min	60°C/140°F
Beef (well done)		180°C/350°F/Gas 4	20 min	70°C/160°F
Lamb (pink)		200°C/400°F/Gas 6	15 min	55°C/131°F
Lamb (well done)		180°C/350°F/Gas 4	20 min	70°C/160°F
Pork (cooked)		180°C/350°F/Gas 4	30-35 min	75°C/170°F
Lamb 6lb/2.700kg bone-in				
(medium rare)	250°C/480°F/Gas 10	180°C/350°F/Gas 4	10-12 min	62-65°C/145-150°F
(well done)	250°C/480°F/Gas 10	180°C/350°F/Gas 4	13-15 min	70-73°C/160-165°F
Lamb 4 lb/1.800kg boned leg or shoulder				
(medium rare)	250°C/480°F/Gas 10	180°C/350°F/Gas 4	25-30 min	60-65°C/147-150°F
(well done)	250°C/480°F/Gas 10	180°C/350°F/Gas 4	30-35 min	70-73°C/160-165°F
Pork, boned and rolled Cooked		200°C/400°F/Gas 6	45 min	75-82°C/170-180°F

Boned roasts require 5-10 minutes more than bone-in roasts.
A long thin pork loin requires less time than a hind leg, or a fore-leg
(hand and spring)

Index

Numbers in **bold**
indicate photographs

Acknowledgments

Thanks to

Carolyn Arnold
Hans Baumann
Mary Berry
Marianne Berryman
Jo Barwick
Gerard Besson
Raymond Blanc
John Bott
Dominique Bouchet
Michel Bourdin
Jean Cazals
Xanthe Clay
Claire Clifton
Simon Corringham
Katey Day
Len and Ysabele Deighton
Roz Denny
Mark Dobson
Lorraine Dickey
Karen Elder
Alison Fenton
Vanessa and Andreas Gledhill
Peter Gordon
the Guild of Food Writers' Sparklist
Juliet Harbutt
Alfonso and Ernesto Iaccarino
Charles Jackson
Pat Jacobs
Chi Lam
Christine McFadden
Anton Mosimann
Jenni Muir
Jean-Christophe Novelli
Andrew Nurnberg
Bruce Oldfield
Sri Owen
The La Petite Cuisine Students
    and Team
Sonia Plenderleith
Helen Priday
Thane Prince
Joël Robuchon
Sue Rowlands
Michel and Robyn Roux, brother
    Albert Roux
Nada Saleh
Suzy and Michael and Alex
    Schneidemann
Bob Scott
Nigel Slater
Jeanne and Robin Stainer
Roger Vergé
Amy Willcock
Lorna Wing
Ian Wisniewski
Antony Worrall Thompson
Alexander Wrighton at Bulthaup
and to all the chefs and teachers who
    have taught me to cook